D1264265

FRIEDRICH HEBBEL

Oxford University Press, Ely House, London W. 1

GLASGOW NEW YORK TORONTO MELBOURNE WELLINGTON
CAPE TOWN SALISBURY IBADAN NAIROBI LUSAKA ADDIS ABABA
BOMBAY CALCUTTA MADRAS KARACHI LAHORE DACCA
KUALA LUMPUR SINGAPORE HONG KONG TOKYO

FRIEDRICH HEBBEL

Portrait by KRIEHUBER, *1858*

FRIEDRICH HEBBEL

A STUDY OF
HIS LIFE AND WORK

BY

EDNA PURDIE

OXFORD UNIVERSITY PRESS

'Zu dichten, dramatisch zu gestalten, werde ich erst aufhören, wenn mir der Schädel mit einer Axt oder einem Kolben zerschmettert ist . . . Es ist meine innerste Natur, mein Ausathmen, nicht Resultat eines Willensacts.'

HEBBEL: 'SÄMTLICHE WERKE', ed. R. M. Werner. 3te Abteilung 'BRIEFE', Vol. IV, pp. 118–9. Letter to FELIX BAMBERG, 15 June 1848.

FIRST PUBLISHED 1932
REPRINTED LITHOGRAPHICALLY IN GREAT BRITAIN
AT THE UNIVERSITY PRESS, OXFORD
BY VIVIAN RIDLER
PRINTER TO THE UNIVERSITY
1969

PREFATORY NOTE

THE claim of Friedrich Hebbel to be included among the greater German dramatists will now hardly be disputed, though it has not perhaps been fully recognized in England. The attempt to present a picture of his life and work to English readers, therefore, may not be regarded as superfluous. The intimate history of creative work has seldom been more fully revealed than in the documents of Hebbel's life; in this particular he seems to make a peculiar appeal to modern readers—but an appeal which is not without its danger, if interest in the poet's processes of thought be allowed to outweigh appreciation of his poetic achievement. Such a danger, however, may be avoided by turning to the tragedies themselves: to suggest this is the main purpose of the present study.

My warm acknowledgements and thanks are due to Professor J. G. Robertson (University of London) for much helpful advice, as well as for his constant kindness and encouragement during the writing of this book. I also gratefully acknowledge the kindness of Herr Rudolf Kardel (Curator to the Hebbel-Museum in Wesselburen) in supplying items of bibliographical information and in arranging for photographic reproductions.

E. P.

UNIVERSITY COLLEGE OF NORTH WALES
BANGOR, N. WALES

1931

CONTENTS

I. EARLY YEARS 1

II. HAMBURG AND MUNICH 12

III. LYRIC AND 'NOVELLE' 35

IV. HAMBURG AND COPENHAGEN. FIRST PLAYS. 'JUDITH'—'GENOVEVA'—'DER DIAMANT' 56

V. YEARS OF TRAVEL. COPENHAGEN—PARIS —ROME. 'MARIA MAGDALENA' . . 92

VI. LIFE IN VIENNA. MINOR DRAMAS. 'HERODES UND MARIAMNE'—'AGNES BERNAUER' 127

VII. LAST YEARS. 'GYGES UND SEIN RING'— 'MUTTER UND KIND'—'DIE NIBELUNGEN' —'DEMETRIUS' 181

VIII. DRAMATIC TECHNIQUE 235

IX. CONCEPTION OF TRAGEDY 255

CHRONOLOGICAL LIST 270

SELECT BIBLIOGRAPHY 272

INDEX 274

LIST OF ILLUSTRATIONS

Friedrich Hebbel. Portrait by Kriehuber, 1858. By permission of the Hebbel Museum at Wesselburen. *frontispiece*

Christine Hebbel. Portrait by Kriehuber, 1855. By permission of the Hebbel Museum at Wesselburen. *facing p.* 128

I

EARLY YEARS

BORN in 1813, the year which heralded the triumphant issue of the 'Wars of Liberation', at Wesselburen in Norderdithmarschen in the duchy of Holstein, Christian Friedrich Hebbel seemed at first destined to a situation far apart from the main movements of German life and letters. Holstein was at that time a Danish state, a fact not without influence on his subsequent career; Dithmarschen was and is at all times a country singularly remote and unlike the inland districts of Germany and Austria which afterwards he learnt to know. Situated in the western part of Holstein, and bounded on the west by the North Sea, it stretches northwards from the estuary of the Elbe until the Eider marks the beginning of Schleswig. Prosperous as its flat, extensive fields and pastures look—the farm-houses disproportionately handsome to the amount of land attached to them—they have no air of sleek satisfaction, as have rich inland pastures. All along the extensive belt of 'Marsch' dividing the open moorland on the eastern side of Dithmarschen from the westerly expanse of shore, an artificially constructed dyke stands as a perpetual sign of man's struggle against the encroaching sea. Crowning the grass-grown dyke is a flat path; along this men and cattle pass, their actual size reduced to toy dimensions by the contrasting background of illimitable space. Isolated farms and clustered buildings dot the 'Marsch' at intervals; but they too, on a clear day, sink into insignificance when the least distance intervenes. Mists, on the other hand, enhance the effect of spaciousness pervading all the 'Marsch', and give a ghostly character to the vast stretch of mud-flats when the tide is at the ebb. Nowhere is it more evident that man's success is dependent on his power to control; and not even in the high mountains does his figure, by comparison with the elements, appear more insignificant. 'Eine Ebene', Hebbel once wrote amid the charms of the Heidelberg landscape, 'selbst die Dithmarsische, hat etwas Unendliches.'[1]

Wesselburen, one of the two towns of Northern Dithmarschen, was even in the early nineteenth century a place of some little importance in the 'Marsch'. Its church spire, of a pattern strange to Holstein, dominates the landscape; and from the church as centre its quaint streets radiate in all directions, much as they did in Hebbel's early years. More important than its size, however, was the fact that it was the centre of a 'Kirchspiel', or parish, and as such offered opportunities which played a considerable part in his career.

The student of Hebbel's life is singularly fortunate in the amount of biographical material available. For nearly twenty-eight years, from 1835 to 1863, diaries with more or less regular entries exist, and the collected correspondence supplements the diaries. Previous to 1835 there are few direct documents; but an autobiographical fragment[2] gives a vivid picture of the conditions in Wesselburen, while much in the Life written by Emil Kuh is evidently derived from first-hand knowledge and direct information. Moreover, the admirably arranged Hebbel-Museum at Wesselburen contains much valuable material, and not only for the early years.

Christian Friedrich was the elder of the two sons of Klaus Friedrich Hebbel, a mason, and his wife, Anje Margarete. The birth of his brother Johann in 1815 brought a poverty-stricken family still nearer to the boundary line which divides poverty from destitution, so that his mother had to take charge of a foster-child with her own infant, in order to eke out their scanty income. A characteristic incident is recorded of Hebbel at the age of two:[3] his mother had told him to rock the stranger in his cradle, but Friedrich replied 'Meinen Bruder will ich wiegen, aber den fremden Bruder nicht!' and took his stand beside Johann.

The whole of Hebbel's childhood was governed by the

[1] *Tagebücher* (*Sämtliche Werke*, ed. cit., 2te Abteilung), vol. i. 269, 6 Aug. 1836.

[2] *Aufzeichnungen aus meinem Leben. Werke*, ed. cit., vol viii, pp. 80–116.

[3] v. Emil Kuh, *Biographie Friedrich Hebbels*, 3te Auflage, Wien und Leipzig, 1912, vol. i, p. 122.

sense of poverty, by the constraints and shifts due to insufficient means. In the autobiographical fragment there is an account—idealized in retrospect—of the physical and mental conditions of his early years; in *Maria Magdalena* a sterner picture of the rigid narrowness of a small household owes without a doubt much of its realism to his actual experience in childhood. Yet as long as the family were quartered in part of the house they owned in the Norderstrasse (now the Hebbelstrasse), his childhood was not altogether an unhappy one. There was a garden, where the children played, and in it a pear tree (to remain in Hebbel's memory as a proof of the calculating nature of childish friendships), whose fruit formed a staple portion of the family means. There were too the other inmates of the house, whose portraits survive in the poet's reminiscences—Meta, the narrator of gruesome ghost and witch stories, and Klaus Ohl, the poverty-stricken ex-mason, who never failed to welcome and amuse the children with a song, or a game of his invention. 'Der Hauptreiz der Kindheit', Hebbel writes in the retrospect upon his childhood, 'beruht darauf, dass Alles, bis zu den Hausthieren herab, freundlich und wohlwollend gegen sie ist, denn daraus entspringt ein Gefühl der Sicherheit, das bei dem ersten Schritt in die feindselige Welt hinaus entweicht und nie zurückkehrt. Besonders in den unteren Ständen ist diess der Fall.' The feeling of the friendliness of animals Hebbel never lost—his little dog figures constantly in his diary, and the hardships of its long tramp from Munich to Hamburg were as much felt as Hebbel's own; the conviction of the 'feindselige Welt' of humanity, however, was early borne in upon him. It began, in fact, with the enforced removal of the family from their own house to rented rooms—a removal all the more bitter since it was due, not to Klaus Friedrich Hebbel's failure, but to that of a friend, for whom he had, on his marriage, become surety. That he had not been called upon before to surrender his small property was merely due to the fact that his creditor was serving a sentence of imprisonment for arson; on the latter's release, the postponed catastrophe occurred. By this time, Friedrich had been for two years, from the age of four to six, in a dame's school kept by a spinster called Susanna, and his experience of the world in little had begun. Susanna was anything but impartial in the distribution of her favours, and the children of poorer parents, who could make no return in kind, realized to the full the dame's interpretation of the text: 'To him that hath, shall be given.' Among his fellow-scholars too the boy early learnt the lesson of distrust—their petty meannesses and tormenting pranks impressed themselves upon a mind already too sensitive for happiness. But he learnt to read in the little school—though he was considered too young to attempt the art of writing, carefully reserved by Susanna, as the highest stage of attainment, to the end.

Towards the end of his sixth year, educational reforms in Holstein brought with them the erection of a primary school in Wesselburen, and Hebbel was transferred to it, just at the time when his family were compelled to exchange their own house for sadly restricted quarters. From the enjoyment of a certain position—though a modest one—among his schoolfellows, he was now deposed; and although capable of maintaining some independence by his fists, he experienced nevertheless a pang of disillusionment. Nor was there any compensation for such trials in the conditions of their family life. Narrow as these conditions had now become, the lack of privacy, as of means, might have been more tolerable had Hebbel's father been of a less forbidding temper. But his disposition, originally dour, was still further embittered by these reverses, and in Hebbel's own poignant phrase: 'a slave of marriage, bound with iron fetters to poverty . . . he hated joy'.[1] Friedrich and his brother were his 'wolves', Hebbel continues, and seldom could eat a piece of bread without being told they had not earned it. 'Dennoch war mein Vater . . . ein herzensguter, treuer, wohlmeinender Mann; aber die *Armuth* hatte die Stelle seiner *Seele* eingenommen.'[2]

From his own account of her, the poet's mother was of a very different temperament.[3] Though it is evident, from

[1] *Tagebücher*, ed. cit., vol. i. 1323, 22 Nov. 1838. [2] Ibid.
[3] Ibid. 1295, 18 Sept. 1838.

many of his reminiscences, that she had a quick temper and was given to sudden impulses of anger, she was full of kindness, and often stood between the children and their father's severity. Especially with Friedrich, her favourite, was this necessary, for the boy's imaginative, susceptible nature made relations with his father particularly difficult. Through her exertions he was sent regularly to school, decently if poorly clothed, and saved, for a time at least, from being forced into distasteful labour.

The primary school, which Hebbel attended until 1825, had for its head a man to whom he alludes later with gratitude, and who did indeed play a notable part in his intellectual development—Franz Christian Dethlefsen. Himself a rather narrow moralist, whose education was by no means extensive, Dethlefsen nevertheless realized the boy's unusual parts, and made two contributions of incalculable importance —the loan of books to read, and encouragement to read them. Later he gave him private tuition, and, moreover, assistance towards the cost of candles for reading in the evenings. Even so, however, it was difficult for Hebbel to avoid his father's reproaches concerning such useless waste of time and money. Similarly, although a good-natured artist gave him drawing lessons without fee, his father condemned the pursuit as a luxurious squandering of time unfitting for a poor man's son. But scenes of anger and reproach, though they undoubtedly embittered the boy's life, could not deprive him of his native privilege—the joy in observation, assimilation, and reproduction, which thus early forecast the artist's development. He was still able to recall, in later years, the joy with which he completed his first drawing—a garden in autumn, with a girl standing behind the gate: 'Mir war wirklich, als müsste die von mir gemalte Pforte sich aufthun, sobald ich nur auch das Mädchen fertig gemacht.'[1] And a similar feeling of ecstasy accompanied the first reading, with a comrade, of Bürger's *Lenore*: 'Wonne, Wehmuth, Leben, Tod, Alles auf einmal: ein Urgefühl!'[2] For music he early developed appreciation. Church music was performed in Wesselburen

[1] *Tagebücher*, ed. cit., vol. ii. 2646, 6 Feb. 1843. [2] Ibid.

during Advent and at other high festivals, and in 1843, on the occasion of a Berlioz rehearsal in Paris, he is so vividly reminded of his early musical impressions that a detailed description of them follows in his diary.[1] He became a chorister in course of time, and thus received (presumably without parental opposition) some practice in this art.

In 1825 Hebbel's father determined that he should learn to be a mason, and no protests served to turn him from this purpose. The experiment, however, was completely unsuccessful; anger and punishment alike were unavailing, since Friedrich seemed unable to acquire even the rudiments of dexterity in handling his materials and tools. Soon it became apparent that the task was hopeless, and on the occasion of a quarrel at their work, the boy refused to continue any longer at the trade. His father, from now onwards, considered him a ne'er-do-weel, and no doubt felt justified in his previous dislike for his son's favourite occupations. No plan for him to enter on a definite career seemed to offer promise of fulfilment; he ran errands and delivered letters, and thus earned a few pence to contribute to the household. His mother alone seems to have made this time endurable, and to have preserved for him his meagre amount of freedom—which he employed in reading books borrowed from Dethlefsen.

When Hebbel was fourteen, his father died. By this event, their small income was still further diminished, although his mother kept the household going by her own labour of various kinds. An opening which suddenly presented itself for Friedrich was therefore all the more welcome. The chief official of the district,[2] a man called Mohr, offered to take the boy (who had frequently run errands for his household) and employ him, giving him board, lodging, and part of his

[1] *Tagebücher*, ed. cit., vol. ii. 2867, 17 Nov. 1843.

[2] The term 'Kirchspielvogt' has no exact equivalent. The executive officer of the 'parish', or rural district, carried out many of the duties of a magistrate, and was responsible to the higher authority of the 'Landvogt' in cases which went beyond his jurisdiction. The taking down of evidence was one of the duties of the clerk attached to the 'Kirchspielvogtei'. For a description of the duties of the 'Kirchspielvogt' in Hebbel's province v. *Verordnung in Hinsicht des Justizwesens und des modi procedendi in der Landschaft Norderdithmarschen*, Kiel, 21 Dec. 1765.

clothing in return. He went to live in the house, shared a bed with the coachman, and had his meals in the servants' quarters.

For a period of over seven years Hebbel lived in this manner and worked for Mohr, gradually becoming a confidential clerk and deputizing for him on occasion. As his usefulness to his employer increased, and as his mind developed, his sense of the indignity of the situation grew, until at last it reached an intensity which is reflected, many years later, in as bitter an indictment as could well be addressed by one man to another. The letter to Mohr, of which a copy appears in Hebbel's diary in 1854,[1] is such that one cannot but wish it unwritten, though the provocation was great. There is no doubt that Mohr took advantage of Hebbel's situation, and kept him in conditions entirely unsuited to the work he gradually came to do, which was that of a salaried confidential clerk. There could be no excuse for such conduct as Hebbel more than once describes in later reminiscences; that he was expected, for instance, to continue sleeping with the coachman even during the latter's recovery from an infectious fever, is sufficient indication of the situation. But by 1854 Hebbel was a great dramatist at the height of his creative power, and it seems incongruous to find him replying with such vehement resentment, even to a provocative allegation. Perhaps it would also be true to say that this very fact gives us the measure of the humiliations of his youth—they were too bitter to lose, with the passage of the years, their power to wound.

One privilege he enjoyed during his time as Mohr's assistant which outweighed many drawbacks—the free use of his employer's library. He took full advantage of this permission and read widely. Schiller and Klopstock, Kleist and E. T. A. Hoffmann, soon became familiar to him. The first poem that he read of Uhland's, above all, made a lasting impression on his mind.[2] His own lyrical attempts had been

[1] *Tagebücher*, ed. cit., vol. iv. 5300, 15 July 1854.

[2] The poem was *Des Sängers Fluch*; R. M. Werner (*Hebbel: ein Lebensbild*, 2te Aufl., Berlin, 1913, p. 46) dates Hebbel's acquaintance with Uhland's poetry in the winter of 1830–1.

in Schiller's manner, and general reflections had seemed to him hitherto an important part of lyric poetry. Uhland's simplicity—'dieses reine, harmonische Glockenspiel'—was a revelation of an unsuspected law: 'dass der Dichter nicht in die Natur *hinein-* sondern aus ihr *heraus* dichten müsse';[1] his power of reducing everything to 'das Einfach-Menschliche' led Hebbel, as he tells us in a vivid image, on to a peak, whose height at first he only realized from the fact that there seemed no air to breathe. How far he still was, he adds, from comprehending the first and only law of art—that it has to present the infinite by means of the individual phenomenon—could hardly be calculated.[2] That Uhland, whose poetic work is in most respects the complete antithesis of Hebbel's, should have caused this original revolution in his mind is one of the pleasant surprises of literary criticism. But Hebbel was always capable of appreciating methods different from his own, provided he could perceive an underlying general principle which he was able to respect. It was the seeing eye, together with the power of vivid presentation revealed in Uhland's work which conquered him, and he never lost his admiration for these qualities.

The first poem which he published in the *Dithmarser und Eiderstedter Bote* (entitled *Sehnsucht: An L.*) had appeared in 1829, and during the next three years several of his poems were printed in that journal—on occasion too, critical rejoinders and satirical sketches found acceptance. As with most young poets, lyric verse was his first means of expression, and the youthful poems are remarkable chiefly for the command of form to which they bear witness. But Hebbel's partiality for a dramatic interest in the subject-matter may also be noted—as, for example, in *Kains Klage* (1829). In 1832, under the pressure of growing impatience with his circumstances, Hebbel addressed a letter to the poet Uhland, sending him some specimens of his poetic work and asking whether he could help him to obtain a post in Stuttgart, and thus escape from the distasteful restrictions of life in Wessel-

[1] *Tagebücher*, ed. cit., vol. i. 136, 5 Jan. 1836.
[2] Ibid.

buren. Uhland sent an answer, stating his inability to help and preaching patience—its coolness mitigated by an allusion to the fact that Hebbel had obviously found opportunity, even in confined surroundings, 'Geist und Gemüt auszubilden'. This was indeed the case. He had made great efforts to fill the gaps in an education which had left many, hoping thereby to prepare himself to enter, by some means, on a University course. He could not supply all that was missing, but it is clear from the problems he discusses in the first book of his diary, in 1835, that he must have assimilated an amazing amount of additional knowledge. He also took part in local activities, and was the centre (at least as far as literary efforts were concerned) of a circle of young men interested in art and literature. Inspired by acting companies, Hebbel founded amongst them an amateur theatre, of which he was the director; he even had the hope, at one time, of escaping from Wesselburen by becoming a professional actor, but a secret visit to Karl Lebrun, then director of the Stadttheater in Hamburg, brought disillusionment. Lebrun's advice was friendly but decisive, and that gate into the larger world was permanently closed.

Not wholly discouraged by the ill-success of his appeal to Uhland, Hebbel decided on the bold stroke (as he termed it to a friend) of writing to Oehlenschläger in Copenhagen in a similar strain, enclosing some of his poems as proof that he was a serious applicant for support. He was of course a Danish subject, and the Kings of Denmark had been noted for their assistance to artists and men of letters; he therefore hoped for Oehlenschläger's good offices in promoting his interest with the King. But here too disappointment was his lot. No answer appears to have been received from the Danish poet.[1]

Indirectly, however, the state of Denmark was to give some involuntary assistance. The question of the dependent states of Schleswig-Holstein had been causing trouble for some

[1] v. Letter to H. A. Th. Schacht, 12 Apr. 1835, in *Briefe*, ed. cit., vol. i, p. 33 and A. Sergel, *Oehlenschläger in seinen persönlichen Beziehungen zu Goethe, Tieck und Hebbel*, Rostock i. M., 1907, pp. 71–2, where the statement of Emil Kuh concerning Oehlenschläger's answer is disputed.

years. The publication, in 1830, of a pamphlet by a Frisian from the island of Sylt, entitled *Über das Verfassungswerk in Schleswig-Holstein*, proved a storm-centre, and although the author was arrested and punished, the effects of his protest continued to be felt. It was a time of emotional political unrest in Holstein, and although Hebbel, preoccupied with his own troubles, was by no means a political enthusiast, a poem which he wrote at this period on a subject taken from Dithmarschen history[1] produced an unexpected result. He sent it, with others, to the *Pariser Modeblätter*—a Hamburg journal edited by Amalia Schoppe—where it was published. The consequence was a communication from the editress, thanking him in encouraging terms for his contributions, and suggesting that he should continue them, at the same time mentioning the interest roused in Hamburg by the subject. To this appreciation Hebbel replied by asking for help, as he had asked for Uhland's and Oehlenschläger's. This time, the appeal was to meet with greater success. Dr. Amalia Schoppe was an energetic woman of forty-one, busied about the affairs of numerous protégés—obscure young men of letters whom she hoped to mother into fame. She bestirred herself effectually to seek help for Hebbel, whom she advised meanwhile to continue industrious in the pursuit of knowledge, to acquire the Latin tongue, and to content himself for the moment with remaining in his present position.

That this position was growing more unendurable as the years went by there is ample testimony. Hebbel's poetic powers were increasing with incredible rapidity; his resentment at the menial conditions of his life grew proportionately, and he withdrew himself more and more from the circle of his friends. Early in 1834 a plan for placing him in a Hamburg business was broached, but nothing further came of the negotiations, until in July of that year he received an enthusiastic letter from Amalia Schoppe, saying that an influential acquaintance had been moved to collect money enough for him to study in Hamburg. Other patrons were secured by her continued efforts; promises of free meals at

[1] *Die Schlacht bei Hemmingstedt.*

certain houses were obtained, and two trustees were appointed to supervise the use made of the fund for his support.

It is worth recording that Mohr, when applied to by Hebbel's protectress for a small contribution, refused to help, but wrote him a laudatory testimonial. We can be sure that it was with no little satisfaction that Hebbel crossed the threshold of the Kirchspielvogtei for the last time, when in the February of 1835 he finally set out on his journey to Hamburg, there to pursue a course of academic study.

II

HAMBURG AND MUNICH

WITH Hebbel's arrival in Hamburg, a new era begins, not only for him but for his biographers. Within a month after he had begun to lead the unfamiliar life of a poor scholar, he decided to keep a diary, and on 23 March 1835 the *Tagebücher* open with a delightful prefatory note, half solemn, half ironical. The new venture, he states, is not undertaken solely from the wish to assist his future biographer—that one will arise is certain 'bei meinen Aussichten auf die Unsterblichkeit'—but it is also to be 'ein Notenbuch meines Herzens'. For while other instruments sound ever the same notes, though in different combinations, the feelings of the human heart, once past, are gone for ever; each hour is a world, complete and self-contained. 'Und wer kann gleichgültig so manche tausend Welten in sich versinken sehen und wünscht nicht, wenigstens das Göttliche, sey es Wonne oder Schmerz, welches sich durch sie hinzog, zu retten?'

Hebbel's own wish, expressed in the year of his death, was that his 'Remains'—correspondence, diaries, and memoirs—should be published posthumously in his collected works; he recognized that they formed an integral part of his life-work, and would serve to illuminate the more public achievement already open to the world. Acute psychologist as he was, Hebbel was not likely to deceive himself on such a point; and even a cursory reading of the *Tagebücher* supplies abundant proof of their importance in any study of the poet and the man.

Indeed, few more fascinating original sources can be found than Hebbel's diaries. In them the whole man stands revealed—his strength and sturdy independence, his weaknesses and tender susceptibilities, his moods of depression, his moments of the poet's dream. In conversation, however intimate, between two persons, there seems ever a slight veil of separation; confession or revelation possesses a touch of the artist's detachment only lost under the stress of very strong emotion. Hebbel's conversation with his diary seems to achieve the impossible: it *is* the reflection of a mind and spirit, free from artistic shaping—the raw material of drama; yet only on comparatively rare occasions do the entries reveal emotional stress. For the most part, the impression is that of a thinker thinking aloud, an artist feeling audibly, a man living, as it were, on the screen, where pictures in rapid sequence follow one another.

From their very beginning, the diaries reflect Hebbel's dominant interest in literature, and in the problems which underlie artistic creation. They also reveal a striking fertility of invention: in March and April 1835—months of adjustment to entirely new conditions—ideas are already noted for a novel, a short story, and a comedy. From the entries we can follow the course of his reading, and watch a mature mind in the process of self-education. Throughout the diary of the Hamburg period indeed, there is an element of pathos in the miscellaneous items of information on widely differing subjects which are scattered over the pages, interspersed with quotations from poets, critics, and historians, or with sage reflections upon life. Knowledge and self-knowledge are acquired rapidly, and side by side; as early as July 1835 entries on Byron, Schiller, and Goethe show critical appreciation and a power of analysis applied equally to the processes of his own and to those of other minds. The man who can write at 22: 'Sehr oft ist das Wiedersehen erst die rechte Trennung. Wir sehen, dass der Andere uns entbehren konnte . . .'[1] and 'Der Tag vor dem Abschied ist das Kreuz über'm Grabe; er trägt die Grabschrift'[2] has not to await a further apprenticeship to suffering to stimulate his critical awareness of life. Such apprenticeship, however, did await him, and combined with the intensity of his perceptions, it threatened to overwhelm him. That it did not do so is perhaps solely due to the force of the creative impulse; without the expression of his experience in lyric verse Hebbel

[1] *Tagebücher*, ed. cit., vol. i. 24, 20 Apr. 1835.

[2] Ibid. 30, 4 May 1835.

might well have ceased to assert himself against the pressure of personal, social, and economic difficulties.

For the incongruity inherent in the situation soon made itself evident. A young man ripening into a poet, with a poet's quick response to life, and with years of experience behind him, set to study Latin under a tutor and to acquire sufficient information to enable him to pass the 'Maturitäts-examen' demanded of every intending University student—this was a difficult enough affair. But when in addition he was dependent for his bread on the favour of several patrons, had to eat his meals gratefully at different houses in turn throughout the week, and to render account to a supervisor appointed to administer the funds available, the position was a peculiarly unpleasant one. Nor was his patroness of a character to ease the situation. Dr. Amalia Schoppe was warm-hearted but exacting in her patronage, and of an emotional temperament; and Hebbel was not an easy protégé. The immediate cause of disagreement was the conduct of his friend Leopold Alberti, who played a treacherous part between them, but probably in any case a conflict would have arisen. The bitterness of experience inspires a later entry in the diary: 'Schwerer, als dankbar zu seyn, ist es, die Ansprüche auf Dank nicht zu übertreiben'.[1]

One solace only was Hebbel's in the uncongenial surroundings of Hamburg—the love and sympathy of a seamstress, Elise Lensing, with whose stepfather he lodged for a few weeks in the spring of 1835. Over eight years older than Hebbel, and without obvious attractions, she gave him a passionate and self-sacrificing love which he never returned in equal measure. She alone kept him upright, and by her sympathy encouraged him to continue when difficulties pressed most closely upon him. From her small earnings she gave him substantial material assistance, both in Hamburg and, later on, elsewhere. Clearly the seeds of conflict were sown in this relationship, which was from the first unequal. Elise was necessary to Hebbel, but her devotion could not obliterate the fundamental differences between them. His

[1] *Tagebücher*, ed. cit., vol. i. 222, 1 July 1836.

love would have been the only satisfying return for her self-sacrifice, and this—in the fullest sense—she never had.

For his introduction to her Hebbel had to thank Amalia Schoppe. The story—coloured no doubt by later experience of his protectress—is told four years later, in a retrospective survey of the account between them.[1] Dr. Schoppe had stepped in when Hebbel was in difficulties about a lodging and had temporarily secured a room 'bei der Mamsell Lensing', at the same time warning him—on the authority of a washerwoman, Hebbel avers—that her character was doubtful. After a short time, he moved to another lodging, but continued to visit Elise, whose kindness and single-mindedness had meanwhile dispelled the effects of initial prejudice. Malicious allusions to the friendship were frequently made by Dr. Schoppe; of all her quarrels with Hebbel, this appears to have been the most productive of the petty warfare which he so bitterly resented. The contrast between Amalia Schoppe's role of censorious benefactress and Elise's unconditional surrender of her heart and all she had was no doubt a factor in the situation: Hebbel was grateful for her love, and also for the fact that it was uncritical. Only later did he grow to demand of her a critical judgement incompatible with this. Meanwhile he turned to her in reaction against the petty trials of existence as a poor dependent; drinking coffee with her of an afternoon, in surroundings that she knew how to make cosy, he could forget that in return for other meals he was expected to be grateful, and learn Latin. The relationship was firmly established, and when Hebbel left Hamburg, he constantly wrote to Elise the most detailed accounts of his life and his affairs. She alone was privileged —if it was, as Hebbel considered it, a privilege[2]—to know intimately the hopes of achievement, the despair of failure, the shifts of destitution which he experienced on his departure from Hamburg.

For after a year spent in the effort, Hebbel felt that the task of filling in the gaps in his early education and qualifying

[1] *Tagebücher*, ed. cit., vol. i. 1701, 16 Oct. 1839.

[2] Letter to Elise Lensing, 19 Dec. 1836, *Briefe*, ed. cit., vol. i, p. 136.

himself for an academic course was still discouragingly far from completion, while the conditions of his benefaction made it increasingly hard to endure the situation. Matters came to a head in the spring of 1836; he decided to leave Hamburg and move to Heidelberg, in company with his friend and teacher Gravenhorst. His plan was to attend courses in Law at the University there, and when Dr. Krafft of the Johanneum in Hamburg refused to give him the testimonial of attainments ('Zeugnis der erlangten Reife') required of an intending University student, Hebbel determined to dispense with it and hear lectures without matriculating. After some delays and hesitations, and only after proof was forthcoming that Dr. Amalia Schoppe had been brought to agree, Pastor Schmalz, the supervisor of the fund for Hebbel's maintenance, acceded to his urgent request for the 230 Marks remaining from that fund. At the same time, however, Hebbel's protectress, disappointed at his decision, and influenced by the machinations of Alberti, wrote in curt terms to state that she would take no further interest in his affairs. That Hebbel had as yet no suspicion of the part played by Alberti is evident from the tone of a long paragraph about the latter's future in a letter written to Elise from Wesselburen in February 1836. The two friends had travelled together to their native country, that Hebbel might see his mother before leaving on his southward journey. Shortly before his departure from Hamburg at the end of March, the intrigues of Alberti were discovered by Amalia Schoppe, and she made amends, at least in form. But that her friendly feelings for Hebbel were not wholly restored we know from her subsequent behaviour, and from his own summary of the matter in Munich, three years later.[1]

Meanwhile, at least a hope of freedom from irksome conditions lay before him; and so, in spite of some misgivings, he set out on his journey by Braunschweig and Frankfurt to Heidelberg, where he arrived on Easter Eve; by Easter Day he was installed in a comfortable lodging near the University.

Hebbel's letters from Heidelberg, where he remained five

[1] *Tagebücher*, ed. cit., vol. i. 1494, 14 Feb. 1839.

months, do not in general suggest that he found the life congenial. He was often melancholy. Naturally, perhaps, this state of mind is more frequently reflected in the letters to Elise than elsewhere; but it is also evident in a letter to a Wesselburen friend, where we may take it to be more than a passing fit of nerves or a flatteringly regretful memory.[1] Student life did not attract him—nor, with rare exceptions, did his student companions. He felt older, maturer than they—concerned, as they seldom were, with the serious problems of life: 'Die tollen Wellen des academischen Lebens rollen an mir, wie an einem Felsblock, vorüber und reissen mich selten mit sich fort. . . . All mein Bestreben ist auf poetisches Schaffen und practisches Wirken gerichtet; was damit nicht nach irgend einer Seite hin zusammen hängt, das ist für mich nicht da.'[2]

He made efforts, nevertheless, to take some small part in community life and attended the 'Kneipe' once a week. After some tribulation on account of his long hair and unfashionable wardrobe, he gained the reputation of an 'original' by composing some occasional verses, and was thereafter left in peace. One great friendship, however, was begun in Heidelberg—Emil Rousseau, a young man of twenty with some poetic talent, attached himself ardently to Hebbel, and the friendship survived even Hebbel's conception of his duty as Mentor to Rousseau's youthful efforts and opinions. The latter was also responsible for another companionship—he gave Hebbel a dog, Hänschen, henceforth the inseparable comrade of all his walks and journeys: 'ein schönes, braunes, wohlgenährtes Thier mit weissen Pfoten und dem appetitlichsten Gesicht.'[3]

The diary gives little more information than the letters. There were moments when the mountain landscape charmed him, as when he climbed the Königsstuhl at night to await the sunrise,[4] saw a sunset reflected in the Neckar,[5] or watched

[1] Letter to Kirchspielschreiber Voss, 14 July 1836, *Briefe*, ed. cit., vol. i, p. 77.
[2] Ibid. p. 70.
[3] Letter to Voss, 14 July 1836, *Briefe*, ed. cit., vol. i, p. 72.
[4] *Tagebücher*, ed. cit., vol. i. 192, 27–8 June 1836.
[5] Ibid. 314, 31 Aug. 1836.

a storm break over the hills.[1] But at other times the neighbourhood was 'trist', the mountains disappointing in contrast to their imagined grandeur, and he thought regretfully of the northern plain. He attended lectures assiduously enough, but there is little reflection of enthusiasm in the journal. There are, however, a number of entries recording facts evidently new to him—in particular such as he retained from the discourses of the physicist Munke. The few lectures in Law which, as a non-matriculated student, he was permitted to attend, did not arouse in him any desire to continue in this study; for the abstractions of legal theory he had no taste, though concrete illustrations instanced by a lecturer would seize on his imagination, and be noted in the diary. A conversation with Thibaut, whose courses on Roman Law he had attended regularly, and who advised him to follow his own bent, finally determined him to abandon jurisprudence. Throughout the Heidelberg time literary plans and hopes for the future were his chief interest and consolation; soon after his arrival he had begun to revise and copy out his poems, with the idea of publication in a volume,[2] and in July had written to Uhland, enclosing some lyrics and asking for permission to dedicate the collection to him, should it be published. To this letter he received no answer; later it appeared that it had not reached its destination. Meanwhile Hebbel, though chagrined, did not allow himself to be discouraged; indeed his measured judgement of the episode contrasts most favourably with his usual acute susceptibility to personal or social slights.[3] Where poetry was concerned, he felt sure of himself.

Fruitless efforts to find a publisher for five short prose tales, however, caused him more discouragement. Two were sent to Hauff, the editor of the *Morgenblatt* in Stuttgart, but there was no reply. (Hebbel discovered in the autumn that this letter and manuscript had also gone astray.) Other attempts were equally without result;[4] and the 'Reisebeschreibung' from

[1] *Tagebücher* ed. cit., vol. i. 327, 2 Sept. 1836.
[2] Letter to Elise Lensing, 3 May 1836, *Briefe*, ed. cit., vol. i, p. 55.
[3] Letter to Elise Lensing, 3 Sept. 1836, *Briefe*, ed. cit., vol. i, p. 91.
[4] *v. infra*, pp. 48–9.

which he hoped to earn at least a small sum was not completed.

Everything seemed to urge him to try his fortune elsewhere. For a time he had the notion of going, by way of Hamburg, to Kiel or Berlin and of continuing his studies. But the decision to give up jurisprudence and devote all his energies to literary activities, combined with his dislike of returning to Hamburg without having accomplished his aim, soon caused him to abandon the idea. Only Elise drew him northwards; and this attraction weighed little against the hopes he cherished of literary work in Munich. Rousseau had recommended Munich, and Hebbel wrote on 20 August to Elise, stating his reasons for deciding to go there. At the same time he accepted a loan she had already offered, and hoped soon to earn enough, by work for the Bavarian journals, to repay it.

On 12 September he left Heidelberg, and with a knapsack on his back made the journey on foot to Munich. On the way he visited Strassburg and Stuttgart, where he had an interview with Hauff, and was told that correspondence from Munich would be welcomed for his paper. From Stuttgart he went on to Uhland in Tübingen, and was deeply disappointed to find no trace of the magnetic personality he had expected. 'Ich werde nie wieder eine menschliche Persönlichkeit zu einem Focus ihrer geistigen Hervorbringungen machen und—dies ist ein sehr grosser Gewinn!—nie wieder vor irgend einen Menschen mit Befangenheit hintreten.'[1] One satisfaction, however, resulted from the interview: Uhland's silence was explained by the discovery that Hebbel's letter and manuscript had miscarried. Little could thus be expected from the visit, since Uhland, Hebbel realized, knew nothing of his poetic work. He left Tübingen with an illusion lost, but perhaps with some assurance gained, and proceeded by Ulm to Munich, where after an eighteen days' journey he arrived at the end of September.

The years that Hebbel spent in Munich (September 1836 to March 1839) were probably the darkest period of his life;

[1] Letter to Elise Lensing, 30 Sept. 1836, *Briefe*, ed. cit., vol. i, p. 98.

in them also the process of self-education was completed. The hopes with which he set out were high. He was confident that he would be able to pay his way for the winter by articles written for the *Morgenblatt*, since Hauff had welcomed the suggestion;[1] he was determined to study the history of art and the history of nations—both, in his view, essential to the equipment of a serious poet; his head was full of plans for completing works already begun and for embarking on fresh literary enterprises: 'jetzt ergiesst sich mir der Strom des geistigen Lebens durch alle Adern, brausend und überschäumend, als wäre er nie gefesselt gewesen'.[2] He notes in the diary the day on which he saw for the first time a Raphael Madonna, and records his feelings on entering the Glyptothek: 'das Gefühl, was ein Schnitter hat, wenn er das Aehrenfeld betritt'.[3] But it is not long before hope is tempered by misgivings. He realizes his own inability to write quickly, his equal inability to write anything that does not contain his deepest thought and feeling; and fear seizes him by his imagination.

'Jene seltne Fruchtbarkeit, die einigen, auch wahrhaft berufenen, Dichtern gegeben ist, hat mir die Natur versagt; bevor aber die Welt die tieferen Fäden, die sich, will's Gott, durch die besten meiner Arbeiten als befruchtende Adern hindurchziehen, erkennt, kann ich zehnmal verhungern. In der That ist's die Furcht, zu verhungern, die mich jetzt fast stündlich quält. Auf fünf Monate bin ich noch versehen . . . der Himmel mag wissen, wie's dann werden wird.'[4]

The spectre thus raised in the first months of his Munich sojourn was to be his constant companion. Though there is little doubt that it was to a large extent a nervous obsession—perhaps from childhood's days—and that the situation was less alarming than Hebbel painted it, the effects of his apprehensions were real enough. Hunger, in a more literal sense

[1] Letter to Elise Lensing, 17 Oct. 1836, *Briefe*, ed. cit., vol. i, pp. 103–4.

[2] Letter to H. A. Th. Schacht, [19] Oct. 1836, *Briefe*, ed. cit., vol. i, p. 111.

[3] *Tagebücher*, ed. cit., vol. i. 372, 29 Sept. 1836.

[4] Letter to Elise Lensing, 29 Nov. 1836, *Briefe*, ed. cit., vol. i, p. 118.

than he had yet known it, did become an actual experience; ridden by his fears for the future, he contented himself for some time with a diet of bread and coffee at midday—a diet carefully concealed from the household where he lodged, lest they should take advantage of his lack of means.[1] The deficiencies of his wardrobe were more difficult to hide. Visits were at first excluded: 'Das geht nun einmal nicht ohne Garderobe, der Geist . . . ersetzt Alles, nur keine Hosen'.[2] Like a melancholy refrain, the problem of respectable clothes recurs throughout Hebbel's letters to Elise; by March 1837, when he has earned 'at the most 10 Thaler' and the remainder of Elise's loan will only last two months, he confesses that the worst trial of all is the state of his garments. 'Ach, wie glücklich sind die Hunde, dass sie ihre Garderobe mit zur Welt bringen!' 'Woher bei solchem Druck', he continues in passionate protest, 'jene geistige Freiheit, die zur Hervorbringung trefflicher Werke erfoderlich ist, kommen soll, begreifst Du gewiss eben so wenig, wie ich.'[3] And not for the first time, the thought of putting an end to the misery crosses his mind. By the autumn of 1837 he is driven to accept Elise's renewed offers of help, and begs her to use the money in Hamburg to buy him a new coat; '*abgerissen* duldet man mich schwerlich länger im Ausland'.[4] A page of instructions on measurements and economy follows; Elise, however, disregarded the second, and sent him a complete new outfit, a gift for which his gratitude and satisfaction were pathetically intense;[5] he had now 'a wardrobe for two years', and the police would place no obstacle in the way of his permit for further residence in Munich. When such were the difficulties of procuring a new suit of clothes, it was no wonder that the strain began to tell on Hebbel's nerves and physique. Sleeplessness and rheumatic pains—each intensifying the other—had attacked him by the spring of 1837, and throughout the first half of this year a series of bodily ills succeeded one

[1] Letter to Elise Lensing, 29 Nov. 1836, *Briefe*, ed. cit., vol i, p. 120.

[2] Ibid., p. 125.

[3] Letter to Elise Lensing, 14 Mar. 1837, *Briefe*, ed. cit., vol. i, p. 181.

[4] Letter to Elise Lensing, 19 Oct. 1837, *Briefe*, ed. cit., vol. i, p. 236.

[5] Letter to Elise Lensing, 7 Dec. 1837, *Briefe*, ed. cit., vol. i, p. 241.

another. Writing had become more difficult—especially the composition of the articles for the *Morgenblatt*, which alone seemed to promise payment. 'Alles fällt mir gegenwärtig schwer . . . so wie ich eine Zeile geschrieben habe, fühl' ich mich nicht zu der zweiten aufgelegt, sondern dazu, die erste wieder auszustreichen. Wie das enden soll, weiss ich nicht.'[1] By the June of 1837, although his articles had been published in the journal, there was no word of the remuneration due for them; Hauff had not replied either to inquiry on this point or to the manuscripts of the prose tales which Hebbel had submitted to him for publication. In response to a further letter, he did, however, receive his first payment from Stuttgart on 27 June;[2] but the uncertainty meanwhile made it all the more difficult to concentrate on work which at best was not the most congenial to his temper. It grew more and more distasteful to him 'über Nichts viel Worte zu machen und Alltagsgeschichten mit einem gefälligen Ausdruck zu vergolden',[3] while his own work, into which he put all he had, could find no market. For *Barbier Zitterlein*, the one tale already printed elsewhere, he had not received a penny; even to the most sanguine, the attempt to live by his writings would not have seemed encouraging. The frequent moods of despair revealed in letters to Elise are not surprising—rather are we amazed at the creative vitality which in such disappointments could still conceive fresh ideas for treatment in verse or prose, and still evolve plan after plan for the publication of the poems and tales already written. In January 1837 he writes to Elise of an idea for a tragedy—a new *Jungfrau von Orleans*, which should make of the historical figure something worthy of her great achievement. The spirit of Schiller's drama did not appeal to him: 'In der Geschichte *lebt*, *leidet* und *stirbt* sie schön; in Schiller's Trauerspiel—*spricht* sie schön.'[4] But, he adds, such a drama cannot be completed for some years. Although Hebbel did not pursue this idea very far, and although later he retracted part of the judge-

[1] Letter to Elise Lensing, 30 Jan. 1837, *Briefe*, ed. cit., vol. i, p. 161.
[2] *Tagebücher*, ed. cit., vol. i. 771, 27 June 1837.
[3] Letter to Elise Lensing, 19 Oct. 1837, *Briefe*, ed. cit., vol. i, p. 232.
[4] Letter to Elise Lensing, 17 Jan. 1837, *Briefe*, ed. cit., vol. i, p. 145.

ment passed on Schiller's play,[1] there is some evidence to show kinship between his idea of the Maid and his conception of Judith: '. . . ein einfach-edles Mädchen, das, nachdem Gott durch seinen schwachen Arm ein Wunder in's Leben gerufen, vor sich selbst, wie vor einem dunklen Geheimniss, zurück schauderte.'[2]

In February, 1837, he writes of a new idea for a drama, 'ein hoher dramatischer Stoff, dessgleichen noch nie behandelt ist und den auch nur Wenige behandeln könnten'[3] —the character of Alexander the Great, 'who during the whole of his life was in doubt whether he was the son of Philip or of Jupiter Ammon'. It is again the abnormal situation that lures him; but he adds, characteristically, that the poet who desires to portray it must seek its origin in the age and in the thought of the age. Two care-free years—he exclaims—and it might be achieved.

In June he tells Elise that a new novel is begun; after hesitating among three or four subjects, he has chosen one which shall 'mirror the whole age and explain it'. The hero of *Der deutsche Philister* was to be a man who is always in the right, but for the wrong reasons.[4] By November he had planned to deal in this work with the attempts to reintroduce Jesuitism, and had determined that he would need at least eighteen months to finish it;[5] a year later he re-read the two completed chapters with some satisfaction, and half decided to take it up again, but the novel was eventually destroyed in a fit of discouragement.[6]

In March 1838 the first mention in the letters of a comedy, *Der Diamant*, occurs, and coupled with it, a characteristic paragraph of contempt for the standards of the theatre. But as there would be no question of getting it performed 'bei meinem bekannten Glücksstern', he added, there was ad-

[1] Letter to Elise Lensing, 18 June 1837, *Briefe*, ed. cit., vol. i, pp. 215–16.
[2] Letter to Elise Lensing, 15 Feb. 1837, *Briefe*, ed. cit., vol. i, p. 170; cp. also *Tagebücher*, ed. cit., vol. i. 1011, 6 Mar. 1838.
[3] Letter to Elise Lensing, 21 Feb. 1837, *Briefe*, ed. cit., vol. i, p. 174.
[4] Letter to Elise Lensing, 18 June 1837, *Briefe*, ed. cit., vol. i, p. 215.
[5] Letter to Elise Lensing, 26 Nov. 1837, *Briefe*, ed. cit., vol. i, p. 240.
[6] Letter to Gustav Kühne, 4 Mar. 1850, *Briefe*, ed. cit., vol. iv, p. 201.

ditional reason for disregarding the prevailing taste. Progress with the comedy was interrupted, and in September he admitted difficulty with the dramatic form; actually it was not completed until November 1841.[1]

Plain as it is from Hebbel's letters that his creative energies were constantly at work, the diary alone reveals how thickly seeds were sown during the Munich years. Apart from innumerable references to smaller projects and a more or less continuous stream of lyric production, clues to the dramas begin to occur as early as the spring of 1837. Long afterwards, in *Ein Geburtstag auf der Reise*, Hebbel, recalling the years of conflict and travail in Munich, recalled also the shadowy figures that were beginning to take form:

> Hier zeigte, wie im Traume,
> Sich mir die Judith schon!
> Dort unter'm Tannenbaume
> Sah ich den Tischlersohn,
> Da drüben winkte leise
> Mir Genovevas Hand,
> Und in des Weihers Kreise
> Fand ich den Diamant.

And that this was no golden enchantment of memory, obscuring chronological fact, the diary will testify. 'Es giebt keinen ärgern Tirannen, als den gemeinen Mann im häuslichen Kreise'[2] suggests Meister Anton, and not only to the hunter of clues; but 'Klara dramatisch'[3] is unimpeachable evidence. When Hebbel formulates the tragic theme underlying the story of Joan of Arc as the idea that even a divine Power, after disturbing the world order by acting directly on an individual, cannot save that individual from the destruction consequent on its response,[4] we have a mental image of the later Judith; and when in the next entry a picture of Napoleon as a tragic hero (a favourite conception with Hebbel at this time) contains a reference to 'den einen Fehler . . .,

[1] *Tagebücher*, ed. cit., vol. ii. 2392, 29 Nov. 1841.
[2] *Tagebücher*, ed. cit., vol. i. 677, 4 Apr. 1837.
[3] Ibid. 1517, 24 Feb. 1839.
[4] Ibid. 1011, 6 Mar. 1838.

dass er sich die Kraft zutraut, Alles durch sich selbst, durch seine eigne Person, ohne Mitwirkung, ja Mitwissen, Anderer ausführen zu können', Holofernes is irresistibly suggested. The entry 'Durch Dulden Thun: Idee des Weibes'[1] is marked by a marginal note of reference to Judith; it applies equally to the figure of Genoveva, as Hebbel had outlined it in a criticism of Maler Müller's drama three weeks previously: '. . . himmlische Schönheit, die durch sich selbst, durch ihren eignen Glanz, ihren göttlichen Adel, in Marter und Tod stürzt'.[2]

These were the figures that stirred into life while Hebbel was in Munich—too shadowy, perhaps too precious, to be confided to any save the diary. It is only on realizing such a background that we can understand either the determination which carried him through the privations and misery of these years, or the amazing productivity of the years which immediately succeeded them. But when such was the seed-time, what wonder if the harvest were tragedy?

Sometimes, however, the skies were blue in Munich. The diary—in this a more unbiased witness than the letters—records that Hebbel was not without his consolations. As early as December 1836, an entry runs: 'Morgens 6 Uhr mit der liebsten, theuersten Beppy eine Adventsmusik . . . gehört. Der Morgen in der Stadt ganz, wie der Abend. . . . Die herrliche Musik, nach und nach durch die Fenster erst das bestimmtere *Blau* des Himmels, dann die zitternde Helle des Tags'.[3]

The 'liebste, theuerste Beppy', to whose simple religious ardour Hebbel owed this moment of splendour, was Josepha Schwarz, daughter of Anton Schwarz, a carpenter. Hebbel had made her acquaintance soon after his arrival in Munich, for in October he quotes her in his diary; by mid-December it is obvious that they have become intimate. The liaison lasted until he left Munich, with moments of quarrel and estrangement, and outbursts of nervous irritability on his part such

[1] *Tagebücher*, ed. cit., vol. i. 1516, 24 Feb. 1839.
[2] Ibid. 1475, 2 Feb. 1839.
[3] Ibid. 460, 3 Dec. 1836.

as those nearest him had always to endure. Josepha was artless and affectionate, simple alike in thought and dealings; she had nothing to offer to his intellect, but she would prattle to him of the practices of her religion, or describe to him her extraordinarily vivid and varied dreams. Hebbel noted many of these *obiter dicta* in the diary, and through the bare record his pleasure in her naïveté can be felt. Generous and devoted, she forgave him when he tormented her and himself by bitter words and irritable scenes. Once, according to an entry in the diary, she had made up her mind, after a quarrel, to have no more to do with him; then she thought of all the holes there were in his stockings, and changed her mind.[1] Hebbel might well comment on her patience and endurance; like Elise, and even Rousseau, she paid the penalty of his power to dominate her heart. But in the circumstances, it is less difficult to forgive him for wounding her by his nervous outbursts than for taking up a censorious attitude towards a previous love affair of hers. Beppy may have been insignificant, but she gave him some kind of companionship, and warm affection; she mended his linen and did him many small services—especially after the spring of 1838, when he went to lodge with the Schwarz family on her account. There were moments when he appreciated her devotion: in June 1838 he promised to send her 100 Gulden within two and a half years after his return to Hamburg. 'Dies soll meine heiligste Schuld seyn!' he adds.[2] Josepha, it appears, took their connexion more seriously than Hebbel; but it was foredoomed to oblivion as soon as he lost sight of her. Later on, when he left Munich in the spring of 1839, she accompanied him for two hours on his road; and with innumerable tears they drank their farewells at a wayside inn. So she fades out of the diary, and out of Hebbel's life.[3] At the other end of that journey, Elise came to meet him.

It is probable that Beppy's affection, more than anything

[1] *Tagebücher*, ed. cit., vol. i. 1458, 20 Jan. 1839.

[2] Ibid. 1178, 9 June 1838. No record of such a payment appears to exist.

[3] A subsequent reference occurs in a letter to Elise Lensing, 25 July 1840: 'Das Verhältniss in München *muss* ich aufheben, es geht nicht länger' (*Briefe*, ed. cit., vol. ii, p. 91).

else, helped to tide Hebbel over the early months in Munich, when apart from her he was solitary. From 13 April 1837, however, he had the company of his Heidelberg friend, Emil Rousseau; on that day he writes with a pleasure engagingly naïve: 'Heute ist ein glücklicher Tag für mich gewesen. 1. erhielt ich heut morgen 8 Louis d'ore aus Berlin. 2. kam Rousseau. 3. kam er 1½ Tag früher, als er mir geschrieben hatte. 4. liess ich heut Abend mein Licht zu Boden fallen, ohne dass es zerbrach.'[1] The friendship, which at Heidelberg had been unduly one-sided, had by means of an intimate correspondence developed into a real intercourse. Rousseau's ardent attachment was no less, but Hebbel now found in him a maturer mind and a steadier discipleship; and during the time they were together in Munich a relationship of intimate affection was established. Rousseau put his library at his friend's disposal—in the circumstances a considerable service; he persuaded him to eat a reasonable meal at midday, for which, Hebbel admits, it was 'high time';[2] and in the autumn of 1837, it was Rousseau who made a fair copy of 113 lyric poems to be sent to Uhland. For Hebbel had determined to make a second attempt to enlist the latter's aid towards publication of the lyrics, and in November 1837 he wrote, recalling their meeting in Tübingen, and asking for permission to dedicate the poems to Uhland, should a publisher be found. The answer, eagerly awaited, did not arrive until February 1838. It was friendly and—as far as the lyrics were concerned—encouraging; but Uhland gave small hopes of publication. Cotta, whom he had approached, feared that he had undertaken to print too much lyric poetry; and a fire which subsequently broke out at the printing house gave him an extra reason for refusal. Hebbel received a polite letter of excuse in February, together with an offer to consider separate poems for the *Morgenblatt*. Characteristically, he was more cheered by Uhland's favourable opinion than discouraged by Cotta's refusal; and on the very day he received his manuscript again, he dispatched it to Campe in Hamburg for

[1] *Tagebücher*, ed. cit., vol. i. 685, 13 Apr. 1837.
[2] Letter to Elise Lensing, 24 May 1837, *Briefe*, ed. cit., vol. i, p. 205.

consideration. Should Campe accept the poems, he wrote to Elise, the way would be clear until another work, more likely to find favour with a publisher, should be finished.[1] Then, in a year's time, he and Rousseau would move to Hamburg; by that time, the latter would have taken his doctor's degree and literary activities would employ them both. But Campe refused to publish the lyrics. His answer, however, was in terms which, to Hebbel at least, compensated for the disappointment. The poems had been sent to Gutzkow for criticism; his judgement was favourable, and his observations unexpectedly appreciative. But from a practical standpoint neither could foresee profit from a volume of lyrics by an unknown poet, and advised gradual publication for at least a year. Gutzkow added a promise to accept some for the *Telegraph*; Campe offered to advance half of the sum asked for by Hebbel for the volume.

Of Gutzkow and the opinions of his circle, however, Hebbel had a distrust so great that he decided not to write direct in answer to the offer of publication in the *Telegraph*, but to reply in general terms to Campe; he wished to be free, in literary matters as in others, to take his own way unhampered by obligations. It was a characteristic attitude—equally characteristic was his acceptance, even if reluctant, of Elise's very considerable sacrifices. The one constituted for him an intellectual, the other an ethical obligation; and, unmindful of the practical considerations involved, he could least easily endure to contract the former. Plans were formed, at this time, of active critical warfare; Hebbel was to write a series of criticisms on 'die gerühmten Productionen der modernen Literatur',[2] and he and Rousseau were to set up a critical journal in Hamburg in the following year.

Meanwhile Rousseau had been preparing with untiring diligence to take the degree of D.Phil. in Munich. He did so in August 1838, and Hebbel, whom he called on to oppose his theses, had the novel experience of speaking before a large and critical audience. Rousseau then left for his home in

[1] Letter to Elise Lensing, 23 Feb. 1838, *Briefe*, ed. cit., vol. i, p. 266.
[2] Letter to Elise Lensing, 14 Aug. 1838, *Briefe*, ed. cit., vol. i, p. 293.

Ansbach; Hebbel was to follow him in a short time and spend some weeks there with him. But two swift calamities intervened. On 16 September, only a few days after he had first heard of her illness, Hebbel had news from Wesselburen of his mother's death. On 17 September, he heard from Rousseau's father that Emil was seriously ill; a gastric fever turned to typhus, and on 2 October Rousseau succumbed to it. Two days later, Hebbel knew that he had lost his friend as well as his mother. 'Erst jetzt', he wrote to Elise, 'ist die Welt mir öde'.[1]

The immediate effect of the double blow was overwhelming—though it may be surmised that the second grief dulled, to some extent, the acuteness of the first. Hebbel had seen little of his mother since leaving Wesselburen, but one of his bitterest trials had been the inability to do anything to help her in her extreme poverty; here too Elise had stepped in and had sent money in his name. It had been his constant hope that a turn of fortune would soon enable him to give her substantial aid and so repay, in some small degree, her firm belief in him. Now he felt that much of the purpose had gone out of life; the future fame in which at moments he still trusted would no longer bring with it that satisfaction. If at the same time he debated whether her death were not an omen that the future held no promise, the reflection was hardly surprising.[2] Rousseau's death meant the loss of an actual and constant companion, whose absence vividly affected almost every daily activity. Hebbel was conscious, too, of the rare quality of that devotion which had kept their intercourse so free of friction, in spite of his own difficult temperament and frequently overstrung nerves. He may have divined that he would never meet with another friend like Rousseau, and the world seemed very empty.

His first reaction to the changed conditions was the impulse to leave Munich at once, instead of in the spring as he had planned. The dreary prospect of the winter's solitude, and the conviction that in such a state of mind and nerves he

[1] Letter to Elise Lensing, 5 Oct. 1838, *Briefe*, ed. cit., vol. i, p. 326.
[2] Letter to Elise Lensing, 17 Sept. 1838, *Briefe*, ed. cit., vol. i, p. 312.

would be incapable of writing, drove him to consider an immediate departure for Hamburg. But he was determined, in order to save expense, to do the journey across Germany on foot; and on practical grounds, to begin such an adventure with the advent of winter seemed highly inadvisable. An added reason for delay was the fact that at this time he was suffering from rheumatism in the chest. Moreover, he was anxiously awaiting a letter from Tieck, to whom he had sent *Schnock* in August, with a request to recommend it to a publisher. Tieck's silence gave Hebbel hope that some efforts were being made on his behalf, and he was reluctant to change his address before receiving a reply. All these arguments were marshalled in a series of letters to Elise, in which his painful indecision of mind is very evident. She was to give the casting vote; but it was impossible for her to do anything but urge him to come, and then let the decision rest with him. Eventually he decided to winter in Munich and travel on foot to Hamburg in the spring. Reasons enough were available for convincing Elise; but it may be surmised that an unacknowledged one existed, perhaps only in Hebbel's subconscious mind. The one problem above all others that awaited him in Hamburg was one he had not yet adequately faced—the problem of his relations with Elise, whose love he did not return in kind, and without whose help, as far as one can see, he would have starved. He might paint as darkly as he chose the difficulties that would attend his return—the mistaken kindnesses of Amalia Schoppe (with whom by this time relations had been resumed and who wished him to become a private tutor until he could afford to take his doctor's degree), the social problems of intercourse with former patrons, the lack of sympathy he felt with the leading men of letters in Hamburg. The greatest problem he ignored, or assumed that it had long ago been solved; and his last letters are full of references to the pleasure of seeing Elise, who at his urgent request was to come as far as Harburg to meet him.

The constant letters of the Munich period afford the first real opportunity for measuring the relationship of Hebbel and

Elise Lensing. One-sided as is the extant correspondence of these years, it reveals something of her as well as much of him. 'Dein ganzes Leben, Deine Art, zu seyn', he writes on one occasion after receiving a letter from her, 'tritt mir daraus entgegen; Leidenschaftlichkeit und Ruhe in buntem Gemisch'.[1] A curious fate seems to have attended the correspondence of these two actors in a drama which in its complex psychological reactions rivals Hebbel's own creations. We are compelled, during the whole period of their intimate relationship, to deduce from Hebbel's letters what Elise's contained, since none of hers are extant; on the other hand, Elise's letters to Hebbel and his wife, from 1847 to 1854,[2] are equally one-sided documents, though the light they throw on her temperament and character is of great value. Generosity and the impulse to service are the motives of her being, and Hebbel is not slow to recognize this fact:

'Ich weiss es wohl, Du giebst nicht, um wieder zu empfangen, Du willst durch eine Wohlthat nicht fesseln, sondern befreien, aber um so mehr drückt mich mein Unvermögen, Dir meinen Dank zu bezeigen. Ich darf es wahrlich für das grösste Glück meines Lebens halten, dass ich mit Dir zusammen gekommen bin; . . . und Du warst es ebenfalls, die bis jetzt, wie ein freundlicher Genius, in der Ferne Alles für mich that, was für mich gethan werden kann.'[3]

Only in the warmth and friendliness of her room would Christmas seem a festival, he writes in the same letter; but he adds 'man kann . . . *bei mir nur gewinnen*, wenn unzulässige sogenannte stärkere Gefühle sich in das der Freundschaft verwandeln. Mögtest Du doch dies einmal recht empfinden —wie glücklich wär' ich.'[4] The knot in the tangle lies here. Though Elise did not wish to fetter him, her every benefaction was a rivet in a chain, unacknowledged but not unfelt; though Hebbel was full of gratitude, he resented its implications.

[1] Letter to Elise Lensing, 12 Feb. 1837, *Briefe*, ed. cit., vol. i, pp. 162–3.

[2] *Elise Lensing: Briefe an Friedrich und Christine Hebbel*, herausgeg. im Auftrage des Hebbel-Museums in Wesselburen von Rudolf Kardel, Berlin u. Leipzig, 1928.

[3] Letter to Elise Lensing, 7 Dec. 1837, *Briefe*, ed. cit., vol. i, p. 242.

[4] Ibid., p. 244.

Even in Heidelberg, he writes in the journal: 'Die Weiber wollen keine Verhältnisse, als ewige';[1] three months later, an entry records the characteristic distinction: 'Der Mann hat sich mit Welt und Leben zu plagen, das Weib mit dem Mann',[2] and in December of that year occurs the sudden statement: 'Die Weiber kennen keinen Gott, als den Gott der Liebe und kein Sacrament, als das Sacrament der Ehe'.[3] Four days later, Hebbel answers a letter from Elise by expounding his views on marriage, in relation to his own life. Though recognizing the necessity of the social institution, he stresses his aversion to such a step:

'Mir wird alles *Unveränderliche* zur *Schranke* und alle Schranke zur *Beschränkung*. . . . Ich kann Alles, nur das nicht, was ich *muss*. Das liegt zum Theil in *meiner* Natur, zum Theil in der Natur des *Künstlers* überhaupt. . . . Nimm es als den höchsten Beweis meiner Achtung auf, dass ich Dir diese dunkelste Seite meines Ichs entschleiere; . . . *Neu* kann Dir das Alles freilich nicht seyn, denn oft genug hab' ich mich über jenen Punct ausgesprochen, aber hier ist's *zusammen gefasst*'.[4]

The individual may avoid the social necessity, Hebbel claims, if he is prepared to make some sacrifice for his freedom. The question that rises in our minds, however, may have risen in Elise's: whose, in such a case, is the sacrifice?

It is fairly evident from the letters of this period that the question of marriage was raised by Elise. In June 1837 Hebbel writes in harsh reproach that it is repellent to him to think '. . . dass Du der Humanität bloss darum geopfert hast, um die Göttin von ihrem Altar zu verdrängen und Dein eignes Bild hinauf zu setzen';[5] a little over a fortnight later the diary records that there are cases where the fulfilment of a duty is a sin.[6]

Equally plain is Hebbel's emphasis on the idea of 'friendship' in his letters to Elise. A conflict between two points of view is suggested by his insistent striking of this note.

[1] *Tagebücher*, ed. cit., vol. i. 162, 4 June 1836.

[2] Ibid. 343, 5 Sept. 1836.

[3] Ibid. 502, 15 Dec. 1836.

[4] Letter to Elise Lensing, 19 Dec. 1836, *Briefe*, ed. cit., vol. i, pp. 131–2.

[5] *Tagebücher*, ed. cit., vol. i. 772, 27 June 1837 (not in the *Briefe*).

[6] Ibid. 805, 14 July 1837.

'Mögest Du an jenem Abend recht klar und innig fühlen, ... dass Du in mir ewig Deinen *wärmsten Freund* haben wirst, der Dich an seinem höchsten würdigsten Leben Antheil nehmen lässt und Dir den Blick in die Tiefen seiner Seele frei stellt, dafür denn aber auch wohl verlangen darf, dass Du nimmer von ihm foderst, was er, als all seinem Denken und Empfinden widerstreitend, nicht gewähren kann. Was Deine Zukunft betrifft, so ist sie freilich nicht sicherer, aber jedenfalls eben so sicher, als die meinige, und wenn ich einst etwas hab', so werd' ich gewiss nicht vergessen, dass Du mit mir theiltest, als Du hattest. Dies ist mein Männerwort. Das zwischen uns bestehende Verhältniss ist auf einen sittlichen Felsen, auf gegenseitige Achtung, gegründet; trat ein Sinnen-Rausch dazwischen, so wollen wir das nicht bedauern, denn es war natürlich, ja, bei der Lage der Dinge, unvermeidlich, aber noch weniger wollen wir's bedauern, dass er vorüber ist.'[1]

The conclusion can hardly be evaded that Hebbel saw what he wished to see, and that his feelings differed profoundly from those of Elise on the terms of their relationship. In material affairs, she had to contend with the drawbacks of marriage without its advantages; not only did she supply funds, but she undertook the conduct of Hebbel's business in Hamburg, fulfilling endless commissions with publishers, editors, correspondents, and friends. He did not hesitate to protest when she did not devote enough attention to these demands in her replies, and instead wrote at tedious length—as remained her habit—on the minute affairs of indifferent acquaintances.[2] The real reliance which he placed on her zeal and her exertions may have compensated—as Hebbel suggested—for these efforts; it could not make up for the gulf that existed in the heart of their relations with each other. Ignore it as he would, Hebbel's return was bound to raise the problem with insistence; and to the sadness with which he left Munich there was added this doubt of what awaited him in Hamburg. For in spite of the anxieties and sorrows he had known there, Hebbel came to leave Munich with regret. The journal records his melancholy farewells to a town he

[1] Letter to Elise Lensing, 19 Dec. 1836, *Briefe*, ed. cit., vol. i, pp. 135–6.
[2] Letter to Elise Lensing, 14 Aug. 1838, *Briefe*, ed. cit., vol. i, pp. 289–92.

had loved even while he endured privations there. It was here that, in his own words, he had come to possess his personality;[1] here too, treasures of art had been his for the seeking, and the joys of companionship, at least for a while. 'Freilich hab' ich in München viel verloren, aber ich habe darin doch auch viel besessen'.[2] He left it on 11 March 1839 with a hope, recorded in the diary, of returning in the future, and set out on a journey that might have daunted the sturdiest of walkers. By way of Ingolstadt, Nürnberg, Coburg, Gotha, Göttingen, Hanover, Celle, and Soltau he reached Harburg on 30 March, where Elise arrived by steamer that same afternoon. On 31 March they proceeded to Hamburg, whose towers, when he first caught sight of them on the previous day, had caused Hebbel a 'feeling of suffocation'.[3] The privations of the long tramp had told upon him, and he had a feverish cold; the meeting with Elise was 'schmerzlich-süss . . . denn auch wir standen nicht zu einander, wie wir sollten und schlecht vergalt ich ihr ihre unendliche Liebe, ihre zahllosen Opfer, durch ein dumpfes, lebefaules Wesen'.[4]

If the return to Hamburg had looked dark from Munich, the omens of arrival did nothing to lighten the gloom.

[1] *Tagebücher*, ed. cit., vol. i. 1494, 14 Feb. 1839.
[2] Ibid. 1528, 10 Mar. 1839.
[3] *Tagebücher*, ed. cit., vol. ii. 2654, 'Reisejournal März 1839', 14 Feb. 1843.
[4] Ibid.

III

LYRIC AND 'NOVELLE'

For the first eight years of Hebbel's efforts at self-expression lyric verse was the medium to which he turned by instinct. It was his chosen form; through it he became convinced of his poetic vocation. And although the output of lyrical poems diminishes after 1839, with his growing absorption in the drama, it never ceases; throughout his life the lyric impulse recurs, in moments of energy and of emotion. The short prose tale, a *genre* which he also early essayed, plainly took second place, and the 'Novellen' shew a greater struggle with the form, an infinitely less spontaneous impulse than the poems. Lyric and 'Novelle' dominate the early period from 1831 to 1839, so that it seems natural to consider Hebbel's achievement in them here, although chronological sequence must of necessity be disregarded when the body of his lyric poetry is considered as a whole.

The picture of Hebbel's early development as a lyric poet is one of slowly growing independence. From the first Wesselburen poems, such as *Vor dem Reiten* or *Kains Klage*, there is a marked transition to a poem like *Der Knabe* (1833) The cadences of the first are almost purely Schillerian:

> Drum frisch, Kam'raden, und spornt das Ross,
> Hier gilt's, den Preis zu erringen—
> Muthvoll hinein—dem feigen Tross
> Der Sklaven wird's nimmer gelingen.
> Wer nicht freudig opfert den höchsten Glanz—
> Nie schmückt den würdig des Glückes Kranz!
>
> (*Vor dem Reiten.* 1829)

So too, in simpler vein, is the second:

> Und du wagst es, noch zu leben?
> Und du hoffst auf Gottes Huld?
> Niemals wird er dir vergeben,
> Denn zu gross ist deine Schuld.
>
> (*Kains Klage.* 1829)

Not only can definite similarities of expression and cadence be traced, but there is resemblance to Schiller's poetry in the generalized images, the vaguely musical words without a concrete picture, and the partiality for ethical exhortation. The second period of the Wesselburen lyrics, from 1831 to 1835, marks the influence of Uhland, and offers a striking contrast to the first. Extreme simplicity of phrase and metre, elliptical indication of a ballad-like situation, characterize the poems of this stage.

Die Mutter ist erblichen,
Arm Kindlein weint nach ihr.
'Sie ist zum Nachbar gangen
Und bringt viel Schönes Dir!'

Arm Kindlein legt sich gläubig
An eine fremde Brust,
Doch nimmer kehrt die Mutter
Und nimmer kehrt die Lust.—

Aus meiner armen Seele
Schwand mir jedwedes Glück,
Doch, klag' ich, ruft die Hoffnung:
'Es kommt erhöht zurück!'

Nun wohl! Will's aus dem Grabe
Auch nimmermehr ersteh'n,
So will ich, wie das Kindlein,
Doch hoffend untergeh'n.

(*Mein Glück.* 1831)

The reflective parallel is here clothed in a folk-song image, while in the final stanza the ethical application suggested by the picture is expressed in personal form; the method recalls Uhland, the reflection Schiller. But in a poem such as *Der Knabe*, written two years later, the influence of Uhland is seen at its highest point. The simple harmony of the language, the vivid pictures emphasizing the kinship between man and Nature, the way in which a mood of folk-tale and legend is evoked, all suggest the manner of the Swabian poet. Even more fundamental is the partiality of both lyrists for a dramatic type of subject, for a kind of emotion or reflection which can be expressed through an event of dramatic significance. The ballad form appeals to Hebbel, as it appealed both to Uhland and to Schiller; but Hebbel's treatment henceforward is pictorial and suggestive, rather than reflective and explicit.

By 1836 he had passed beyond the primarily imitative stage; in such a poem as *Bubensonntag*, written in that year, a personal method has already been evolved. A child's emotional reaction to the mystery of God is the subject of this poem. Nothing is presented but the supremely natural picture of the child who, disregarding the playthings and the pets of every day, hastens to church to be alone with God and see Him face to face, and each returning Sunday is convinced of His bodily presence by the awe and fear that make him close his eyes:

Kam mein Hündchen froh gesprungen,
Schalt ich: Komm mir nicht zu nah!
Kaum dass ich, zur Seite schielend
Nach der Vogelfalle sah.

Fiel die Kirchenthür nun knarrend
Hinter meinem Rücken zu,
Sprach ich furchtsam-zuversichtlich:
Jetzt allein sind Gott und du!

. . . .

Drang ein Schall zu mir herüber,
Dacht' ich: jetzt wirst du ihn schau'n!
Aber meine Augen schlossen
Sich zugleich vor Angst und Grau'n.

But in this picture of the child, where each outward incident carries forward the process of the spiritual drama, Hebbel succeeds in suggesting the whole attitude of mind whereby the human spirit supports its conviction of religious experience:

Und dies Zittern, dies Erbangen,
Und mein kalter Todesschweiss—
Dass der Herr vorbeigewandelt,
Galt mir Alles für Beweis.

Still und träumend dann zu Hause
Schlich ich mich in süsser Qual,
Und mein klopfend Herz gelobte
Sich mehr Muth fürs nächste Mal.

The restrained, allusive art of *Bubensonntag* showed Hebbel to have assimilated and transformed into a highly individual method that which in the earlier years he had so visibly learnt from others. With his singular self-knowledge, he realized the fact: '*Bubensonntag*', he wrote to Elise Lensing in 1838 when the poem had appeared in the *Morgenblatt für gebildete Leser*, 'ist vielleicht das Beste, was ich jemals gemacht habe'.[1]

The feeling of kinship with Nature, the appreciation of her phases and processes, already visible in some of the Hamburg lyrics, are more frequently reflected in the poems written in Munich between 1836 and 1839. Rarely, however, do we find a poem such as *Vorfrühling*, where both the lyric form and the impressionist picture of Nature in action recall the method of Goethe:

Wolkenmassen ballten
Sich der Sonne entgegen,
Doch durch tausend Spalten
Dringt der befruchtende Segen.

It is more characteristic of Hebbel to link the image of Nature to his mood, as in *Spaziergang am Herbstabend*. Still more suggestive of his later development is the poem *Winter-Landschaft*, where without definite comparison, and mainly by the force of the 'glaub' ich', the living figure of the bird relates the frozen landscape to the poet's cheerless heart:

Unendlich dehnt sie sich, die weisse Fläche,
Bis auf den letzten Hauch von Leben leer;
Die muntern Pulse stockten längst, die Bäche,
Es regt sich selbst der kalte Wind nicht mehr.

Der Rabe dort, im Berg von Schnee und Eise,
Erstarrt und hungrig, gräbt sich tief hinab,
Und gräbt er nicht heraus den Bissen Speise,
So gräbt er, glaub' ich, sich hinein in's Grab.

[1] Letter to Elise Lensing, 30 Sept. 1838, *Briefe*, ed. cit., vol. i, p. 321.

Die Sonne, einmal noch durch Wolken blitzend,
Wirft einen letzten Blick auf's öde Land,
Doch, gähnend auf dem Thron des Lebens sitzend,
Trotzt ihr der Tod im weissen Festgewand.

It is in this passionate fusing of the world outside and the human spirit of the poet that Hebbel's true gift as a lyrist seems to lie. Not by any means in all his lyrics—perhaps hardly even in the majority—does he succeed in producing such vivid awareness of relationship as will at once convince us; but his power to create the significant symbol grows. At its best, his lyric poetry is reflective, but indirectly so; reflection is the outcome and not the origin of the poetic conception. The first stanza of *Sommerbild* (1844) is a typical example of reflection issuing from an emotional awareness:

Ich sah des Sommers letzte Rose steh'n,
Sie war, als ob sie bluten könne, roth;
Da sprach ich schauernd im Vorübergeh'n:
'So weit im Leben ist zu nah am Tod!'

On the other hand *Blume und Duft*, written six years earlier, shows a less spontaneous impulse and more deliberate reflection:

In Frühlings Heiligthume,
Wenn Dir ein Duft an's Tiefste rührt,
Da suche nicht die Blume,
Der ihn ein Hauch entführt.

Der Duft lässt Ew'ges ahnen,
Von unbegränztem Leben voll;
Die Blume kann nur mahnen,
Wie schnell sie welken soll.

'Das ganze Gefühlsleben', Hebbel wrote in 1840, in a note on lyric form, 'ist ein Regen, das eben heraus gehobene Gefühl ist ein von der Sonne beleuchteter Tropfen.'[1] The individual moment of emotional life is the essence of the lyric: the more individual the poem, he says elsewhere, the more certainly will it have a general as well as a particular significance.[2] Feeling, not reason, is fundamental to it; the perfect lyric

[1] *Tagebücher*, ed. cit., vol. ii. 1953, 28(?) Mar. 1840.
[2] *Tagebücher*, ed. cit., vol. i. 1017, 7 Mar. 1838.

reveals the poetic idea to the spirit, not the intellect.[1] But the particular emotional moment must not be entirely dominant; for months after the death of Emil Rousseau, Hebbel could not write a poem in memory of him—the grief was too vivid and too sharply focussed. Not until 1841, in the *Alte Widmung dieser Gedichte*, did he succeed in giving form to the emotional impulse, and even so, the quality of the poem is uneven. The opposite extreme is shown in *Das abgeschiedene Kind an seine Mutter*, written to comfort Elise after the death of her little son, which leaves an impression of coldness mainly due to its curiously intellectualized character. Small wonder that it failed to comfort the mother in her grief; but the poet himself was too much in earnest over the argument to realize that the poem did not make that appeal to the 'Gemüth' which, in his critical theory, he considered essential. Hebbel's problem as a lyrist was the problem which faced him as a dramatist—the interdependence of thought and feeling; and in the best of the lyrics, as in the great plays, the fusion is complete. Such a poem as *Herbstbild* (1852) shows this serene and certain balance:

Diess ist ein Herbsttag, wie ich keinen sah!
Die Luft ist still, als athmete man kaum,
Und dennoch fallen raschelnd, fern und nah,
Die schönsten Früchte ab von jedem Baum.

O stört sie nicht, die Feier der Natur!
Diess ist die Lese, die sie selber hält,
Denn heute lös't sich von den Zweigen nur
Was vor dem milden Strahl der Sonne fällt.

Lyrics in which there is no element of dramatic narrative do not form the major part of Hebbel's verse. Even in a poem such as *Das Grab* (1837) the purely lyric note is modified by the dream basis; situation and characterization are dramatically conceived to bear the irony of the final stanza:

Mir war, als müsst' ich graben
Und grub gar tief hinab;
Grub in die Läng' und Breite,
Am Ende ward's ein Grab.

[1] Letter to Elise Lensing, 18 Jan. 1838, *Briefe*, ed. cit., vol. i, p. 253.

War, weiss nicht wie, gezwungen,
Hab's nimmer gern gethan,
Doch sollt' ich, was ich wünschte,
Zuletzt als Lohn empfah'n.

Das Grab war aufgeworfen,
Matt sank mir Arm und Bein,
Ich hatte Nichts mehr zu wünschen
Und legte mich selbst hinein.

It was indeed natural that Hebbel, with his bent towards the drama, should tend to clothe thought and sentiment in dramatic narrative, and from the early Wesselburen poems onwards, ballads and tales in verse form a considerable section of his poetic work. In a letter to Elise written in 1837, he draws the parallel between verse-tale and drama: 'Die Idee einer echten Romanze, die bloss in der Länge, aber nicht in der Würde, dem höchsten Drama nachsteht . . . kommt so selten, wie die Idee zu einem Faust oder einem Macbeth';[1] and *Schön Hedwig* (1838) was written by way of protest against Halm's *Griseldis*, on the theme of Kleist's *Käthchen von Heilbronn*—'womanhood in conflict with itself'.[2] The poem is attractive in its simplicity of expression and rapidity of movement, but Hebbel's power at this time lay in the treatment of sombre rather than of cheerful themes. *Der Haideknabe* (1844) with its mood of foreboding gradually deepening into horror, gives more scope to his gift for creating atmosphere. In this poem too are seen a mastery of form, a command of swift, significant, elliptical dialogue, which show Hebbel as a ballad-writer of distinction. The dream motif recurs, but with an unusual intensification—the boy's vision fulfils itself by means of his very efforts to avert it.

We are plunged straightway into the dramatic situation by the first two stanzas:

Der Knabe träumt, man schicke ihn fort
Mit dreizig Thalern zum Haide-Ort,
  Er ward drum erschlagen am Wege
  Und war doch nicht langsam und träge.

[1] Letter to Elise Lensing, 14 Mar. 1837, *Briefe*, ed. cit., vol. i, p. 183.
[2] Letter to Elise Lensing, 20 Nov. 1838, *Briefe*, ed. cit., vol. i, p. 361.

Noch liegt er im Angstschweiss, da rüttelt ihn
Sein Meister, und heisst ihm, sich anzuzieh'n
Und legt ihm das Geld auf die Decke
Und fragt ihn, warum er erschrecke.

Three verses of dramatic dialogue follow, and the boy is driven to obey. His instinctive cry:

'Ach Meister, mein Meister, sie schlagen mich todt,
Die Sonne, sie ist ja wie Blut so roth!'

is taken up and amplified in the description of the heath:

Hinaus aus der Stadt! Und da dehnt sie sich,
Die Haide, nebelnd, gespenstiglich,
Die Winde darüber sausend.
'Ach, wär' hier Ein Schritt, wie tausend!'

He begs the company and protection of a shepherd's servant from a lonely cottage, for fear his dream should come true; but at sight of him shudders and takes flight. Overtaken, he is induced to sit down and rest and relate his dream; and at each point of the narration, he is confronted with the reality:

'Nun sprich, du träumtest'—'Es kam ein Mann—'
'War ich das? Sieh mich doch näher an,
Ich denke, du hast mich gesehen!
Nun weiter, wie ist es geschehen?'

'Er zog ein Messer!'—'War das, wie diess?—'
'Ach ja, ach ja!'—'Er zog's?'—'Und stiess—'
'Er stiess dir's wohl so durch die Kehle?
Was hilft es auch, dass ich dich quäle!'

And the end of the tale is known to the raven and dove who were sitting there:

Und fragt ihr, wie's weiter gekommen sei?
So fragt wohl zwei Vögel, sie sassen dabei,
Der Rabe verweilte gar heiter,
Die Taube konnte nicht weiter!

Der Rabe erzählt, was der Böse noch that,
Und auch, wie's der Henker gerochen hat,
Die Taube erzählt, wie der Knabe
Geweint und gebetet habe.

Here is unquestionably the art of objective, dramatic ballad-writing. As in the old ballads, a wealth of suggestion underlies the simple phrase—we know at once the scene over which the raven lingered, the action accompanying the man's final words. So too the nature background skilfully enhances the impression of the child's increasing fears, and the brisk, impatient answers of the master act as a foil to the boy's timidity. There are no wasted words, no intrusions of reflection into the compressed action, which develops logically and with a sombre irony. *Der Haideknabe* is perhaps the most concentrated example of Hebbel's art as a ballad-writer: its salient features of dramatic compression, ironic contrast and suggestive ellipsis are to be found in other poems—*Die Kindesmörderin* (1832), *Todes-Tücke* (1832), *Vinum Sacrum* (1837), or *Das Haus am Meer* (1838)—but in none does the tragic interest rise to the height of that in *Der Haideknabe*. It is noteworthy that in 1837, seven years before the composition of this poem, Hebbel wrote down in his journal an extract from the *Allgemeine Zeitung* relating that the Bishop of Autun, against whose life an attempt had been made, had dreamt of the figure of the assassin and at sight of him covered his face.[1] Two years later he wrote in the diary under the heading 'Mord aus Traum' a detailed story of a timorous Hamburg apprentice, tallying in many respects with the narrative in *Der Haideknabe*.[2] Five years later, the ballad was written. This procedure is as characteristic of Hebbel as is the poem itself.

Among the narrative poems of a non-tragic character, *Das Kind am Brunnen* (1841)—where tragedy is averted by the unconscious action of the child—stands out by the delicacy of its treatment and the flexibility of its form. There is a delightful lilt about the opening verses, with their picture of a smiling scene:

Frau Amme, Frau Amme, das Kind ist erwacht!
Doch die liegt ruhig im Schlafe.
Die Vöglein zwitschern, die Sonne lacht,
Am Hügel weiden die Schafe.

[1] *Tagebücher*, ed. cit., vol. i. 770, (?) June 1837.
[2] Ibid. 1582, 6 May 1839.

With the mellowing passage of the years, indeed, warm sunny pictures are more frequently evoked. The *Dithmarsischer Bauer* of 1853 is not as grey and rugged as he might have been in Hebbel's youth; strength is there, but serenity as well, in the figure of the peasant, sparing of his words but unsparing of his giant frame. Hebbel's gift of allusion, of suggesting a wide vista in few words, combines in the opening stanza of this poem with a ringing quality of simple verse, so that the image of the autumn harvest haunts the reader's memory:

> Der warme Sommer scheidet
>   Mit seinem letzten Stral;
> Der Sohn des Südens schneidet
>   Das Korn zum zweiten Mal;
>
> Man bäckt's am Donaustrande,
>   Man mahlt's am Rhein und Main,
> Und führt's am fernsten Rande
>   Des Reichs zum Dreschen ein.

Indeed, to the conception of Hebbel only as the stern exponent of inexorable tragic destiny, the lyrics are a useful antidote. Their variety of form and subject, their wealth of imagery reveal both the author of *Maria Magdalena* and the poet of *Gyges und sein Ring*; in addition, they show the Hebbel who in later life delighted in the affectionate antics of his squirrel, or in the tranquil domesticities of his tiny Gmunden cottage. Effects of colour and radiance on the one hand, and of twilight and obscurity on the other, play a large part in the natural settings of the lyrics; he loved the first as well as the second, and it is no insignificant juxtaposition that we find in the short Heidelberg poem *Erleuchtung*:

> Da thust du in die dunkeln Risse
>   Des Unerforschten einen Blick
> Und nimmst in deine Finsternisse
>   Ein leuchtend Bild der Welt zurück.

A contrast may suffice to show the range of suggestion in Hebbel's poetic vocabulary: the imagery of the second *Waldbild*, entitled *Böser Ort*, and that in a verse of *Das Opfer des Frühlings*, where the morning winds are working the magic of spring. In the former, the deep red flower in the mysterious wood symbolizes for the poet the hidden evil that he feels is in the place:

> Die Blumen, so hoch sie wachsen,
> Sind blass hier, wie der Tod,
> Nur Eine in der Mitte
> Steht da in dunklem Roth.
>
> Die hat es nicht von der Sonne,
> Nie traf sie deren Glut,
> Sie hat es von der Erde,
> Und die trank Menschenblut!

Dominated by the impression of evil, he plucks the flower and casts it down. A bird sings mockingly:

> Jetzt lässt der Ort dich weiter,
> Da ihm sein Recht geschah,
> Du hast die Blume getödtet,
> Es war nichts Anders da!

The irony of the situation is complete—by the very act of resistance, the evil is done, just as, in different circumstances, the boy in *Der Haideknabe* brings about his own undoing, and in *Die Kindesmörderin* the mother commits her crime at the very moment when it is made of no avail.

The contrasting verse from *Das Opfer des Frühlings*, written in Rome two years later, conjures up a picture of radiant vitality:

> Flugs nun auf den leichten Schwingen
> Eilen sie durch Hain und Thal,
> Und vor ihren Küssen springen
> Spröde Knospen ohne Zahl.
>
> Jeder Busch, wie sie ihn streifen,
> Wird zum bunten Blütenstrauss,
> Und die Wurzeln, die noch steifen,
> Treiben erstes Grün heraus.

Imagery and movement together create the sense of springing, joyous life; colour and swiftness are made visible to the mind's eye by the choice of words and metrical pattern.

In face of such varied achievement, few would deny Hebbel's claim to be ranked among the lyric poets, or would consider unjustified the sentiment that inspired the following poem, written in 1838 during the dark period in Munich:

Und ist ein blosser Durchgang denn mein Leben
  Durch Deinen Tempel, herrliche Natur,
So ward mir doch ein schöner Trieb gegeben,
  Vom Höchsten zu erforschen jede Spur,
So tränkt mich doch, bin ich auch selbst vergänglich,
  Ein Quell, der ewig ist und überschwänglich!

To turn from Hebbel's Hamburg and Munich lyrics to his early prose tales is to exchange the craftsman for the apprentice. While the poems grew like flowers in a rich meadow, the ground had to be sedulously cultivated for the rearing of the 'Novellen'. Labour was prodigally spent on every one of those that are extant, and Hebbel's letters contain references to others which were not preserved, and some of which, no doubt, were never finished. In later years, he himself considered the Tales to be chiefly documents of his development,[1] and as such they have an interest greater perhaps than their intrinsic literary value.

The six tales dating from the Wesselburen days—*Holion*, *Des Greises Traum*, *Der Brudermord*, *Der Maler*, *Die Räuberbraut*, and *Die einsamen Kinder*—may be regarded simply as experimental excursions. Hoffmann was the first of Hebbel's models in this *genre*, and to him they owe many of their features. But in the summer of 1835 Hebbel contributed to one of the weekly gatherings of the *Wissenschaftlicher Verein von 1817* a critical paper on *Theodor Körner und Heinrich von Kleist*, in which he analysed the art of Kleist, commenting in particular on the dramatic and psychological power of *Michael Kohlhaas*; and it is not difficult to trace the influence of Kleist on the first of the Hamburg 'Novellen'—*Barbier Zitterlein*. Lacking in dexterity as it is, and often unsure in its effects, this tale yet shows, in the logical development of a pathological study, a certain ungainly strength. Hebbel is not concerned with outward incident or marvellous event; Zitterlein alone is the

[1] Letter to Karl Gutzkow, 15 Nov. 1857, *Briefe*, ed. cit., vol. vi, p. 80.

centre of his interest, even to the exclusion of the two other characters. Agatha and Leonhard are lifeless; but in the father's growing madness and recognition of madness, there are life and vigour enough. The constrained atmosphere of the narrow home, too, is well conveyed, and faintly suggests the future author of *Maria Magdalena*. The matter of the tale, however, is better than its manner. The stiff dialogue and the anxious detail of the narrative show that Hebbel still had much to learn, though the dramatic division of his material holds promise of achievement. According to an entry in the journal, *Zitterlein* was begun on 27 June and finished on 1 August 1835.[1] On 9 June 1836 he writes that *Anna* is completed, and adds a note indicating satisfaction: 'Zum ersten Mal Respect gehabt vor meinem dramatisch-episch in Erzählungen sich ergiessenden Talent'.[2] The influence of Kleist is still more evident in *Anna*, where a concatenation of circumstances, all issuing from the maid's submission to her master's unjust treatment, leads to a disaster in which, by her own act, both she and her lover are involved. The logic of *Anna* recalls an earlier entry of Hebbel's in the diary: 'Wen ein grosses Schicksal zu Grunde richtet, ist klein, *wen ein kleines vernichtet, der kann gross seyn*'.[3] In this tale, as in *Zitterlein*, the idea is better than the execution, but there are moments when they are more nearly matched. Anna is the first of Hebbel's passive heroines, who kindle fires that only their death can extinguish. As yet, however, there is not the quality of passion in her delineation to endow the tragic outcome with significance.

Meanwhile, it is plain that Hebbel had written other tales. In a letter to Elise he mentions five short stories which he has offered to Engelmann for publication in a small volume. Three of them, he writes, she already knows: *Herr Weiss*, *Johann*, and *Gertrud*; two she has not read: *Anna* and *Eine Nacht im Jägerhause*.[4] Clearly the first three must date from the Hamburg period and were written before *Anna*; clearly,

[1] *Tagebücher*, ed. cit., vol. i. 87, 1 Aug. 1835.
[2] Ibid. 178, 9 June 1836.
[3] Ibid. 53, 14 July 1835.
[4] Letter to Elise Lensing, 20 Aug. 1836, *Briefe*, ed. cit., vol. i, pp. 82–3.

too, the date which Hebbel later assigned to *Eine Nacht im Jägerhause* (1837) was inaccurate. R. M. Werner, in the preface to the Tales, identifies *Herr Weiss* by the evidence of the manuscript with *Herr Haidvogel und seine Familie*, which was revised in 1847 and dated accordingly by Hebbel; he also concludes that *Johann*—of which no further mention is made —is *Pauls merkwürdigste Nacht.*[1] *Schnock*, a tale begun in Hamburg and finished at the end of 1836 (though not published until 1849), was subjected to a revision which evidently caused Hebbel some anxiety and which extended to the spring of 1837; and in May of that year Hebbel submitted three manuscripts to the *Mitternachtszeitung* (where *Zitterlein* had already been published). These were *Ein Abend in Strassburg* (the only portion he completed of his intended 'Reisebeschreibung'), *Die Obermedicinalräthin* and *Der Schneidermeister Nepomuk Schlägel auf der Freudenjagd*, which he had finished in January 1837. The fragment *Die beiden Vagabunden* also belongs to this year; and in May he finished *Der Rubin* ('die beste meiner bis jetzt entstandenen prosaischen Arbeiten'.[2]) Two years later *Matteo* was written, and in 1849 *Die Kuh*—already planned in 1843. This completes the list of Hebbel's prose tales; virtually, his absorption in the drama put an end to his experiments with the 'Novelle'.

After the publication of *Zitterlein* in the *Mitternachtszeitung für gebildete Stände* in 1836, and of the two very slight sketches *Die Obermedicinalräthin* and *Ein Abend in Strassburg* in the same journal a year later, Hebbel sought for some years in vain for a publisher willing to accept the Tales. In 1836 Engelmann had already refused the offer of 'Novellen' for a small volume;[3] a similar fate attended attempts from Munich to induce first Campe and then a Berlin publisher to accept *Schnock*.[4] Hebbel then sent *Schnock*, *Anna*, and *Der Rubin* to Tieck and asked

[1] *Werke*, ed. R. M. Werner, vol. viii, pp. xx–xxii; v. also Letter to Elise Lensing, 12 May 1837, *Briefe*, ed. cit., vol. i, p. 201, where the name Paul appears instead of Johann.

[2] Letter to Elise Lensing, 23 May 1837, *Briefe*, ed. cit., vol. i, p. 203.

[3] Letter to Elise Lensing, 20 Aug. 1836, *Briefe*, ed. cit., vol. i, pp. 82–3, and 3 Sept. 1836, *Briefe*, ed. cit., vol. i, p. 90.

[4] Letter to Elise Lensing, 11 Apr. 1837, and (?) Jan. 1839, *Briefe*, ed. cit., vol. i, p. 190 and p. 382.

for his assistance, but Tieck, though complimentary, could do nothing.[1] In 1840, according to an entry in the diary, he offered these three tales to a Leipzig publisher, but received no answer.[2] Even the excision of *Schnock* could not induce Campe to publish the rest, though Hebbel wrote urgently, first from Paris, then from Italy. Finally *Schnock*, the initial stumbling-block, found a publisher in 1850, when it appeared in Leipzig; but Weber did not consent to print the other tales. Seven were at last published in 1855 by Gustav Heckenast, through the good offices of Kolbenheyer. Meanwhile, *Matteo* in 1841, and *Eine Nacht im Jägerhause* in 1842, had appeared in the *Morgenblatt für gebildete Leser*, and in 1843 *Der Rubin* was printed in *Der Freihafen*, edited by Mundt in Altona. *Der Salon*, edited by Sigmund Engländer in Vienna, took *Anna*, *Nepomuk Schlägel*, and *Die beiden Vagabunden* in 1847, while *Pauls merkwürdigste Nacht* appeared in another Viennese journal in the same year. In 1848, *Herr Haidvogel und seine Familie* was published in *Poetische Bilder aus der Zeit* (Leipzig), and *Die Kuh* appeared in the year of its completion in *Die Presse*. No doubt the normal difficulty of finding a publisher for the work of a young and unknown author was increased by the uncompromising character of most of Hebbel's tales. They were likely to be anything but popular; and it was not until he had made a name for himself with *Judith*—however much disputed it might be—that the journals began to find space for the 'Novellen'.

Many of the tales are concerned with characters dominated by some one trait or motive. Zitterlein is a man obsessed by the desire of possession and led by his dark jealousy to insanity; Haidvogel is the complete egoist, the boastful spendthrift who with a perpetual grievance against others manages never to bear his own burdens; Paul is a coward who under the pretence of caution yields to the wildest fears; Schnock is the very embodiment of apprehensiveness, while Nepomuk Schlägel bears a grudge against every man for his

[1] Letters to Elise Lensing, 18 Nov. 1838, 12 Dec. 1838, 12 Jan. 1839, *Briefe*, ed. cit., vol. i, pp. 356, 366, 379, and Letter from Tieck to Hebbel, 23 June 1839, *Briefe*, ed. cit., vol. ii, pp. 365–6 (Anhang).

[2] *Tagebücher*, ed. cit., vol. ii. 2225, 21 Jan. 1841.

better luck, and finds, with incredible ingenuity, something to envy in every life except his own. Equally characteristic is Hebbel's partiality for those swift turns of circumstance which change the complexion of a narrative. Matteo, in desperation planning murder, is saved by the trust placed in him by a man and a child; then in obedience to the orders of his rescuer, is driven to kill another, but unintentionally, in self-defence. In *Pauls merkwürdigste Nacht*, craven fear leads a man to magnify the harmless incidents of a night journey, until he is convinced that an assassin is pursuing him. At the end of a headlong flight, when he has given his supposed pursuer into custody, he discovers him to be the friend for whose company he had been longing through the terrors of the night. Similarly, in *Eine Nacht im Jägerhause*, the mind, once started on a line of suspicion, turns every incident into a confirmation of its fears. A thin line divides horror from farce, and the grave from the ludicrous. 'Unter Ironie', Hebbel wrote to Emil Rousseau in 1838, 'versteht er (muss er, Solger, verstehen) nichts Anderes, als den Blick auf das Ausgleichende, das in Zeit, Zufall und Schicksal liegt und das den Dichter, der es schon im Voraus mit dem geistigen Auge erfasst hat, das Ungeheuerste der Gegenwart leicht und leichtsinnig betrachten und behandeln lässt'.[1]

The prevailing tone of Hebbel's Tales is sombre. Injustice, fear, envy, malice are dominant themes; where comic incongruity occurs, there is an element of grimness in the swift reversal of events. Some light is thrown on Hebbel's mode of treatment by entries in the first volume of the diary on 'Humor' and 'das Humoristische'. 'Humor ist Erkenntniss der Anomalien'.[2] Or later: 'Humor ist Zweiheit, die sich selbst empfindet. Daher das Umgekehrte von Form und Inhalt.'[3] Plainly such entries reflect the mood of many of the Tales, but the connexion is made most clearly in a note of 1837, in which the following story is quoted from the newspapers: A miser, on being told by his doctor that he is

[1] Letter to Emil Rousseau, 5 Mar. 1838, *Briefe*, ed. cit., vol. i, pp. 271–2 (from *Tagebücher*, ed. cit., vol. i. 1009, 6 Mar. 1838).

[2] *Tagebücher*, ed. cit., vol. i. 118, 24 Oct. 1835.

[3] Ibid. 1566, 16 Apr. 1839.

doomed, rises from his sick-bed and burns the papers which represent his very considerable fortune. On returning to bed, he falls into a deep sleep; so that when the doctor comes again, he tells him the crisis is over and there is no further danger. In despair at the sacrifice of his wealth, the miser hangs himself. Hebbel's comment on the story is 'Wunderbar-herrlicher Humor der Nemesis'.[1]

As might be expected, the Tales in general are written with a complete detachment—in this the 'humorist' and the dramatist in Hebbel coincided. Only in one do we find the personal touch of the satirist. *Nepomuk Schlägel* indeed can hardly be entitled a 'Novelle'; it is devoid of narrative incident, and recalls the 'Characters' of an earlier age. It had, we may suppose from an entry in the journal of 4 April 1837, something of a personal application; Hebbel's own experience gave him insight into dark places of the heart where envy and bitterness could flourish. Nepomuk has these feelings without justification; he is a poor creature at best. In Hebbel there was a strength of mind and spirit which could balance—for the most part—the bitter revolt against his situation. But that there is something of Hebbel's darker spirit in Schlägel there is little doubt.[2] The study suffers, however, from too elaborate an accumulation of detail without a corresponding cumulative effect, and leaves the reader with a feeling of frustration.

Schnock, on the other hand, in which the central character is equally dominated by one motive, is a pleasant sketch, skilfully imagined as an episode of travel, and thus ending naturally and effectively with the departure of the traveller. It stands alone among the Tales in its cheerful humour and

[1] *Tagebücher*, ed. cit., vol. i. 728, 13 Apr.–26 May 1837.

[2] Cp. *Tagebücher*, ed. cit., vol. i. 672, 4 Apr. 1837: 'Jener edlen Gift-Einsaugungskunst . . . hab' auch ich mich befleissigt. . . . Es kommt aber hinzu, dass ich . . . das Gift recht geschickt wieder von mir geben kann, freilich nicht sowohl, um Anderen, was nur nebenbei geschieht, ihre Stunden zu verderben, als um mir manche durch das süsse Gefühl, einmal des Stricks und Schandpfahls zugleich würdig gewesen zu seyn, recht zu würzen. *Hierin ist nicht die geringste Uebertreibung.* Wollt' ich mich von diesem Punct aus einmal schildern, so gäb' es gewiss eine Art Character, von dem Jeder, der ihn bedauerte, zugleich bedauern würde, dass er sich nicht überwinden könne, ihn anzuspeien. Vielleicht ist's meine Pflicht, es zu thun.'

its delight in eccentric situations; through all the variety of incident, however, the development of the condition of fear is strictly logical. 'Furcht ist kein Gefühl', Hebbel wrote in 1836, 'es ist der einzige Zustand, der den Menschen aufhebt.'[1] The picture of Schnock, with his broad shoulders and his childish face, is vivid from the first: 'ein Mann . . . breitschultrig, von gewaltigem Knochenbau, aber mit einem Gesicht, worauf das erste Kindergreinen über empfangene Ruthenstreiche versteinert zu sein schien; ein Bär mit einer Kaninchen-Physiognomie;' and every incident narrated by him points this contrast between appearance and reality. There is an unforced humour in the initial situation, where Schnock has most unwillingly effected the capture of an escaped criminal, and is reluctantly congratulated by the village officials for his deed. The skilful transition from this scene to the autobiographical reminiscences of the hero himself is rather surprising—for such technical dexterity is not characteristic of the early 'Novellen'—until the difficult and extensive revision of the whole work is recalled.[2] The henpecked husband then gives an account of his enforced courtship and marriage, and of his vain attempts to make upon his wife the requisite impression of prowess; incidentally he relates a number of anecdotes, among the best of which are his reluctant visit to a travelling menagerie, and his strange experience one night when he attempted to burgle his own larder for the sake of a square meal. The final scene, where the silent Schnock is eating and drinking for a wager and the landlord is vainly endeavouring to make him speak or laugh and thus forfeit double the value of the viands, is well conceived; and in the middle of the landlord's lengthy threats of the persuasions he will yet employ, the horses are whipped up and the traveller's carriage drives off.

[1] *Tagebücher*, ed. cit., vol. i, 207, 1 July 1836.

[2] v. Letter to Elise Lensing, 8 Dec. 1836, *Briefe*, ed. cit., vol. i, p. 127: 'Die meiste Mühe macht mir der *Schnock*. Die letzten hier in München entstandenen Scenen wage ich Allem, was jemals im Komischen auf Deutschem Grund und Boden geleistet worden, an die Seite zu setzen. . . . Aber das meiste des in Hamburg fertig Gewordenen . . . bedarf fast gänzlicher Umarbeitung, die in keiner, als in der besten Stunde, wo man doch so leicht zu ganz neuer Arbeit greift, gelingen kann.' v. also *Briefe*, ed. cit., vol. i, p. 130.

The influence of Jean Paul Richter upon *Schnock* is very plain. Hebbel himself alludes to it in 1839, in a letter to Elise:

'Ich habe in diesen Tagen den Schmelzle von Jean Paul, der mir zum Schnock die erste Anregung gab, einmal wieder gelesen und mich überzeugt, dass Schnock nicht der bloss fortgespielte hasenherzige Feldprediger, sondern ein ganz neuer Character ist. Ich fürchtete wirklich, das Vorbild möge stärker eingewirkt haben, als mir lieb seyn könnte, doch meine Furcht war Gott Lob ungegründet. Nur Böswilligkeit kann mir Nachahmung vorwerfen, Schnocks Feigheit ist eine ganz andere, als Schmelzles'.[1]

That Hebbel was absorbed—and for the first time with real delight—in Jean Paul's works during the period when he was at work on *Schnock* is also amply proved by passages in his letters and in the diary.[2]

But although many resemblances can be traced, in episodes and situations, between the two tales, and although the basic idea of Jean Paul's *Schmelzle* recurs in the figure of Schnock, the difference in characterization and structure warrants Hebbel's feeling of independence. His way was not one of facile construction or imitation; he was always striving to penetrate the inmost minds of his characters.

'Es ist unendlich schwer', he writes to Elise in illuminating comment, 'einen Character der Art aus dem Innersten heraus zu erschaffen; nicht allein lieber, sondern auch leichter baut der Mensch sich einen Vergrösserungsspiegel, als einen verkleinernden; dort gilt es bloss ein Ausdehnen, hier aber ein Einspinnen, ein völliges Verkriechen in das Hirn eines Regenwurms. Den Conflict selbst, in den z. B. der furchtsame Schnock mit Welt und Natur gerathen muss, hinzustellen, ist mehr, als leicht; wie aber das All in seinen Augen sich bricht und malt, und wie *dasselbe* Schraubenwerk, das Napoleon nach Muskau windet, diese Raupenseele vor einem kalekutschen Hahn in die Flucht treibt, das zu erfassen und zu zeichnen, ist die Aufgabe.'[3]

That the figure of Schnock owed its inception to outside influence no doubt made this probing the more necessary; it is

[1] Letter to Elise Lensing, (?) Jan. 1839, *Briefe*, ed. cit., vol. i, p. 382.

[2] v. Letters to Elise Lensing, 18 Dec. 1836, and 19 Dec. 1836, *Briefe*, ed. cit., vol. i, pp. 131 and 134, and the numerous passages quoted from Jean Paul in the *Tagebücher*, 1836–7.

[3] Letter to Elise Lensing, 15 Dec. 1836, *Briefe*, ed. cit., vol. i, p. 130.

a process we shall see repeated, especially in connexion with those of Hebbel's dramas which derive their material from legendary or literary sources.[1] In *Schnock* he has not yet acquired that certainty with which the later dramatic characters are drawn; he is still feeling his way, still learning to build 'from the inside outwards'; but the tale marks nevertheless an advance in psychological presentation.

The 'Märchen' *Der Rubin*, composed in 1837, is chiefly important for its subsequent history. As the author himself turned to drama, so the Eastern fairy-tale, twelve years later, became a 'Märchen-Lustspiel'. The story of the princess, imprisoned by enchantment in a ruby ring and only to be released if the possessor of the ring should voluntarily cast it away, is slight enough; but the implication in Hebbel's treatment is weightier. In the dramatic version it might be formulated as 'Wirf' weg, damit du nicht verlierst'. This moral cannot be pursued too far, for Assad's renunciation is made in order to prevent another man from acquiring the ring, which he himself had only gained by force. But all is justified by Assad's courage in facing death through following his intuitive conviction that the ruby has some special message for him—an intuition supported by the miraculous appearance of the sage, who reveals the secret of its prisoner. The idea of the tale may have been suggested to Hebbel by a passage in Hoffmann's *Das öde Haus*, where there is a similar notion of a being imprisoned in a diamond, and thereby lending it a supernatural brilliance.[2]

After 1841, only one short story was composed—*Die Kuh*, which was not finished until 1849, although the material was noted in the journal in 1843.[3] In January 1849, an entry records the completion of the tale, and Hebbel adds: 'Ich habe mich seit meinem letzten Aufenthalt in Hamburg damit getragen, so klein sie ist!'[4] A comparison of the bare facts in the newspaper story with Hebbel's arrangement of them in the 'Novelle' reveals much of his constructive method. It

[1] v. *infra*, and Hebbel's discussions of the characters of Judith, Mariamne, and Kriemhild.

[2] v. *Werke*, ed. cit., vol. viii, p. xlii.

[3] *Tagebücher*, ed. cit., vol. ii. 2701, 20 May 1843.

[4] *Tagebücher*, ed. cit., vol. iii. 4513, 18 Jan. 1849.

shows above all how dependent upon significant detail is the massive effect of logic so characteristic of his work. To the actual incidents, only two are added: the father lights his pipe by twisting a piece of paper and holding it in the flame of the lamp, and thus the child only imitates his action when it burns the paper money in order to see the glow; and at the end the cow, for whose arrival the peasant is looking when the accident occurs, shares the fate of the house and its inmates and is destroyed in the fire. These additions are trivial in themselves. But how greatly they enhance the irony of the situation! Where the newspaper report conveys merely the impression of haphazard, casual disaster, the tale reveals a sequence of events, leading to a catastrophe equally unmerited, but seemingly inescapable. Instead of relegating to a final paragraph the explanation of the incident—the purchase and impending arrival of the cow—Hebbel sets it in the centre of the tale, leading up to it with great skill and effectively springing it upon the reader: 'Brüllt's nicht schon?' . . . 'Nichts da'—sagte er zurückkehrend—'das kam aus dem Stall des Nachbars! . . . Na, Junge . . . Die Kuh ist schon unterwegs! Du musst das Pferd schaffen, wenn Du gross wirst! Hörst Du?' Das Kind nickte, als ob es verstände, was es doch noch nicht verstehen konnte.' The impatience of the father, his pleasure in achievement—how dearly bought by toil we know from his previous recollections, as he counts his money, of the way in which each bill was earned —the child's innocent absorption, and the father's proud hopes for the future—all these set the key for the tragedy, when in frenzied rage at the shattering of his dreams, Andreas seizes the innocent cause of the misfortune and hurls him to the ground. Here was the fact needing motivation, and all Hebbel's skill is used to prepare the reader's mind and emotions for this turning-point, after which every act in the tragic concatenation inevitably follows. We recognize in the author of *Die Kuh* the creator of Mariamne. This is not surprising, for by the time Hebbel wrote it, he had become a dramatist before all else; and the tale which shows him master of the short story is also his farewell to it.

IV

HAMBURG AND COPENHAGEN. FIRST PLAYS 'JUDITH'—'GENOVEVA'—'DER DIAMANT'

AFTER the first mood of depression that accompanied Hebbel's arrival in Hamburg in 1839, affairs seemed to run more smoothly for a while. Elise's home provided a refuge; Dr. Schoppe and others of his former circle showed themselves more friendly than he had expected; relations were established with Campe, the Hamburg publisher, and even (though with reservations on Hebbel's part) with Gutzkow. Work seemed to be available: 'Arbeit genug, ich darf nicht länger klagen, die Pforte ist mir geöffnet.'[1] But the hopeful mood did not last long. In May he fell ill, and at the beginning of June a relapse brought about a dangerous crisis, which he was only just able to surmount. Elise nursed him through the illness, and his comparatively rapid recovery was due largely to her care. But in the weakness of convalescence gloom and doubt invaded his spirit, and life in Hamburg no longer seemed to offer promise. After a letter from Cotta refusing his poems for publication, even the impulse to write lyrics failed: 'Arbeiten kann ich nicht mehr, ich bin ein Baum, der vertrocknet; zuweilen noch ein Knospenansatz, welcher der Wurzel die letzten Säfte raubt, ohne der Krone Schmuck zu verleihen.'[2] A favourable though belated verdict from Tieck on *Schnock* had caused a momentary break in the clouds, but the tale was once more refused when Hebbel offered it to Aue, a publisher in Altona. Relations with Amalia Schoppe were again becoming difficult; a dispute with Campe in October led to a temporary break in their negotiations; Hebbel distrusted Gutzkow and disliked the new literary doctrines; Hamburg, in short, in spite of reviews and articles published in the *Telegraph*, was rapidly becoming intolerable. 'Es tritt immer deutlicher

[1] *Tagebücher*, ed. cit., vol. i. 1550, 11 Apr. 1839.
[2] Ibid. 1631, 27 Aug. 1839.

hervor, dass ich Recht hatte, wenn ich mir in München die Hamburger Verhältnisse als unleidlich ausmalte.'[1]

But in this same month of October, the decisive moment in Hebbel's poetic activity occurred. In spite of despondency and foreboding, he found his medium: on 3 October an entry in the diary records: 'Gestern fing ich meine Tragödie *Judith* an und schrieb ein Paar Scenen, die mir gefielen.'[2] 'Gott', he adds, 'wenn das ginge!' And through the moods of the late autumn months in Hamburg *Judith* did progress, and with her, at intervals, a new spring of hope arose in her creator. In his usual retrospect on New Year's Eve, Hebbel could write of two acts that were finished, and of a plan 'in's Kleinste hinein vollendet'; and on 28 January 1840, he wrote the final scene,[3] thus completing his first tragedy in something under four months.

Judith was printed in February for private circulation, and immediately Hebbel wrote to Uhland, sending him a copy, and asking for his verdict. A marginal note dated 29 September 1840 records, however, that Uhland sent no answer: 'Dies ist der schlagendste Beweis dafür, dass zwischen Jugend und Alter kein Verhältniss möglich ist.'[4] A more fruitful approach was made to Frau Stich-Crelinger. Through the agency of Dr. Schoppe (with whom a fresh reconciliation had taken place) Hebbel sent a copy of the play to this well-known actress in Berlin. His resentment was aroused afresh by the subsequent discovery that his patroness had seized the opportunity to send a 'jämmerliches Rührspiel' of her own as well; but the consequences were not such as he feared. Frau Stich-Crelinger's verdict was encouraging, and negotiations for the performance of *Judith*—with alterations—were begun. It was played in July 1840, in a mutilated theatre version, and was well received. For the first time Hebbel began to experience the pleasures of success. While criticism veered between high praise and scathing censure, the performances found favour, and the name of the author

[1] *Tagebücher*, ed. cit., vol. i. 1693, 12 Oct. 1839.
[2] Ibid. 1677, 3 Oct. 1839. [3] *Tagebücher*, ed. cit., vol. ii. 1893, 28 Jan. 1840.
[4] Ibid. 1913, 17 Feb. 1840; v. also 1992, 26 Apr. 1840.

could henceforth no longer be considered 'obscure'. Yet it was still hard to find a publisher—it was not until March 1841 (by which time *Genoveva* also had been written) that Campe bought *Judith* for 10 louis-d'or.

Meanwhile, literary success was tempered by private cares. The serious illness of Elise in the spring of 1840 was succeeded by the discovery that she was to bear a child in the late autumn. This news coincided with a quarrel with Dr. Schoppe—originating, as ever, in a trivial cause of offence, but assuming formidable dimensions owing to her vehement reproaches and Hebbel's state of mind. His lack of money was made worse by the reflection that Elise's small savings had been spent, and that he was in no position to make restitution. It was small wonder that the success of *Judith* only half occupied his mind, and that the journal frequently reflects a 'grässliche Stimmung'.[1]

Yet it is in these circumstances that one of the strangest moments in Hebbel's life is recorded in the diary, and in his correspondence. Elise had left Hamburg for a time towards the end of June; and Hebbel, burdened as he was with new responsibilities and open to new apprehensions, fell in love with Emma Schröder, a young Hamburg beauty whom he met in July for the first time. And not only did he record his feelings in the diary,[2] but with an almost incredible egotism wrote to Elise of this new passion, adding the comment: 'Liebe knüpft sich an Schönheit und Jugend.'[3] We hear little of Emma Schröder in the journal; their relations were broken off by accidental circumstances and in any case, as things were, would probably have had little prospect of permanence. But it is difficult not to regard the comments to Elise at such a time as matter for regret, even when they were succeeded in September, on her second departure from Hamburg, by an outpouring of remorse. On 5 November, Elise gave birth to a son, and Hebbel's anguished anxiety in her difficult confinement is recorded in the diary. By

[1] *Tagebücher*, ed. cit., vol. ii. 1973, 13 Apr. 1840.
[2] Ibid. 2045 and 2047, 20 July and 27 July 1840.
[3] Letter to Elise Lensing, 26 July 1840, *Briefe*, ed. cit., vol. ii, p. 90.

mid-November she was out of danger, and Hebbel wrote: 'Ich habe es bisher immer für etwas gehalten, wenn Einer sagte: lieber will ich selbst leiden, als ein Geliebtes leiden sehen; aber es ist blosser Egoismus. Viel lieber selbst mit dem Tode kämpfen, als ein Geliebtes mit dem Tode kämpfen sehen.'[1] For the time, a common suffering and a common responsibility brought a closer union between them, and the year ended on a note of resolution and of hope.[2]

In the September of 1840, *Genoveva*, Hebbel's second tragedy, was begun; by the beginning of the New Year three acts were written, and by 1 March 1841 the play was finished—the virtue of the long seed-time was becoming clear in the swift harvest. And although the work on *Genoveva* was more intermittent than that on *Judith*, this was compensated for by a short period of intense creative achievement 'in einer Begeisterung, die mir Schlaf und Alles raubte',[3] so that seven years later, working on *Herodes und Mariamne*, Hebbel could look back on the *Genoveva* period as one of great poetic fervour.[4] This high mood brought its reaction, however; and in spite of Campe's acceptance of *Judith* in March, the inertia—partly due to indecision about the new drama—lasted till the early summer. 'Jetzt wieder ein Pflanzenleben. Genoveva liegt noch immer unfertig da. Aendern muss ich, aber kaum weiss ich was, noch weniger, wie.'[5] Finally, however, he completed the revision, 'nach langen Wehen',[6] and sent the manuscript to the Berlin Theatre; but in October a polite refusal reached him, stating that Raupach's *Genoveva* was already in the repertory.

Meanwhile, pressed as he was for money, Hebbel had accepted the offer of a Hamburg publisher and undertaken to write two short historical works on the Thirty Years' War and the Maid of Orleans for a popular series. These were completed in 1840 in a few months, and brought him in a small remuneration, but they were published under a pseudonym ('Dr. J. F. Franz') and never acknowledged.

[1] *Tagebücher*, ed. cit., vol. ii. 2193, 16 Nov. 1840.
[2] Ibid. 2203, 31 Dec. 1840.
[3] Ibid. 2267, 11 Feb. 1841.
[4] *Tagebücher*, ed. cit., vol. iii. 4431, 9 Aug. 1848.
[5] *Tagebücher*, ed. cit., vol. ii. 2337, 29 May 1841.
[6] Ibid. 2376, 27 Aug. 1841.

Campe had at length accepted the collected lyrics for publication in a volume, and in September 1841 Hebbel completed the necessary revision—'eine schwere Aufgabe', he records. The book was not actually published until July 1842, when he transcribed the date of composition of each poem in the journal, before destroying the remaining manuscript versions. The lyrics in their published form were not chronologically arranged; Hebbel sought to create the impression of variety, while at the same time grouping together poems related in subject-matter or in treatment. The meticulous care with which he sorted, grouped, and polished the lyrics, finally destroying (and asking others to destroy) all versions but those in final form, was characteristic of a mind which in its sense of detail singularly refutes the accepted fiction that the artist is incapable of organization.

Lyric and short tale, prose tragedy and verse tragedy—all these Hebbel had now produced. One important form remained; and in November 1841 a sudden entry in the diary records the completion of his first comedy: 'Heute Abend habe ich das Lustspiel: *Der Diamant* beendigt.'[1] Work on this play, begun in Munich, evidently occupied the autumn months; but there is no continuous record of its progress in the journal as there is for the other plays. Later, Hebbel propounded a theory of comedy; later still, in 1847, he sent *Der Diamant* to Campe, with the observation: 'Es ist doch in Form und Gehalt mein bedeutendstes Werk und man muss die Pfeile nicht im Köcher rosten lassen.'[2] In 1841, however, the comedy served a different purpose; Hebbel sent it in for a prize to be awarded in Berlin. His anticipation of the result was fulfilled: '[Mein Stück wird wohl] so wenig den ersten als den zweiten Preis in Berlin erhalten'—although, he says in the same breath: 'Dessen glaube ich gewiss zu seyn, dass in Deutschland, da Tieck alt ist, kein ebenbürtiges Komödien-Talent neben mir auftreten wird. . . .'[3] At least a partial explanation of both

[1] *Tagebücher*, ed. cit., vol. ii. 2392, 29 Nov. 1841.
[2] *Tagebücher*, ed. cit., vol. iii. 3961, 5 Feb. 1847.
[3] *Tagebücher*, ed. cit., vol. ii. 2397, 10 Dec. 1841.

statements may be found in the significant phrase that accompanied the completion of *Der Diamant*: 'Komödie und Tragödie sind ja doch im Grunde nur zwei verschiedene Formen für die gleiche Idee.'[1]

On this period of intensive activity the usual depression followed. Although 'Klara' and 'Moloch' were stirring into life, a new work could not be begun so soon, and while the fate of *Genoveva* and *Der Diamant* was still uncertain: 'da kehrt sich denn, wie gewöhnlich, das Bischen Kraft, das ich sonst auf künstlerische Objecte verwende, gegen mich selbst, wie die Zähne, die Nichts zu beissen haben, sich in das eigene Fleisch hinein graben, das sie ernähren sollen.'[2] Throughout the months of January, February, March, and April the customary inertia after active creation lay heavily upon him, only lightened by the gradually developing impulse to write sonnets. But during the whole winter of 1842–3, the references to Elise show an increased warmth, and gratitude—more constantly expressed than hitherto—not only for her help but for her patience and devotion. Moreover, with all the moments of despondency and the insistent doubts concerning *Genoveva*, Hebbel's self-confidence was growing. He consoled himself for the anticipated failure of *Der Diamant* by the feeling that the 'power and ecstasy' of creation were his, an inalienable gift—for the defects of his disposition by the conviction that at least he knew no temptation to carelessness in his poetic work. Though the black moods were there—as indeed throughout his life they were always to recur—he was able to detach himself a little more, and to await their passing with a less complete absorption in himself.

Relations with Campe were not altogether satisfactory to Hebbel through the winter—though it is easy to perceive that much was due to his own extreme susceptibility. But when in May 1842 the disastrous fire broke out which destroyed the central part of Hamburg, including Campe's printing-house, the publisher showed generosity and gave him 'the 10 louis-d'or which he had not sent from Leipzig'.[3]

[1] *Tagebücher*, ed. cit., vol. ii. 2393, 29 Nov. 1841.
[2] Ibid. 2408, 28 Dec. 1841.
[3] Ibid. 2548, 13 May 1842.

Hebbel saw 'a few care-free months' before him, and his mood grew perceptibly lighter. He was pleased, moreover, with the edition of the poems, which at length appeared in July. It was dedicated to the memory of Emil Rousseau, and Hebbel took the opportunity of its publication to send a copy to Rousseau's mother and thus renew relations with the family. This had important results. On 3 September he received from Emil's father a loan of 20 louis-d'or, and with the record of this loan there occurs in the diary the first mention of a project which rapidly took form—a journey to Copenhagen. In the hope of obtaining, as a Danish subject, that support which the Kings of Denmark had been known to extend to men of letters, Hebbel determined on a personal application to influential figures in the Danish capital, trusting thereby to obtain an audience of King Christian VIII himself. Preparations went forward swiftly; Campe advanced 20 louis-d'or; the omens were so favourable that Hebbel, apprehensive as he ever was, distrusted them the more. On the eve of departure he was uncertain of his aims, and of himself; but any prospect, any possibility, seemed better than remaining quiescent in Hamburg. On 12 November he set out, and travelled by Kiel (where a vacant chair of aesthetics seemed to offer the possibility of a permanent position) to the Danish city, where in a fit of melancholy he made the first Copenhagen entry in the diary.

With this journey began the period of that wider experience of travel and society which had hitherto been lacking in Hebbel's education. He was fully conscious of the deficiency: '. . . ich muss mit Menschen verkehren und es ist gewiss Zeit, dass ich dies endlich lerne. Der Dichter in mir hat seine Bildung erlangt, aber der Mensch ist noch weit zurück.'[1] And if the entries in the journal often afford evidence of his defective social development, at the same time the triad of dramas dating from the second Hamburg period substantiates his claim to have attained poetic maturity.

The three plays are very different in form and content; yet in all we find the mode of treatment characteristic of

[1] *Tagebücher*, ed. cit., vol. ii, 2586, 8 Sept. 1842.

Hebbel's dramatic work—the logical development of character, the fusion of passionate experience and intellectual problem, the sharp dialectic of the psychologist combined with the imagination of the poet.

Judith, the first in time, is in some ways the most interesting and characteristic. Stimulated, as he so often was, by a previous interpretation which seemed to him inadequate, Hebbel took the old Apocryphal tale of Judith and Holofernes, and fashioned it anew. From the sixteenth century onwards many German plays on the story of Judith had been written. Playwright after playwright was drawn to the theme for its dramatic quality; but none saw in it what Hebbel saw—a woman essaying a task outside her field of action, and in the moment of achievement stricken by the realization that in her act she has transgressed, since her motives have been touched by personal desire, where she had thought them pure. The single-minded victor of the Apocrypha, a softer Jael, singing paeans to her God for granting her the strength to conquer—even if by guile—is here transformed into a woman, mystery-ridden, who in the conflict attains perilous self-knowledge, and at the end remains, though outwardly victorious, inwardly destroyed.

The Apocryphal tale is a simple one. The Jewish city of Bethulia is besieged by the mighty Assyrian general Holofernes, who has vowed utter destruction on the Jewish nation for being the last to yield to his conquering army. Threatened with starvation, the citizens are inclined to listen to counsels of surrender. But Judith, the beautiful widow of Manasses, full of piety and faith, persuades them to wait five more days. Meanwhile, trusting in the Lord, she resolves to attempt the impossible; and she leaves the city with her maid for the camp of Holofernes. Her beauty stirs the passions of the Assyrian, and beguiled by her plausible words, he allows her to remain in the camp, and even to pass in and out to pray. The Jewish God, she avers, will be wrathful against the Bethulians when they sin against Him, as they propose to do by eating the firstfruits of the Lord, and she—having therefore fled from the doomed city—will learn in prayer when they have thus incurred His anger. Then Holofernes may destroy them at the moment of their disobedience, when their God is turned away from them.

On the fourth day of her sojourn the Assyrian holds a feast, to which he bids Judith. She awaits her opportunity, and when he is drunk with wine and with desire, she slays him as he lies asleep within his tent, and with his head wrapped in a covering, passes out with her maid, as if to prayer. In the morning, the head of Holofernes is hung high upon the walls of Bethulia, the Assyrian armies, struck by fear, are put to flight by the attacking citizens, and Judith sings a hymn of praise to the Lord for His gracious aid in their tribulation.

It is difficult to say with certainty what directed Hebbel's attention to this story. His statement (in the preface to the private print of 1840) that he was first reminded of it by Giulio Romano's picture of Judith in the Munich Art Gallery seems open to some doubt; but possibly he did see a picture, and disliked the suggestion of triumph in it as he undoubtedly detested the triumphant victor of the Apocryphal tale.

Die Judith der Bibel kann ich nicht brauchen', he wrote in the diary. 'Dort ist Judith eine Wittwe, die den Holofernes durch List und Schlauheit in's Netz lockt; sie freut sich, als sie seinen Kopf im Sack hat und singt und jubelt vor und mit ganz Israel drei Monde lang. Das ist gemein; eine solche Natur ist ihres Erfolgs gar nicht würdig, Thaten der Art dürfen der Begeisterung, die sich später durch sich selbst gestraft fühlt, gelingen, aber nicht der Verschlagenheit, die in ihrem Glück ihr Verdienst sieht. Meine Judith wird durch ihre That paralysirt; sie erstarrt vor der Möglichkeit, einen Sohn des Holofernes zu gebären; es wird ihr klar, dass sie über die Gränzen hinaus gegangen ist, dass sie mindestens das Rechte aus unrechten Gründen gethan hat.'[1] And on another occasion: '. . . die Judith der Bibel ist eben Nichts, als eine Charlotte Corday, ein fanatisch-listiges Ungeheuer. . . .'[2]

If the particular occasion of Hebbel's interest in Judith as a subject is not easily defined, much in the character of

[1] *Tagebücher*, ed. cit., vol. ii. 1872, 3 Jan. 1840.

[2] *Mein Wort über das Drama. Werke*, ed. cit., vol. xi, p. 14.

Judith herself—as has already been suggested—is due to his reflections on the problems presented by the *Jungfrau von Orleans*. Indeed an entry in the diary concerning this character might almost refer to Hebbel's own heroine, and there is little doubt that the psychological approach to the latter was by way of the Maid.

'Die Gottheit selbst', he writes in 1838, 'wenn sie zur Erreichung grosser Zwecke auf ein Individuum unmittelbar einwirkt und sich dadurch einen willkürlichen Eingriff . . . in's Weltgetriebe erlaubt, kann ihr Werkzeug vor der Zermalmung durch dasselbe Rad, das es einen Augenblick aufhielt oder anders lenkte, nicht schützen. Dies ist wohl das vornehmste tragische Motiv, das in der Geschichte der Jungfrau von Orleans liegt. Eine Tragödie, welche diese Idee abspiegelte, würde einen grossen Eindruck hervor bringen durch den Blick in die ewige Ordnung der Natur, die die Gottheit selbst nicht stören darf, ohne es büssen zu müssen. (Besser auszuführen).'[1]

While the mission of the Maid of Orleans gave Hebbel a starting-point for reflection on the motives of his Judith, there is some suggestion of Holofernes in the following comment on Napoleon, written at the same time:

'Napoleon könnte allerdings der Held einer echten Tragödie seyn. Der Dichter müsste ihm all die grossen, auf das Heil der Menschheit abzielenden Tendenzen, deren er auf Sct Helena gedachte, unterlegen und ihn nur den einen Fehler begehen lassen, dass er sich die Kraft zutraut, Alles durch sich selbst, durch seine eigne Person, ohne Mitwirkung, ja Mitwissen, Anderer ausführen zu können. Dieser Fehler wäre ganz in seiner grossen Individualität begründet und jedenfalls der Fehler eines Gottes; dennoch aber wäre er, besonders in unserer Zeït, wo weniger der Einzelne, als die Masse, sich geltend macht, hinreichend, ihn zu stürzen'.[2]

The traditional Holofernes was a full-blooded Oriental tyrant, mighty in battle and uninteresting, if also dangerous, elsewhere. Hebbel's figure, though not free from the defect of exaggeration, has something of daemonic force behind his huge self-confidence. He *is* a 'grosse Individualität'—and it is

[1] *Tagebücher*, ed. cit., vol. i. 1011, 6 Mar. 1838.
[2] Ibid. 1012, 6 Mar. 1838.

no empty fear of Judith's that she may really yield her spirit to his magnetic power. In fact, the conflict between two representative figures of Judaism and paganism suggested in the Apocryphal tale has become individualized. It does not thereby lose its larger meaning; rather is its content enriched. The more or less symbolical opposition of Jewish woman and heathen warrior is a superficial one, compared with this tragic opposition of a man and woman with a fundamental affinity, which but sharpens the conflict in the given circumstances. Hebbel's experience of sex relationship bore the tinge of tragedy; and in his first drama, as in later ones, the dominant note of such relationship is tragic. In the conflict of Judaism and paganism he saw the time-setting for his two antagonists; a background suggesting a crisis of world-history was entirely congenial to his conception of tragedy. The motivation of Judith's decisive act in killing Holofernes binds the two conflicts together; she first sees herself as the saviour of Bethulia, then realizes that she has acted from personal motives, as an injured woman. Thus the circle completes itself: it is in Judith's own soul, in the confusion of her feelings, that the tragic conflict centres. She is the tragic individual, who by her act of self-assertion has disturbed the cosmic process: believing herself to be the channel of the divine purpose, she has unwittingly superimposed upon her mission individual feelings and desires. The balance can only be restored by her renewed surrender to the general will (or, in her terms, the Will of God); the disturbance of the cosmic process inherent in any act of self-assertion of the outstanding individual necessarily implies the destruction of that individual—'die Zermalmung durch dasselbe Rad, das es einen Augenblick aufhielt oder anders lenkte'.[1] This sequence recurs again and again in Hebbel's dramas: it is fundamental to his tragic conception. As long as Judith remains inactive, she incurs no tragic guilt, either as an individual unit in the world-organism or as a woman; as soon as she asserts herself in action, she transgresses the bounds set to the activity of both. 'In der

[1] *v. supra*, p. 65.

Judith zeichne ich die *That* eines *Weibes*,' Hebbel wrote, 'also den ärgsten Contrast, dies Wollen und Nicht-Können, dies Thun, was doch kein Handeln ist.'[1] By this transgression of the limitations of her womanhood, she incurs her fate; the actual form in which fate overtakes her is the confusion of her own motives and feelings which ensues, and which she can only overcome by reverting to passivity, by leaving all personal desire behind her, and by placing the issue once again in the hands of a higher power. In so doing, she regains her poise, but at the sacrifice of individual being; no personal life remains to her: 'Die Waage muss, weil keine irdische Ausgleichung denkbar ist, in beiden Schaalen gleich schweben, und der Dichter muss es unentschieden lassen, ob die unsichtbare Hand über den Wolken noch ein Gewicht hinein werfen wird, oder nicht!'[2]

If Hebbel's treatment of his subject stands in striking contrast to that accorded to it by his predecessors, the formal mastery of his drama is almost equally arresting. The structure of the play is clear and logical; the two parallel actions are conducted, and finally interwoven, with great skill.

The first act shows the camp of Holofernes, and the Assyrian general in his most despotic humour. Passionately absorbed in his own greatness, he is yet bored by the monotony of power. 'Hätt' ich doch nur einen Feind, nur Einen, der mir gegenüber zu treten wagte! Ich wollt' ihn küssen, ich wollte, wenn ich ihn nach heissem Kampf in den Staub geworfen hätte, mich auf ihn stürzen und mit ihm sterben!' Nebucad Necar, his overlord, he despises as a weakling incapable of using his enormous power; for the servile homage of the ambassadors from conquered lands he has only contempt. But when he hears of the Hebrews, a small people worshipping an invisible God and strong in their obedience to His commands—a mere handful defying the mighty armies of Assyria—his attention is at once attracted. 'Ich achte ein Volk, das mir Widerstand leisten will. Schade, dass ich Alles, was ich achte, vernichten muss.' And sending Achior,

[1] *Tagebücher*, ed. cit., vol. i. 1802, 24 Nov. 1839.
[2] *Tagebücher*, ed. cit., vol. ii. 1958, 3 Apr. 1840.

the Moabite chieftain who tells him of the Hebrews, to share their fate as a reward for his warnings, he ends the audience (and the act) with a call to arms against Bethulia.

The second act takes place in the Hebrew city. Not, however, in the streets or in the market-place, but in the apartments of Judith—the true centre of the Bethulian action. For only through the mind of Judith can we apprehend the force measured against Holofernes, or realize the nature of the tragic conflict. So, in conversation first with Mirza, her attendant, and then with Ephraim, her suitor, the picture of Judith's state of mind reveals itself, and at the conclusion of the act we know that she has become aware of the desire to meet, and combat, this unknown and powerful personality.

The motives of Judith's subsequent action are clearly indicated in this second act. Her mind is prepared by a singular experience for a decision most women would have found it difficult to take; in telling Mirza of the mysterious vision seen by Manasses on their wedding night, she reveals the profound psychological effect produced upon her by the unconsummated marriage. 'Unselig sind die Unfruchtbaren, doppelt unselig bin ich, die ich nicht Jungfrau bin und auch nicht Weib!'[1] A further impulse to action springs from her conversation with Ephraim, which occupies the second half of the scene. Thinking to frighten Judith into turning to him for protection (and in so thinking, showing his fundamental ignorance about her) Ephraim vehemently describes the terrible might of Holofernes, and his treatment of those who are in his power. 'Ich mögt' ihn sehen!' she

[1] Hebbel was much preoccupied with the problem of Judith's position, v. *Tagebücher*, ed. cit., vol. ii. 1872, 3 Jan. 1840: 'Nur aus einer jungfräulichen Seele kann ein Muth hervor gehen, der sich dem Ungeheuersten gewachsen fühlt.... Die Wittwe muss daher gestrichen werden. Aber — eine jungfräuliche Seele kann Alles opfern, nur nicht sich selbst, denn mit ihrer Reinheit fällt das Fundament ihrer Kraft. . . . Ich habe jetzt die Judith zwischen Weib und Jungfrau in die Mitte gestellt und ihre That so allerdings motivirt; es frägt sich nur, ob Judith nicht hiedurch ihre symbolische Bedeutung verliert, ob sie nicht zur blossen Exegese eines dunklen Menschen-Characters herabsinkt.' A curious parallel to Hebbel's solution is to be found in a drama, otherwise quite unimportant, published at Zerbst in 1818 (v. *The Story of Judith in German and English Literature* (Bibliothèque de la Revue de Littérature Comparée, XXXIX, Paris, 1927, p. 90).

replies—and in an aside: 'Was sagt' ich da!' And when Ephraim answers that Holofernes would sack the city on her account alone, did he but know her there, she smilingly replies: 'Mögt' es so sein! Dann braucht' ich ja nur zu ihm hinaus zu gehen, und Stadt und Land wäre gerettet!' But the half-jesting answer turns to earnest as Ephraim argues with her; until finally she offers him the chance to win her by going out himself and slaying Holofernes. 'Wie es möglich ist?' she says in answer to his recoil: 'Weiss ich's? Dann thät' ich's selbst! Ich weiss nur, dass es nöthig ist.' To Ephraim's ineffectual protests she opposes fiery scorn. 'Und ist Deine Feigheit die Deines ganzen Geschlechts, sehen alle Männer in der Gefahr Nichts, als die Warnung, sie zu vermeiden—dann hat ein Weib das Recht erlangt auf eine grosse That, dann—ha, ich hab' sie von Dir gefordert, ich muss beweisen, dass sie möglich ist!'

Thus the first and second acts set the stage for the scene of Judith's great resolve. The third act completes its motivation. Skilfully divided into two sections, it first shows us Judith, sunk in a sombre trance, but waking to an impassioned prayer for light to dispel the darkness of her mind, and finally seizing the inspiration of a thought:

'Ich lauschte in mich selbst hinein, weil ich glaubte, ein Blitz der Vernichtung müsse aus meiner Seele hervorspringen; ich horchte in die Welt hinaus, weil ich dachte: ein Held hat Dich überflüssig gemacht; aber in mir und ausser mir bleibt's dunkel. Nur Ein Gedanke kam mir, nur Einer, mit dem ich spielte und der immer wiederkehrt; doch, der kam nicht von Dir. Oder kam er von Dir?—(*Sie springt auf*) Er kam von Dir! Der Weg zu meiner That geht durch die Sünde! . . . Vor Dir wird das Unreine rein; wenn Du zwischen mich und meine That eine Sünde stellst: wer bin ich, dass ich mit Dir darüber hadern, dass ich mich Dir entziehen sollte!'

The scene changes to the streets of Bethulia, and a great crowd scene intervenes between Judith's conception and its translation into action. From one angle after another, the situation is reflected; one group after another shows terror, greed, selfishness, despair. Blown hither and thither by conflicting counsels, and finally keyed to intense emotional reaction after the episode of the blind and dumb Daniel, who finds his speech to prophesy, the populace is about to insist upon surrender when Judith appears amongst them. She supports the protest of the aged priest against the yielding of the city, but her real interest is reflected in her questioning of Achior concerning Holofernes. Finally, announcing her intention to carry out a plan she has conceived, she passes out with Mirza to the Assyrian camp.

Acts I and II lead up to the decision taken by Judith in Act III; Acts IV and V show its effect in action. With amazing intuition Hebbel thus avoided the crucial difficulty of dramatic structure—the *ritardando* of the fourth act, intervening between crisis and solution. Here the interview between Judith and Holofernes bridges the gulf between resolve and action, and leads up to the catastrophe. In it the necessary preliminaries to action are completed; Holofernes is tested, and Judith finds him adamant in his resolve to destroy the Bethulians, though otherwise open to the lure of her beauty. She beguiles him by her half-true tale, and deceives even Mirza into believing that she has betrayed her people. All is prepared for the clash of the two antagonists in the succeeding act.

The scene opens at evening, on the fourth day of Judith's sojourn in the Assyrian camp. Holofernes commands her presence at his table, and a dialogue ensues of great significance for Judith's state of mind. It is interrupted by the abortive attempt of Ephraim to kill Holofernes, after obtaining from the latter a promise of safe-conduct. The Assyrian's behaviour compels Judith to unwilling admiration: 'Du bist gross und Andere sind klein. (*Leise*) Gott meiner Väter, schütze mich vor mir selbst, dass ich nicht verehren muss, was ich verabscheue! Er ist ein Mann. . . . Ich muss ihn morden, wenn ich nicht vor ihm knieen soll.' Momentarily blinded by the spaciousness of vision he reveals, Judith is unable to see beyond his dominant figure: 'Mensch, entsetzlicher, Du drängst Dich zwischen mich und meinen Gott! Ich muss beten in diesem Augenblick, und kann's nicht!' But at Holofernes' answer: 'Stürz' hin und bete mich an!' clarity returns to her and she realizes that the will to power has become master of him who possesses it. Yet it is not until he makes a disparaging comment on her feminine lack of understanding that she is kindled to resentment; then she announces her resolve to kill him, only to be met by scorn: 'Und es sagt mir das, um sich die That unmöglich zu machen! O Feigheit, die sich für Grösse hält!' and Holofernes takes advantage of the confusion of her feelings to drag her away in triumph to his sleeping-tent. Mirza remains in the outer tent, full of apprehension. 'Ich glaube, dort wird Jemand ermordet; ich weiss nicht, ob Holofernes oder Judith!' She guesses her mistress's design, and trembles—but not only in fear: 'Ich habe keinen Muth, ich fürchte mich sehr; aber nicht die Furcht spricht jetzt aus mir, nicht die Angst vor dem Misslingen. Ein Weib soll Männer gebären, nimmermehr soll sie Männer tödten!' At this moment Judith reappears, and in a passionate relation of events to Mirza spurs herself to the decisive act: seizing Holofernes' sword as it hangs above his head, she contemplates him sleeping—and nerves herself to avenge this added outrage to her feelings: 'Dieser ruhige Schlaf nach einer solchen Stunde, ist er nicht der ärgste Frevel?' But when the deed is done, she is tossed from one revulsion of feeling to another. Mirza, though struck with horror, is still able to seize on the weak point of Judith's passionate arguments. She asks her why she should have come in all her beauty to the heathen camp:

'Hättest Du es nie betreten, Du hättest Nichts zu rächen gehabt.

Judith. Warum ich kam? Das Elend meines Volks peitschte mich hierher. . . . O, nun bin ich wieder mit mir ausgesöhnt. Dies Alles hatt' ich über mich selbst vergessen!

Mirza. Du hattest es vergessen. Das also war's nicht, was Dich trieb, als Du Deine Hand in Blut tauchtest!

Judith. (*langsam, vernichtet*) Nein—nein—Du hast Recht—das war's nicht—Nichts trieb mich, als der Gedanke an mich selbst. O, hier ist ein Wirbel! . . . jetzt muss ich meine That allein tragen, und sie zermalmt mich!'

With the realization of her own motives, her course gradually becomes clear. Bearing the head of Holofernes, they return to the city, and Judith knows that praise and acclamation will be her almost unendurable reward.

Bethulia is in the last stages of despair when the day dawns. As in the third act, groups are passing by, their fragmentary conversations evoking images of horror. The arrival of Judith and Mirza turns their hopelessness to triumph—but a triumph all too consonant with the qualities revealed in their adversity: 'Das ist Schlächtermuth!' Judith cries, as they surge out towards the panic-stricken camp of the Assyrians. Of priests and elders who remain, offering her reward and praise, Judith exacts a promise to grant her her one desire—death, should she ask it of them. To Mirza alone does she reveal her motive, in the final words of the drama: 'Ich will dem Holofernes keinen Sohn gebären. Bete zu Gott, dass mein Schooss unfruchtbar sei! Vielleicht ist er mir gnädig!'

Brevity and force are two outstanding qualities of Hebbel's first tragedy. The vigorous prose of the dialogue endows even the long speeches of Holofernes with a vivid interest, while the dramatic concentration of the exposition in Acts I and II is especially remarkable in an early work. The episodes and minor figures are all closely related to the main action and characters; a group of smaller contrasts heightens the effect of the central opposition of two forceful personalities. Such figures as the old blind Samuel, driven by extremity to disclose sin hidden for long years, Assad and Daniel, whose relationship is suddenly reversed by Daniel's momentary and miraculous recovery of his faculties, or Delia, Samja's wife, with her pitiful lament: 'Weiter haben sie keinen Trost für mich, als dass sie sagen: Er, den ich liebte, sei ein Sünder gewesen', suggest in their transient passage an impressive logic of fatality. Similarly, every episode in the Assyrian camp enhances the sense of superhuman force in Holofernes, and emphasizes the tragic arrogance which brings his fall. If the portrait of Judith herself is Hebbel's most striking innovation in the drama, the dramatic economy of the characterization in general is hardly less remarkable. Only

Holofernes sometimes lacks convincing quality. There is an element of exaggeration in the picture which detracts from its effectiveness; on occasion, his self-confidence overleaps itself, and his speech borders on rhetoric. This is the chief mark of immaturity in Hebbel's play. He never again courted the danger; indeed Golo, in his next play, triumphantly showed his power of portraying a daemonic figure, when such a figure was driven by a deeper passion.

In the theatre version of *Judith*, Hebbel was obliged to modify the end, curtailing the scene in Holofernes' tent, and eliminating much of Judith's psychological conflict. In so doing, he felt that he was destroying the coherence of the drama. 'Diese [Abänderungen] hab' ich heute . . . zu bewerkstelligen versucht, und dabei erfahren, dass es die schwerste Aufgabe ist, etwas *Gutes* schlecht zu machen!'[1] He protested, in reply to criticism, against the acceptance of any but the original version: '[Professor Heiberg] spricht nicht über die Judith, die ich . . . in den Druck gegeben habe und die der Kritik als Object vorliegt, er spricht über eine andere, über eine von mir für die Bühne abgeänderte Judith, die Manuscript geblieben und Manuscript zu bleiben bestimmt ist.'[2] The end is indeed essential to the drama. It alone restores the balance that has been disturbed, and Hebbel rightly felt that the concessions made to public feeling destroyed the tragic solution. The success of the performances of *Judith* was not without its penalty: 'Die Poesie,' he wrote in doubtful mood, 'will ich wohl vertreten, aber das Theatralische macht mir grosse Sorgen.'[3]

Genoveva, Hebbel's second drama, presents in form and content a remarkable contrast to the first. Compressed, vigorous, somewhat angular prose is replaced by blank verse with more than a touch of epic breadth; austere economy in the dramatic structure by length and complexity of action. Whereas *Judith* shows a woman transgressing by active assertion of her individual impulse, Genoveva is a

[1] *Tagebücher*, ed. cit., vol. ii. 1923, 4 Mar. 1840.
[2] *Mein Wort über das Drama. Werke*, ed. cit., vol. xi, p. 11.
[3] *Tagebücher*, ed. cit., vol. i. 1862, 30 Dec. 1839.

passive figure, whose tragic guilt lies only in the saintliness and beauty which release in others untamed passions bringing destruction in their train. And while in *Judith* the sex-conflict produces a confusion of feeling which is in itself the tragic complication, in *Genoveva* that conflict evokes in one of the two central figures a passion pursued with logical coherence to its end, and in this pursuit involving the destruction both of itself and of its object. The absorbing interest thus attached to the character of Golo is at once the strength and the weakness of the drama. Into this character Hebbel poured his poetic store, and none can deny its power as a dramatic portrait. Choosing evil while ever seeing good, Golo rivets attention on himself and holds the imagination in thrall. But in this concentration of interest there is an epic rather than a dramatic quality, which is not lessened by the long speeches and monologues that reveal the progress of his passion. In contrast to the swift tempo, the action and reaction of opposing individualities in *Judith*, the course of *Genoveva* is a single forward movement, slowly gathering force, and culminating in its own long foreseen catastrophe. The character of Golo, therefore, who sets the movement going, governs the whole action. In it, Hebbel found a problem that absorbed him.

As the Apocryphal Judith had stirred him to dislike, so previous versions of the medieval Genoveva legend roused his critical opposition. Twice in the diary the statement occurs that it was Tieck's *Leben und Tod der heiligen Genoveva* which called forth his own play;[1] but its origin is less simple than this assertion would suggest. As early as 1839, in Munich, he had read Maler Müller's *Golo und Genoveva*, and in criticizing the author's treatment of the legend had outlined very fully his own idea of the development of Golo's character.[2] Whatever its demerits—and Hebbel saw many—

[1] *Tagebücher*, ed. cit., vol. ii. 2122, 13 Sept. 1840: 'Habe die *Genoveva* angefangen, weil ich die Tiecksche las, mit der ich nicht zufrieden bin. Die ersten Scenen sind recht geglückt', and vol. ii. 2203, 31 Dec. 1840, '. . . an Genoveva (durch Indignation über Tiecks Drama des Namens hervor gerufen) ist der dritte Act fast fertig.'

[2] *Tagebücher*, ed. cit., vol. i. 1475, 2 Feb. 1839.

Müller's drama at least recognizes the significance of this figure. But the dramatic treatment did not satisfy Hebbel; and before his mind there rose a vision of the character, prefiguring in all essentials the Golo of his own drama two years later. In his criticism he clearly stated the main problem: 'Der dramatische Dichter kann den Golo des alten Volksbuchs nicht brauchen, nur, wenn es ihm gelingt, diesen flammenden, hastigen Character aus menschlichen Beweggründen teuflisch handeln zu lassen, erzeugt er eine Tragödie.'[1] Tieck's play, which he read in 1840, while it might suggest a stronger emphasis on the supernatural element of the old legend, could only stimulate him to greater opposition by its treatment of Golo. And if he had condemned Müller's drama as weak and sentimental, the totally undramatic character of Tieck's was still less satisfactory. Yet the decisive impulse to creation may be sought, not only in the outward occasion that Hebbel suggests, but also in his experience during the latter half of the year 1840. The picture of Golo had been complete enough in 1839; to endow it with life there was only needed what Hebbel now knew in greater measure—the experience of passion, such as Elise had not roused in him, the fuller realization that self-torment creates the desire to inflict torment upon others, and finally, the subsequent perception that in her capacity for passive suffering, Elise was remarkable.

His love for Emma Schröder, as can be seen even from the scanty references he makes to it, was full of youthful fire and energy—a dominant impulse, sweeping him on to disregard the other claims he yet admitted. Relations with Elise were intolerably complicated by this new sensation. The open expression of his feelings to her reveals, not an unimaginative mind so much as a deliberate assertion of his freedom—an assertion the more vehement as he felt, deep in his heart, the fetters of present and coming obligations. To this complex state of mind, succeeded in the autumn by an access of remorse towards Elise, the figure of Golo—revived in memory by the reading of Tieck's play—made a stronger appeal than

[1] *Tagebücher*, ed. cit., vol. i. 1475, 2 Feb. 1839.

it had done in Munich. In Golo Hebbel saw the strange relationship of love to hate and torment; the passion that, baulked of satisfaction, resorts to the power of causing pain. He did not need to feel himself a Golo in order to visualize in him the logical development of an impulse whose daemonic power he realized. And without considering Elise to be a Genoveva, he might well feel—as he repeats in the self-reproachful letters of the autumn—that her patience and long-suffering were phenomenal. Only so, I think, can such passages as the following be interpreted:

> 'Mir ist noch kein menschliches Wesen von so wunderbarer, himmlischer Harmonie vorgekommen, wie sie [Elise]. Ich hätte ohne sie die Genoveva nicht schreiben können.'[1] . . . 'Ich habe das Talent auf Kosten des Menschen genährt und was in meinen Dramen als aufflammende Leidenschaft Leben und Gestalt erzeugt, das ist in meinem wirklichen Leben ein böses, unheilgebärendes Feuer, das mich selbst und meine Liebsten und Theuersten verzehrt.'[2]

And numerous passages in the letters to Elise stress this self-accusation.

The problem of a satisfactory motive for the action of Golo was thus a very living one; and in none of the previous versions of the Genoveva legend could Hebbel find it solved. Here was no finished villain, no Iago; the transition from good to evil had to be made credible. In Maler Müller's *Golo und Genoveva* the problem had been in a measure realized—throughout a play of great length the dramatist endeavours to present the development of Golo, but can only show the motive for his surrender to evil by means of the figure of Mathilde. At once a luring and a dominating spirit, she both tempts Golo to crime and weaves the plot that will ensure success. Müller shows a Golo alternatingly protesting and complying, in neither case free from an exaggeration of sentiment that produces an effect of weakness. But at least the interest of the central problem is recognized. In Tieck's version, on the other hand, no central theme predominates;

[1] *Tagebücher*, ed. cit., vol. ii. 2402, 20 Dec. 1841.
[2] Ibid. 2509, 19 Mar. 1842.

through a play of even greater length the interest is divided among various groups of characters and different actions. Tieck expends his efforts on the semi-lyric figure of the saintly Genoveva; hence the long 'Epilogue' of her forest life, restoration and death is almost expanded into a fresh play. The good and evil in Golo seem incompatible with one another, and it is difficult to gain a coherent picture either of his character or Siegfried's.

The clue to Hebbel's conception of Golo is twice stated in the diary: 'Was Einer werden kann, das ist er schon.'[1] The tragic outcome is implicit in the very nature both of the situation and of the actors in it. In Golo and Genoveva Hebbel sees a fatal combination: passion drawn by its opposite, and goodness unable to comprehend evil. Golo's worst temptation proceeds from the very nature of Genoveva, and it is by his capacity to appreciate her quality that he falls a victim more surely to his own desires. All Hebbel's powers, of poetic vision as of dialectic, are expended on revealing by subtle indications the development of Golo's passion and his gradual enthralment to the powers of darkness. To follow this is to follow the action of the play.

Act I shows the sparks that are ready to be kindled into flame. Courage and impetuosity, the impulse to assert himself and gain the respect of those whom he admires, mark Golo's protest in the opening scene to Siegfried at being left behind when his lord leaves on a Crusade. Even Siegfried's answering words of trust:

> Golo, dem Besten nur vertraut der Mann
> Sein Bestes an, und der seid Ihr. Ihr bleibt
> Und nehmt mein Weib in Obacht und in Schutz.

rouse in him first a thought of self to mingle with his thanks: should he pray that he may earn this trust, or pray God to care for Genoveva? In the one case he would be calling down upon her suffering and danger, that he might free her from them; in the other reposing slothfully, his respon-

[1] *Tagebücher*, ed. cit, vol. ii. 2290, 12 Mar. 1841, and vol. ii. 2600, 7 Oct. 1842.

sibilities removed. Siegfried smiles upon his headlong youth; but to us, a shadow already seems to fall across the path.

The moving farewell between Siegfried and Genoveva in the second scene sheds a new light on her to Golo, who is an unseen spectator of their parting. Revealing, in the tender abandonment of grief, an unsuspected power of love, she thus unwittingly rouses him to passion:

> Denn Genoveva, der ich selten nur
> In's Aug' zu schauen wagte, weil, so oft
> Ich's that, ein Licht durch meine Seele fuhr,
> Das mich erröthen machte vor mir selbst;
> Ja, weil ihr Auge mir ein Spiegel schien,
> So rein, dass Alles drin zum Flecken ward;
> Dieselbe Genoveva liebt und weint,
> Sie ist ein Weib! Sie ist ein Weib, wie keins!

Disguised at first as impatience with Siegfried's self-control, his feelings gradually reveal themselves:

> O Liebe, niemals hab' ich dich erkannt,
> Doch jetzt erkenne ich dein heilig Recht!
>
> . . . .
>
> Du bist nicht Leben, du bist Tod, ja Tod!
> Du bist des Todes schönste, höchste Form,
> Die einzige, die giebt, indem sie nimmt!

until when Genoveva falls unconscious and is left by Siegfried in his care, he yields to the temptation of her swoon and wakes her with a kiss.

Forced to an explanation by her surprise at his presence and her vague memory of the caress, Golo makes his first false statement, in a kind of self-defence. But he is conscious of its weight:

> Wer spricht aus mir? Ich nicht! Schweig', böser Geist!

Swiftly following on the first sense of guilt comes Drago's entry. A trusted servant, he has divined Genoveva's longing for a last message from her husband and has brought back greeting from him. To the tender words he adds Siegfried's final exhortation:

Sie soll in Allem Golo sich vertrau'n!
Er führt an meiner Statt das Regiment,
Denk' ich an ihn, so wird mir leicht um's Herz.

Spurred by self-reproach at Siegfried's message, and still more at Genoveva's innocent endorsement:

Auch weiss ich es ja längst, wie Ihr ihn liebt,
Und wer ihn liebt, den lieb' auch ich!

Golo resolves to test his fate. A reckless climb to the castle tower, to destroy a brood of jackdaws that has long disturbed the inmates with their noise, shall solve his problem for him. He throws the responsibility on a higher power:

Du aber, Gott, beschirm' mich nicht!
Ich fürcht' mich selbst, drum wend' ich mich an Dich!
Brech' ich nicht Hals und Bein zu dieser Stund',
So leg' ich's aus: ich soll ein Schurke sein.

And with this curtain to Act I, we know that Golo cannot now save himself from his own mind. The exposition is complete.

The second act opens with a skilful account of Golo's feat, and his apparently miraculous preservation. While all are praying for his safety, he has dared much to seek destruction; and a similar irony prevails in the succeeding scenes, where the servants, his foster-mother Katharina, and Genoveva in turn express their reproaches and relief. Meanwhile, Golo broods over the meaning of this miracle, and the distorted logic of his mind grows plainer:

Denn mir scheint,
Ich that doch Alles, was ein Mensch vermag.

. . . .

Nicht eines Stosses von des Höchsten Arm
Bedurft' es noch, nur, dass er mich nicht hielt!
Er aber that ein Wunder—und warum?
Damit in mir der Schurke reifen kann.

Almost he would himself have taken the one false step needed for destruction:

dann aber rief ich: Nein!
Ich that genug! Wirft Gott mich nicht hinab,
So will ich auch nicht selbst mein Henker sein!

Golo's habit of long monologues and long asides begins in this second act, and henceforth prevails. Especially in his protracted dialogue with Genoveva in Scene 4 does it become apparent—to the detriment of the dramatic value of the scene. The fluctuations of his mood are shown most clearly here. Vague impulses to good are evoked by the crystal clarity of Genoveva's soul, and culminate in his appeal to her:

O Genoveva, weihe Du mein Schwert!

Her reluctance to bless a weapon of destruction, and her eventual dedication of the sword to that fight against evil which alone will justify its use, are full of a deep irony which finds expression in Golo's final soliloquy:

Nur, weil die Heil'ge Weib ward, lieb' ich sie,
Nur, weil ich's sah, wie süss sie küssen kann!
O, wie verstrick' ich mich! . . .

. . . .

Doch nein! Zu schlimm bedrohter Frauen Schutz
Hast Du mein Schwert geweiht; ich will für Dich
Es zücken auf mich selbst, wenn—Du's gebeutst!

With this renewed attempt to cast the responsibility elsewhere, the transition to the chief scene of the next act is suggested.

While the first two acts display the threads that are ready for weaving, Act III shows the preparation of the web. It is of inordinate length; and it is doubtful whether the sinister figure of Margaretha, who suggests the tissue of lies, is made sufficiently credible by the allusive recital of her history to her sister Katharina. She is the incarnation of evil, worked on by the sight of Genoveva's purity, and without excuse of passion:

Weisst Du nicht,
Warum ein Schwan so weiss ist? Dass man ihn
Mit Koth bewirft.

In a word she points the possibilities latent in Genoveva's concern for Drago's illness; in another she uncovers Golo's passion. Mischief is her goal, as she begs a night's lodging from her sister; and she goes to hide in her chamber 'like a firebrand in the straw'.

Between Margaretha's foreshadowing of the plot and its actual execution two episodes intervene, providing her with opportunity in the resultant state of Golo's mind. Greetings and a letter from her husband are brought to Genoveva by Tristan, a knight journeying from the Holy Land. Her reception of the letter and her anxiety at discovering (in spite of his attempt to conceal it) that Siegfried has been wounded, inflame Golo's mind with images of the latter's return; while the following scene, where a painter brings Genoveva's portrait and accepts a commission to paint Siegfried's likeness from memory, overturns the balance completely. Forgetful of all but the intoxication of his senses, he reveals his passion to her portrait as, paralysed with horror, she stands by. Then, in realization of her recoil from him, he reverts to the idea suggested in their previous dialogue and bids her condemn him to self-destruction:

> Wenn Einer fühlt, dass ihn die nächste Stund'
> Zum ungeheuren Frevler stempeln wird;
> Wenn ein Verbrechen, das die Hölle selbst
> Auf's Neu' entzünden könnt', wär' sie verlöscht,
> Aus seiner Brust hervor bricht, hat er dann
> Das Recht, sich selbst zu tödten? Sprecht für Gott!

Genoveva, being what she is, can give but one reply to this: a man capable of realizing that the choice lies between sin and death will be of noble mind, and will never commit the crime he thus condemns. But no sane argument avails against Golo's logic of insanity; and on Genoveva's refusal to accept the responsibility he would thrust upon her, he plainly shows his overmastering passion and disregards alike her appeal to his honour and her own magnanimity. The decisive moment in Golo is now past:

> Ich bin ein Schurk'. Nun hab' ich Schurken-Recht!
> Denn auch ein Schurk' hat Recht. Er kann nicht mehr
> Zurück, drum muss er vorwärts.

The favourable moment for Margaretha's plot has come,

and she expounds it to Golo in his half-desperate mood. Drago is to be asked to keep watch in Genoveva's room, in order that Golo may refute a slanderous statement that has been made about her. To do this, he must conceal himself. An entry can then be forced—an accusation will be in Golo's hands, and he can use it as he will. Golo consents. Still pursuing his perverted argument, he half persuades himself that it is but a further test:

> Wenn sie erliegt,
> So hatt' ich's Recht zur Jagd! Wenn sie besteht,
> So werd' ich um Nichts schlechter sein als jetzt!

By working on Drago's loyalty, he persuades the reluctant retainer that he will be doing his lady a service. In the last scene of the act, the plot is carried out; Drago is stabbed by a zealous servant before he has time to speak, and Genoveva is led away to be imprisoned in the tower. Golo remains, tossing his thoughts as a conjuror tosses balls:

> Ein Mord! Was ist ein Mord? Was ist ein Mensch?
> Ein Nichts! So ist denn auch ein Mord ein Nichts!
> Und wenn ein Mord ein Nichts ist, dien' er mir
> Als Sporn für das, was wen'ger als ein Mord,
> Und also wen'ger als ein Nichts noch ist!

The fourth act is divided into two sections, of which the first shows us Genoveva's state, and the second Siegfried's reception of the news that Golo brings to him in Strassburg. The first part is purely narrative in character; only through the long dialogue between Katharina and Golo do we learn of the latter's recent illness, of Genoveva's imprisonment and the hardships she has suffered. The child she had told Siegfried would await his home-coming has been born during her incarceration, but as none knows the time of its birth except the plotters, its advent has but strengthened calumny. Starvation and grief for her child's hunger have not availed to break Genoveva's resolution, or lessen her trust in Siegfried; and the news that the latter is in Strassburg, sorely weary of his half-healed wounds but pressing homewards, rouses Golo to a plan of action. So he bears the slanderous tale to Siegfried, and the second section of the act is played in Strassburg, whither Margaretha has meanwhile returned.

The reaction of Siegfried to the news is a crucial difficulty of the story, and Hebbel felt it to be so. It is true that Golo's subtle conduct of the dialogue gains every advantage that can be gained by guile. Yet in the end, Siegfried's belief rests, not on his knowledge of both characters—for this, he surely lacks the faculty of observing and interpreting the data that he already has—but on a deep sex-instinct:

> Ich stelle mich als Mann zum Mann. Ich kann
> Nur steh'n für mein Geschlecht, für ihres nicht.
> Was einem Weibe möglich ist, wer hat's
> Erforscht! Doch, was ein Mann zu thun vermag,
> Das sagt die Ahnung in der Brust mir an. . . .

Thus, having chosen between his 'dearest treasures', he is ready to listen with belief while Golo tells a skilful tale. Turning for aid to Margaretha who, posing as a leech-woman, has been tending his wounds, he bids her use her magic crystal; but when Golo, in a swift access of remorse, attempts to tell the truth—

> Herr Graf, ich log!

Siegfried refuses to believe his recantation:

> Nein, Golo, wenn Du Dich verklagen willst,
> So halte Dich im Menschlich-Möglichen,
> Dann helf' ich Dir vielleicht mit meinem Schwert
> Aus diesem Leben mitleidvoll heraus.

To Golo, this is a further link in the binding chain of argument:

> Mein Widerruf bewirkte Nichts,
> Als dass er mir's nur um so fester glaubt.
> Nur darum, denk' ich, liess die Höll' ihn zu!

Driven to frenzy by Margaretha's lying vision in the incantation scene, Siegfried gives his sword and signet ring to Golo, with orders to kill Genoveva and the child. The act ends with Margaretha's vision of the ghost of Drago, who bids her confess her lies to Siegfried after seven years have passed. In this short epilogue to the Margaretha plot there is an allusion to the significance of Genoveva's figure in the universal scheme: the Lord has promised

> Dass er das arme menschliche Geschlecht
> Nie tilgen will, wenn alle tausend Jahr'
> Auch nur ein Einziger vor ihm besteht.
> Auf Genoveva schaut sein Auge jetzt
> Herab und sieht die Andern alle nicht;
> In sieben langen, langen Jahren wird
> Sie dulden, was ein Mensch nur dulden kann.

Such a prophecy, anticipating as it does the action of the fifth act and the *Epilogue*, enhances the epic impression noticeable from the second act onwards.

Act V opens with the preparations immediately preceding the catastrophe. Golo, after ensuring the obedience of the two servants who are to lead Genoveva to the lonely place appointed for her execution, persuades himself once again that a way of escape is left; writing a confession on his tablet, he weighs his own resolve:

> Weisst Du gewiss, dass es Dein Ernst nicht ist?
> Dass Du, sobald es Noth thut, aus dem Busch
> Hervor trittst, ihr dies Blatt reichst, und Dich selbst
> An ihrer Statt dem Rächer-Eisen beutst?
> Besinne Dich, und trau' Dir nicht zu viel!

But the incalculable intervenes to hinder this final test of will. Genoveva's strength does not endure to carry her and the child to the spot so carefully chosen and insisted on by Golo. And her executioners, on the point of carrying out their orders, are frustrated by the simple Klaus, on whom they try to thrust the deed. Acting as if inspired, he kills the one and threatens the other; so that when Genoveva, intervening, begs her life and the child's, the poor boon is granted her. Cutting off her hair as proof to take to Golo, Balthasar leaves her to the dangers of the forest. Meanwhile Golo, awaiting their arrival at the appointed place, torments himself in vain, and finally Balthasar's concocted story of the execution drives him to accuse himself. Siegfried, riding in haste to pursue them, arrives at the crucial moment of Golo's despair; but the latter's impulse to confession is checked by Caspar, Siegfried's servant, who begs him to spare his master. Golo consents, on condition that Caspar will execute on him the vengeance Siegfried would have taken. Blinding himself with his own hand, he bids Caspar bind him to a tree in the inmost forest and leave him to the destruction of wild beasts; but the servant raises a sword to carry out a more merciful sentence as the curtain falls.

The length and complexity of action in *Genoveva* do not obscure the dominance of Golo's figure. And in spite of its absorbing interest, there is justification for Hebbel's initial feeling that the play would be 'wohl kein Drama für's Theater'.[1] The long monologues and conversations, which reveal every stage of resolution in the development of Golo, tax the dramatic form to the uttermost. The thread of fate, as Hebbel later recognized, is 'zu sehr mit Gemüths-Darstellungen umsponnen'.[2] Yet it is precisely in this new vision of the mind of Golo—as has already been suggested—that the most distinctive contribution of Hebbel's *Genoveva* lies. When we turn to the other chief figure, the difference in tragic interest is apparent. Genoveva herself is, from the nature of the situation, a passive character throughout. But as the play progresses she becomes increasingly so, with the growth of Golo's activity. The charm of her shy response to Siegfried's passion in the first act gives place to a pure light of steadfastness while her hope is still in his return; when that hope too is removed, she becomes a purely suffering figure, stirring not so much interest as compassion. In the drama of Golo's conflict between good and evil, her role is necessarily passive. Her stainless spirit is incapable of imagining even so much as the effect of her beauty upon others.

> O, Sünde ist's, so liebenswürdig sein,
> Dass man durch einen Blick, durch einen Ton,
> Ja, durch ein Lächeln selbst, das ihm nicht gilt,
> Den Mann im Innersten in Fesseln legt,
> Die Kraft ihm bricht, den stolzen Muth ihm raubt—
> (II. 4)

[1] *Tagebücher*, ed. cit., vol. ii. 2122, 13 Sept. 1840.
[2] Ibid. 2464, 10 Feb. 1842.

Golo cries in anger, when her innocent kindness has interpreted to his advantage a move calculated to gain her sympathy. Were she taken from the earth, temptation too would vanish:

> Nimm, Ewiger, nimm sie zu Dir empor!
> Nur, weil es Edelsteine giebt und Gold,
> Giebt's Räuber. O, ich fühl' es, dieses Weib,
> Wenn Du nicht schnell sie unserm Blick entziehst,
> Ruft Sünd' in's Dasein, ausserordentlich,
> Wie ihre Schönheit, einzig, wie sie selbst! (II. 4)

In this, the tragic quality of Genoveva is expressed. Guiltless in any ethical sense, she is the cause of guilt in others; and her very excess of beauty and goodness thus constitutes a tragic fault. Hebbel is here following a line of thought which was to attain increased significance in *Agnes Bernauer.* It is less logically presented than in the later play; for the poet is not here content only to assign a passive role to Genoveva in the tragic human drama which ends in Golo's death. He attempts to combine with this drama a superhuman action in which the figure of Genoveva must play an active part. She incarnates the divine power in the battle of good and evil in the universe; in this contest Margaretha, the opposing force of evil, may triumph for a time, but is finally defeated. The prophecy of Drago's ghost is the turning-point of this action and Klaus the divine instrument of Genoveva's preservation—an instrument itself destroyed. But as soon as Genoveva became not only the passive heroine of the human drama, but also (as in the medieval legend and Tieck's play) the protagonist in a universal drama, Hebbel was involved in conflicting conceptions which he did not entirely succeed in resolving. Whereas Judith could act decisively both as an individual and as an instrument of the divine purpose, Genoveva, by virtue of that passivity which is her essential quality, can only play a central part in the superhuman action. The drama of Golo, with Genoveva placed between him and Siegfried, finds its natural end in Golo's despair and voluntary death. The other, with Genoveva as the positive force, and Golo's soul the battle-ground of good and evil, cannot end with this. If, as Hebbel averred, the Christian idea of vicarious suffering and atonement underlay his version of the story,[1] and if the words of Drago's ghost were to bear their full meaning, a further action was demanded. And when Hebbel, in 1851, looked back upon his early work, he saw its implications more plainly. The result was the *Nachspiel zu Genoveva*. Only by the vindication of Genoveva before her passing, the repentance of Siegfried and the recognition of his child, can the conflict of good and evil issue in that triumph of good foreshadowed in *Genoveva* itself. But the *Epilogue* is illuminating. In it we see how shadowy are the characters in the universal drama—how dependent for interest on a sequence of ideas. Perhaps only in the opening scene, where the gentle doe takes refuge in the cave and interrupts the prayers of Schmerzenreich and Genoveva, does a traditional situation of the legend suggest a dramatic moment of great charm. Otherwise, the figures in the Epilogue move and have their being in a remoter world, where thought and emotion are not wholly interfused. Siegfried—even in the drama a figure for whom it is difficult to feel a real sympathy—is no more compelling in the sequel. In Hebbel's original view, he was the most guilty character: 'Es ist ungleich sündlicher, das Göttliche in uns'rer Nähe nicht zu ahnen, es ohne weitere Untersuchung für sein schwarzes Gegentheil zu halten, als es in weltmörderischer Raserei zu zerstören, weil wir es nicht besitzen können.'[2] And although he endeavoured to motivate Siegfried's guilt with care, Genoveva's indictment when she hears her husband's verdict:

> Er hat mich so geseh'n, wie Gott mich sieht.
> In dieser Stunde fängt mein Elend an. (V. 3)

clings about his figure; it is not materially modified by the picture of his repentance in the *Epilogue*. That Golo is the

[1] *Tagebücher*, ed. cit., vol. ii. 2337, 29 May 1841: 'Das Drama hat den Fehler seiner Idee, mögte ich sagen. . . . Die Idee ist die christliche der Sühnung und Genugthuung durch Heilige. Das Menschliche hat sich in die Charactere hinein gerettet.'

[2] *Tagebücher*, ed. cit., vol. i. 1475, 2 Feb. 1839.

life of the drama of *Genoveva* is thus still further demonstrated by the *Nachspiel*. Without this character, which Hebbel's experience informed with passionate life, Genoveva and Siegfried are but pale reflections. The subjective interest that he felt in Golo might prove a source of weakness as far as dramatic balance was concerned: it was the poetic strength of Hebbel's play.

Genoveva, more plainly than *Judith*, shows the poet experimenting with the possibilities of the dramatic form. One further experiment preceded the attainment of that mastery for which *Maria Magdalena* serves as proof: in *Der Diamant* he attempted to explore the scope of comedy.

The theme which Hebbel treated in this play afforded him opportunity for a type of character-drawing akin to that in his prose tales. Two groups of characters, sharply distinct from one another, are related by the loss of a diamond and the adventures attending its recovery; two different types of action lead to the same end. On the one hand, the shadowy figures of the court are grouped round the Princess, whose mental balance has been disturbed by the loss of the precious stone and the ill-fortune it entails. This fairy-tale action centres in the hope that the diamond may be recovered and the Princess thus freed from her delusion. On the other, a group of comic characters, in different situations, forms a circle round the stone, whose progress from hand to hand, as in a game of hunt-the-slipper, entirely occupies their minds. Their several reactions to the temptation of the precious stone and the large reward offered for its recovery form the true substance of the comedy. But the reactions themselves are singularly uniform; all but the old peasant Jacob are led by cupidity to deceit and to the brink of crime—and he is too simple to use guile. The central figure in this group is Benjamin the Jew, whose original theft of the stone from Jacob sets the action moving. The expedient he adopts to evade discovery—the swallowing of the diamond—leads to situations which amply demonstrate his combination of craven spirit and resourceful mind. His tissue of lies is only equalled in audacity by the plausible adroitness of the penniless doctor; in comparison with these two adepts, the covetous judge Kilian and the common scoundrel of a gaoler are but amateurs.

The process of recovering the diamond, continually retarded by the crossing plots of these seekers after the reward, is hastened by the intervention of the Prince. Seeking news of the lost stone, in despair at a delay which may prove fatal to the Princess's state, he tries to cut the knot by insisting on the immediate performance of an operation on the Jew. Nature, intervening, solves the problem. With poetic justice she restores the stone to Jacob during a scuffle; he claims and receives the promised million from the King, while the Princess, healed of her malady, is ready to reward the devotion of her Prince.

The element of comedy in the fantastic tale consists chiefly in the reversal of purpose and achievement. As with Nepomuk Schlägel, there is a striking discrepancy between the aims of the comic characters and the results which they attain. Only to Jacob, whose modest ambitions do not soar beyond the simplest luxuries, and with whose original act of charity the progression begins, does the process of reversal bring a fortune. But while in this way a comic idea does underlie the action, there are two great obstacles to the comic effect. An over-sharp division exists between the two groups of characters; whereas those in the fairy-tale group are too typical and too passive, those in the active group are too generally contemptible. In several scenes there is effective characterization, but *Der Diamant* as a whole shares the defects of Hebbel's comic tales. That comedy and tragedy were but reverse sides of the same medal was his deep conviction; that the angle of vision must be entirely different for the contemplation of the one side or the other he does not seem to have believed.

The Prologue which accompanied *Der Diamant* when Hebbel sent it to the judges of the prize competition is a remarkable document for such a purpose. Amid the temptations presented by the false Muse, the poet resolves with conscious rectitude to follow the difficult way of the true Muse.

Ich will ihn nicht, den Bastard-Witz,
Der, wie ein nachgemachter Blitz,
Aus Glas und Leder kläglich springt,
Ich will, was aus der Tiefe dringt.

The comedy he aims at is

kein illustrirtes Wort,
Das heute glänzt und morgen dorrt.

It is to present men burning with a vital flame, and hint at a strange governance of their lives:

Und dämmernd über den Gestalten
Will ich ein wunderbares Walten,
Drin, wenn auch ganz von fern, der Geist,
Der alle Welten lenkt, sich weis't.

The false Muse counters these aspirations by the assurance that no reward can be expected for such aims: the world only honours that which is akin to its own spirit. The Berlin prize for the best comedy will undoubtedly be given to a picture of the time:

Ein Spiegel
Der Zeit, ein abgeriss'nes Siegel
Des Lebens, das, geschickt gelöst,
Das Tiefstversteckte fein entblösst.

. . . .

Mit einem Wort: die Gegenwart
Ist, wie Narciss, in sich vernarrt,
Sie will ihr Bildniss, zart umrissen,
Dem lieben Sohn erhalten wissen,
Sie hat sich ihr Portrait bestellt,
Und Du, Du bringst das Bild der Welt.
Für Deine Müh' ist Nichts zu hoffen,
Sie krönt nur den, der sie getroffen,
Und hast Du Gott, den Herrn, gemalt,
So sei er's auch, der Dich bezahlt!

And although the poet in the Prologue protests against the possibility that such motives should govern 'erlauchte Richter', it is plain enough that the author of *Der Diamant* believed in their potency. It was all too plain, no doubt, to the judges in Berlin; and it is a proof the more of that combination of unpractical frankness and dogmatic assertiveness which pervaded all Hebbel's dealings at this time, alike with friends and strangers. The Prologue to *Der Diamant* lacks the wit and lightness of touch that distinguish Goethe's *Vorspiel auf dem Theater*, which may have been its model. As in the comedy itself, Hebbel's earnestness is rather too obtrusive for the form.

At Hebbel's entry into Copenhagen, he thus had behind him two major dramas and a short comedy, besides a volume of lyric verse and a number of prose tales—ample justification for the request he proposed making to the Crown. In spite of poverty and moods of hopelessness, he had in some sense 'arrived'; but he now felt a significant moment of his life was come, for on the outcome of his application depended both material subsistence and spiritual development.

V

YEARS OF TRAVEL—COPENHAGEN—PARIS—ROME. 'MARIA MAGDALENA'

HEBBEL'S stay in Copenhagen opened drearily. In the late autumn rain and mists, the future looked gloomy and remorse assailed him for the past. The diary records his first pleasurable emotion on 25 November, when a letter reached him from Elise; five days later, a mood of intense depression prompts him to write: '30 Jahr alt und schon Alles bergab. Ich glaube nicht mehr an die Zukunft und dieser Glaube allein war es, der mich bisher oben erhielt.'[1] The year's retrospect is one of the most despairing entries in the diary; there was no achievement to look back on, no stirring of the creative spirit to give hope for the future: 'Die inneren Quellen springen nicht mehr. . . . Alles, was ich beginne, misslingt. Wenn ich studire, so füllt sich mein Hirn nicht mit Ideen, sondern mit Dampf. Wozu weiter schreiben!'[2] This mood, however, was for the most part due to solitude and is more evident in the journal than in Hebbel's correspondence. His letters to Elise, though anything but hopeful as to the main issue of his Danish visit, are at first determinedly cheerful in tone and full of detailed descriptions of his experiences in the capital. On occasion he was profoundly dissatisfied with his own social disabilities; but such moments were counterbalanced by others, such as the unexpected pleasure of his intercourse with Oehlenschläger, or the satisfaction with which he observed his own sturdy demeanour in his first audience with the King. His account of this to Elise closes with the characteristic comment: 'Jedenfalls ist es besser, ein eckiges Etwas gewesen zu seyn, als ein rundes Nichts.'[3] The interview did not inspire him with great hopes; the King discouraged him in the matter

[1] *Tagebücher*, ed. cit., vol. ii. 2622, 30 Nov. 1842.
[2] Ibid. 2627, 31 Dec. 1842.
[3] Letter to Elise Lensing, 13 Dec. 1842, *Briefe*, ed. cit., vol. ii, p. 157.

of the professorship in Kiel, and though otherwise gracious, was non-committal in his attitude. For the social obligations attached to the status of a petitioner Hebbel had little liking and less talent. It was only in contact with his intellectual equals, with men of letters and artists, that he felt successful or at ease: in Oehlenschläger's company he could be himself, in Thorwaldsen's studio feel reverence and admiration for a kindred art. Christmas and the New Year passed in a gloomy solitude; but by the end of January a more hopeful mood had come upon him. Oehlenschläger warmly supported his application for financial assistance in an open letter to the King; a second audience, ending with friendly words, encouraged him to hope for some substantial outcome, and a letter arrived from Campe, accepting Hebbel's offer of a Dithmarschen novel he proposed to write, and promising to advance the honorarium. 'Von heute', he writes on 23 January, 'fange ich innerlich ein froheres Leben an, der Himmel ist aufgehellt, die Wolken haben sich verzogen.'[1] Under the influence of this new mood a few lyrics were achieved, which he sent in February to Elise for her comments: 'Sey offen und ehrlich, weitläuftige Auseinandersetzungen verlange ich nicht, sie sind nicht Deine Sache, aber von Niemand kann ich es sicherer erfahren, was die Dinge werth sind, als von Dir, denn Dein Gefühl sagt Dir immer das Richtige'[2]—a tribute of some significance. By the end of the month, however, an attack of rheumatism, casually mentioned in a letter to Elise, had crippled him for a day or two. He went out too early to the library, to avoid the expense of heating in his lodging, and the trouble recurred in an acuter form. By mid-March he had been entirely confined to bed for some days, and fever was upon him. In the beginning, he consoled himself as best he could, and the first act of *Maria Magdalena* was conceived and partly written down. But he soon became obsessed by feverish anxiety and the gloomiest forebodings. The whole of March passed without perceptible improvement, and by April his

[1] Letter to Elise Lensing, 23 Jan. 1843, *Briefe*, ed. cit., vol. ii, p. 192.

[2] Letter to Elise Lensing, 1 Feb. 1843, *Briefe*, ed. cit., vol. ii, pp. 200–1.

spirits—depressed by ennui, solitude, and pain—were at their lowest ebb. On 4 April, however, came the welcome news, brought by Oehlenschläger in person, that the King had granted him a 'travelling allowance' for two years of 600 (Danish) Reichsthaler a year.[1] 'Es hat sich schon mit mir gebessert', he writes on that day to Elise, 'und jetzt wird es sich mit Riesenschritten bessern, da ich, in meinem ganzen Leben zum ersten Mal, frei und ruhig aufathmen kann.'[2] Some days later came the official confirmation, and Hebbel began to think of plans. 'Zwei sorgenfreie Jahre habe ich vor mir, es gilt, diese auf die rechte Weise zu nützen.'[3] Paris and Italy occurred to his mind; at least, he explained, Elise would realize that he must not contemplate a long stay in Hamburg. Berlin, too, was suggested as a more immediate goal, perhaps in her company. Meanwhile his rheumatism was not yielding as quickly as he had anticipated to the new hopes and plans, and the depression of illness and confinement did not wholly vanish. But in mid-April he went out for the first time, and by 27 April he was able at last to embark for Hamburg. Reconciled to Copenhagen at the end, he thus records his departure in the journal: 'Die Sonne vergoldete die Stadt, die mir ewig theuer seyn wird. Wir hatten die herrlichste Reise von der Welt.'[4] And on 1 May the first entry after his return to Hamburg runs: 'Heute morgen den ersten Act vom "bürgerlichen Trauerspiel" geschlossen.'

This statement, however, was no augury for the summer months that Hebbel spent in Hamburg. There are few entries of importance in the diary, and a general impression of aridity prevails. In June he was still undecided whether to visit Rome or Paris;[5] not until August is there any mention in the journal of his plans.[6] By then he was intending to set

[1] The equivalent of 1200 Mk. in Hamburg, or 80 Louis d'or. Cp. C. D. Westphalen, *Ein- und ausländische Wechselrechnung nach dem Hamburgischen Geld- und Wechselcours, wie auch Waarenrechnungen*, 17te Aufl., Hamburg, 1835.

[2] Letter to Elise Lensing, 4 Apr. 1843, *Briefe*, ed. cit., vol. ii, p. 251.

[3] Letter to Elise Lensing, 13 Apr. 1843, *Briefe* ed. cit., vol. ii, p. 259.

[4] *Tagebücher*, ed. cit., vol. ii. 2676, 30 (?) Apr. 1843.

[5] Letter to Eduard Duller, 17 June 1843, *Briefe*, ed. cit., vol. ii, p. 271.

[6] *Tagebücher*, ed. cit., vol. ii. 2751, 9 Aug. 1843.

out for Paris in three weeks' time, and was studying French, apparently with small success. In a letter to Hauff he refers to five weeks of illness on his return from Denmark, but no mention of this occurs in the irregular entries of the journal during May and June. Nor does the warmth of sentiment pervading all Hebbel's thoughts of Elise while he was in Copenhagen find any echo in the Hamburg diary. Four matter-of-fact and incidental references are all the latter has to show, together with one entry which perhaps may serve as commentary: 'Die Menschen, in ihren Verhältnissen zu einander, denken immer nur, wenn sie mit einander über abnehmende Neigungen rechten, an ihr bewusstes Wollen und Thun, niemals aber an die mit der früheren oft im grellsten Widerspruch stehende Entwicklungsstufe ihres Wesens, die sie unbewusster Weise erreicht haben oder auf die sie zurück gesunken sind.'[1] In daily intercourse the daily irritations were apt to prevail; absence—while in a measure it had cast a glamour and restored serenity—had meant growth, and growth divergence. A hint of the tragic issue to their intercourse in the forthcoming separation is surely present in the general observation here recorded in the diary.

From the year's retrospect, written in Paris, we know that the Hamburg time was not a happy one. Hebbel could not work; he was the victim of 'eine tolle Leidenschaft . . . sie gewährte mir selbst keinen Genuss, verfinsterte aber ein Daseyn, das ich billig aus allen Kräften zu erhalten und zu erheitern bestrebt seyn sollte.'[2] The main product of these months was polemical. An article by Hebbel in the *Morgenblatt*, entitled *Ein Wort über das Drama*, had been translated into Danish and had called forth a disparaging counter-article by J. L. Heiberg, a Danish critic who was also a co-director of the Copenhagen Theatre. At the moment when the Danish sovereign had just granted a considerable sum of money to the poet, it was impossible to overlook a damaging attack, which was based on a complete misunderstanding

[1] *Tagebücher*, ed. cit., vol. ii. 2700, 20 May 1843.

[2] Ibid. 2975, 31 Dec. 1843; cp. also ii. 2757, with an unexplained reference, obviously to the same relationship.

of Hebbel's statements, and which, among other things, used for its quotations from *Judith* the theatre manuscript of the play sent privately for consideration to the management.

Hebbel therefore wrote in Hamburg a reply to Heiberg, *Mein Wort über das Drama*, setting out to refute the latter's criticisms and in this process elaborating his own reflections on the nature of tragedy and tragic guilt, and on the relations of drama and philosophy. On the last day of July an entry in the diary records the completion of this article, which was published as a pamphlet in Hamburg and which he subsequently sent to his friends Oehlenschläger and Möller, and to some of the influential persons at the Danish court. The controversy brought him no satisfaction, but he regarded his participation in it as a duty to himself and to his patron; its main interest now lies in the clearer definition of Hebbel's own views which emerged from it.

On 8 September he left Hamburg once again—unconscious, as was Elise, that it was to be a lasting separation—and by Havre and Rouen reached Paris on the 12th.

The year which Hebbel spent in Paris was to contain moments of profound significance for both of them, but it opened uneventfully. The first impressions were on the whole unfavourable: ill advised by an acquaintance, who had engaged a room for him, he first lodged at St. Germain-en-Laye, and found himself, to his dismay, cut off from the city by the distance and the expense of traversing it, and doomed to solitary boredom. At the end of the month, however, he was able to move to a lodging in Paris itself and begin his exploration of the capital. It did not attract him on a first acquaintance. A picture in the diary reveals his initial mood: 'Die Lilie tritt aus der Erde hervor, denn es war ihr in deren Schooss zu finster, aber sie mögte wieder in die Erde zurück, denn draussen ist's ihr zu hell.'[1] As in Copenhagen, he records that his first pleasure in France was the arrival of a letter from Elise.[2] For Notre Dame he had no

[1] *Tagebücher*, ed. cit., vol. ii. 2789, 20 Sept. 1843.
[2] Ibid. 2790, 28 Sept. 1843.

admiration: it was 'schwarz, finster, schnörkelhaft'.[1] Versailles oppressed him with its wealth and abundance, but 'man hat keine Ruhe, einem solchen Reichthum gegenüber'.[2] The Pantheon, on the other hand, in its serenity, moved him to the first unqualified expression of delight.[3] He proposed to return to Hamburg in the spring, and to try his fortune in Berlin: never again, he writes to Elise, will they be separated.[4] 'Ich bedarf des Familien-Lebens, ich muss eine Brust haben, an die ich mein wüstes, müdes Haupt anlehnen darf, ich muss bei Dir seyn.'[5] The completely different mode of life, in an apartment without domestic comforts and in cafés, did not appeal to him, and above all, he missed a sympathizing listener. But gradually his view of Paris changes: 'Ich kam kühl an,' he writes three months later, 'aber meine Theilnahme wuchs von Tage zu Tage.'[6] 'Gott,' he exclaims, 'was ist hier Alles zu sehen!'

It was well that he could find satisfaction in the contemplation of art and in the observation of the city's life, for there was comparatively little pleasurable intercourse available. His inability to master the French language precluded much that would have been of interest, and his circle of acquaintances was confined to Germans, or such as could speak German. He met Heine, who made on him an unexpectedly favourable impression,[7] and with whom (in spite of a subsequent temporary coolness based on trivial causes) he continued to exchange visits and ideas. Felix Bamberg, the later editor of his selected correspondence, attached himself to Hebbel and devoted much time to accompanying him on his sight-seeing excursions. Yet he never entirely lost a feeling of isolation, partly native to him, but also due in part to the busy alien life surrounding him. During October he was busy with *Maria Magdalena*; but a few days after the

[1] Letter to Elise Lensing, 3–4 Oct. 1843, *Briefe*, ed. cit., vol. ii, p. 299.
[2] Letter to Elise Lensing, 3 Oct. 1843, *Briefe*, ed. cit., vol. ii, p. 293.
[3] Letter to Elise Lensing, 4 Oct. 1843, *Briefe*, ed. cit., vol. ii, p. 300.
[4] Letter to Elise Lensing, 17 Sept. 1843, *Briefe*, ed. cit., vol. ii, p. 290.
[5] Letter to Elise Lensing, 16–17 Sept. 1843, *Briefe*, ed. cit., vol. ii, p. 288.
[6] Letter to Elise Lensing, 17 Dec. 1843, *Briefe*, ed. cit., vol. ii, p. 359.
[7] Letter to Elise Lensing, 16 Sept. 1843, *Briefe*, ed. cit., vol. ii, p. 287.

completion of the second act, news of a personal disaster intervened—Elise wrote to tell him of the death of Max, their little son, from cerebritis.

The death of this child was a crucial point in the relations of Hebbel and Elise Lensing. Had he not been so far away, and residence abroad so necessary to fulfil his obligations to the Danish grant, there seems little doubt but that their marriage would have taken place. Elise was expecting another child in the late spring, and her frenzied grief at Max's death was a source of deep anxiety to Hebbel. The anguish which pervades his own comments in the journal was in great part remorse—unavailing remorse indeed, since it was concerned with an attitude and outlook that were part of his very being. Every worry—and there were legitimate worries enough—was magnified into a mountain of difficulty, and anticipatory cares were always able to crush the joy he might have had in the present. So fatherhood had brought him little pleasure. Oppressed by the material cares involved, he had been—he reproaches himself—unloving, and unworthy of the gift of a child's love. This conviction, together with the anxiety for Elise's mental and bodily health, produced in him a feeling of despair and misery only fully revealed in the entries in the diary. In his letters to Elise he was at first mainly concerned to stem the tide of her grief by recalling to her his own claims upon her love. These letters, by themselves, seem on occasion egocentric, and filled with an austere philosophy that must have held little warmth of comfort; but read in conjunction with the entries in his journal, they are poignant documents of a difficult relationship. And in view of the crisis which was so shortly to arise in that relationship, Hebbel's insistence on the claims of their affection, on the sacredness of the tie which bound them, and on Elise's duty to spare herself for his sake, if not for her own, is an example of tragic irony worthy of one of his own dramas. 'Sie! Ginge sie auch dahin, und ich könnte nicht wieder gut machen, was ich an ihr verbrochen habe, könnte ihr nicht wenigstens meinen Namen geben, wenn ich denn Nichts Anderes zu geben habe . . .' runs an entry in the diary.[1] And in the first letter to Elise he offers an immediate marriage. 'Wir heirathen uns, sobald wir uns wieder sehen. Das versteht sich von selbst. Aber wir müssen uns so schnell, als irgend möglich, wieder sehen. Gestern würde ich gleich abgereis't seyn, wenn ich Geld gehabt hätte.'[2] He suggests returning to Hamburg, or Elise's joining him in Paris. 'Du bist meine Frau, sobald Du willst.'[3] Three letters are written in this turmoil of mind; on 6 November a fourth follows in a different key. Calculation of the scanty means available and of their probable joint expenses, in Paris or elsewhere, presents the hard logic of facts as an antidote to impulse and emotion. 'Du weisst', the letter ends, 'wie unendlich gern ich dich in meinem öden finstern Daseyn bei mir hätte, aber Du wirst mit mir zweifeln, ob wir an diesen Wunsch unser Alles wagen dürfen.'[4]

When this letter reached its destination, Elise was almost ready to set out upon her journey. Perhaps to her lasting regret, she yielded to his logic and abandoned her resolve. They decided to wait upon events, and see whether Cotta would publish correspondence from Paris, or the Danish king countenance the use of a travelling allowance for residence in Germany. 'Gewiss ist der Entschluss, den wir nun Beide gefasst haben, vernünftig, das Schreckliche liegt nur eben darin, dass wir auf diese Weise vernünftig seyn müssen. Aber das ist der Fluch der Armuth, man darf keiner menschlichen Empfindung folgen.'[5] In the same letter he expresses a half wish that Elise had carried out her first intention, and hints that the decisive calculations were perhaps a little pessimistic, but at the same time reports a refusal from Cotta which seems to confirm the wisdom of their renunciation.

This moment is a turning-point in their drama. The decision once taken, the temperature of the letters falls; the

[1] *Tagebücher*, ed. cit., vol. ii. 2805, 24 Oct. 1843.
[2] Letter to Elise Lensing, 23 Oct. 1843, *Briefe*, ed. cit., vol. ii, p. 305.
[3] Ibid., p. 307.
[4] Letter to Elise Lensing, 7 Nov. 1843, *Briefe*, ed. cit., vol. ii, p. 324.
[5] Letter to Elise Lensing, 21 Nov. 1843, *Briefe*, ed. cit., vol. ii, p. 326.

warmth of anxious sympathy is replaced, to some extent, by argument, reflection, and advice. Hebbel's own mind found satisfaction, if not consolation, in a philosophy of life: 'es giebt nur eine Nothwendigkeit, die, dass die Welt besteht; wie es aber den Individuen darin ergeht, ist gleichgültig, ein Mensch, der sich in Leid verzehrt, und ein Blatt, das vor der Zeit verwelkt, sind vor der höchsten Macht gleich viel, und so wenig dies Blatt für sein Welken eine Entschädigung erhält, so wenig der Mensch für sein Leiden, der Baum hat der Blätter im Ueberfluss, und die Welt der Menschen!'[1] He realized now, only too clearly, the practical difficulties standing in the way of a career. He could never, he writes, fill a professorial chair; his knowledge would be too defective, the constant expression of his reflections utterly alien to his nature. He could envisage the gradual production of six or seven dramas—provided only that they were able to 'mature slowly in the depths';[2] but he was now convinced that he was a poet only, and would never be 'ein Gelehrter'. So he persuades himself and her that they have acted wisely, and through December endeavours to distract her mind by reflection and description, until in the Christmas letter he encloses a poem for her consolation: *Maximilian Friedrich Hebbel an seine Mutter. Zu Weihnacht, 1843.* In the diary he records with satisfaction the completion of this poem, which was to bring comfort to Elise by its picture of the boy, speaking to her in philosophical reflections from a remote abode of bliss. It was hardly surprising that to the lonely mother, longing for the physical presence of her child, such abstract consolation seemed utterly unreal. Hebbel, on his side, was bitterly disappointed at its ineffectiveness: 'Ich hatte mir von meinen Briefen und von dem tiefen Terzinen-Gedicht einige nachhaltige Wirkung versprochen, aber trotz ihrer Worte sehe ich wohl, dass Alles Nichts hilft; es ist, als ob man ihr nach Welt-Untergang wieder eine Hütte zusammen flicken wollte. Zustände, kaum zum Ertragen! Mein Talent hat sich in der letzten Zeit wieder

[1] Letter to Elise Lensing, 21 Nov. 1843, *Briefe*, ed. cit., vol. ii, p. 329.
[2] Ibid., p. 333.

so schön geregt . . . aber wie soll man sich solcher Eindrücke erwehren!'[1] His own grief by this time had subsided into resignation—not without some misgivings on his part: 'Bei dieser ungeheuren Reizbarkeit . . . woher die jetzt in mir schon eingetretene Beruhigung über den Tod meines Sohnes? Ist das Kraft des Geistes, oder Schwäche des Herzens? Ich wage nicht, Ja oder Nein zu sagen, aber ich habe schon oft darüber gedacht.'[2] There is little doubt that after the first shock of feeling, the pressure of circumstances went far to reconcile him to the loss. Moreover, Hebbel had sources of consolation which Elise could not have. He was at a distance, and although at first this seemed a hard condition, it spared him much that she endured. He was a man who had contracted the burden of family cares because he could not resist the solace of sympathy and passion, but who was singularly unfitted to endure the pressure of such cares. He was, above all, a poet; and in the last months of 1843, while Elise mourned in Hamburg, he had transmuted his emotion into the final scenes of *Maria Magdalena*, which he completed early in December. The difference in their reactions to this common sorrow left its mark. Elise's absorption in her maternal feelings no doubt contributed to Hebbel's returning conviction that their marriage would condemn him to an existence of struggle and responsibility sufficient to stifle all poetic inspiration. The reiterated emphasis in subsequent letters on their 'marriage of conscience', and on the example of other writers—Lessing and Hamann, apart from Goethe (whose case, he felt was different)—does little to dispel the impression.[3] Clearly Hebbel disliked the idea of a return to Hamburg, even should his advices from Copenhagen not preclude such a step: 'Mein Wille ist, zurück zu kehren, es handelt sich einzig und allein darum, ob ich darf. Gern thue ich es nicht, das versteht sich von selbst, denn so sehr ich mich sehne, Dich wieder zu sehen, so fürchterlich ist mir Hamburg mit allen meinen dortigen Verhältnissen zuwider;

[1] *Tagebücher*, ed. cit., vol. ii. 2989, 19 Jan. 1844.

[2] Ibid., 2960, 23 Dec. 1843.

[3] Cp. letters to Elise Lensing, 2 Jan., 21 Jan., 13 Feb., 6 Mar., 12 Apr. 1844, *Briefe*, ed. cit., vol. iii, pp. 3–4, 19, 35–6, 45, 77–8.

aber das kommt, wenn ich an das denke, was auf dem Spiel steht, nicht in Betracht.'[1] Later in the same letter he declares: 'Ich bleibe, auch wenn ich zurückkehre, auf keinen Fall in Ham[burg]. Kein Nest in der Welt ist mir so zuwider.'[2]

Oehlenschläger's reply, dated 18 February, did not reach him until the end of April, and by this time its exhortation to caution was scarcely necessary. It was clear from it, however, that any chance of a renewal of the Danish grant would be sacrificed if he returned to Germany. Oehlenschläger added a counsel echoing Hebbel's own fears: 'Was hilft es gleich Ehegatte zu seyn, wenn Sie Frau und Kinder nicht versorgen können?'[3] *Maria Magdalena* had been refused for performance at the Berlin Theatre; the Preface, completed early in March, had been sent to Campe with a letter asking for the establishment of their relations on a different financial basis, but by May Hebbel was still awaiting a reply. Compelled by the fear of losing their only stable income to remain abroad, he received in Paris on 21 May the news of Elise's safe delivery of another son; and from the time when his anxiety concerning her was eased, his indecision also lessened. On 19 June he announced his resolve to carry out the plan of going to Rome, and in an access of hopefulness began to study Italian.[4] Meanwhile he took steps to obtain a doctor's degree at Erlangen, and sent in a thesis on dramatic theory to this end; the considerable expenditure was to be met in part by a sum of money from Campe, who was publishing *Maria Magdalena*; but part of the payment had to be postponed and the actual diploma only reached him later. In September he urged Elise to give up her separate quarters in Hamburg and return to her family's house, as the expense even of her small household was more than he could bear. Spectres of want once more rose up in his mind: 'All die Gespenster, die ich in München

[1] Letter to Elise Lensing, 6 Mar. 1844, *Briefe*, ed. cit., vol. iii, pp. 44–5.

[2] Ibid., p. 49.

[3] *Friedrich Hebbels Briefwechsel*, ed. F. Bamberg, Berlin, 1890, vol. i, p. 245.

[4] Letters to Elise Lensing, 19 June and 8 July 1844, *Briefe*, ed. cit., vol. iii, pp. 112 and 119.

sah, jetzt sind sie da!'[1] At length, on 24 September, he writes that a copy of *Maria Magdalena* has reached him, and that in two days he will be on his way to Rome. Meanwhile, he sends Elise instructions for rectifying a printer's error, for dealing with Campe and for sending complimentary copies of the play to Copenhagen. On the 26th he left Paris with regret; the sun was shining, as if to imprint the city in her fairest form upon his memory: 'Das ist unnöthig, Paris wird immer der Mittelpunct aller meiner Wünsche bleiben. Lebe wohl, Du schöne, herrliche Stadt, die mich so gastfreundlich aufnahm! Empfange meinen wärmsten Segen!'[2] He would feel content, he wrote to Elise, if he found in Rome as much as he was leaving.[3]

He arrived on the evening of 3 October, and with an interval of sixteen weeks in Naples he remained in Rome until October 1845. But this sojourn had not for Hebbel the significance of an 'italienische Reise'. Rome—apart from the glamour of the thought that he was there—drew him, as a city, less than Paris. Plastic art had not the attraction for him that it had for Goethe; he could not rebuild in the mind's eye splendid temples from the Roman ruins. 'Rom ist nur als Ganzes etwas für mich und die höchste Poesie, die ich daraus mit wegnehmen werde, ist der Gedanke, da gewesen zu seyn.'[4] (Its natural beauties, on the other hand, gave him intense delight; he never ceased to wonder at the amazing blue of the Italian sky.) A fortnight after his arrival he writes: 'Warum steht noch Nichts über Rom in diesem Tagebuch? Weil etwas ganz Besonderes darin stehen sollte!'[5] and this sense of oppression seems to have persisted. It was no doubt increased by illness; the Roman climate did not suit him, and three attacks of fever, of which the first came upon him in the second week, left him void of energy. 'Mein Kopf ist nicht dumpf, aber unfruchtbar. Kein Gedicht, geschweige ein Drama. . . . Einmal kommt die

[1] Letter to Elise Lensing, 7 Sept. 1844, *Briefe*, ed. cit. vol. iii, p. 149.
[2] *Tagebücher*, ed. cit., vol. ii, 3241, 26 Sept. 1844.
[3] Letter to Elise Lensing, 24 Sept. 1844, *Briefe*, ed. cit., vol. iii, p. 163.
[4] *Tagebücher*, ed. cit., vol. iii. 3318, 20 Feb. 1845.
[5] *Tagebücher*, ed. cit., vol. ii. 3251, 18 Oct. 1844.

Zeit, wo das Talent mich verlässt. Wenn sie schon da wäre?'[1] The familiar spectre looms once more; and once again the letters to Elise contain gloomy financial calculations. Provision, of the scantiest, can be made till March, he writes to her; meanwhile a petition has to be sent to Copenhagen asking for a renewal of his allowance for another year, the reply and, even in a favourable event, the actual payment, have to be awaited. 'Diese Gedanken machen mich zu Allem unfähig, zum Geniessen, zum Arbeiten. Wahrscheinlich wird mein Drama, wegen des Vorworts, auch bei der Kritik schlechte Aufnahme finden. Nein, nein, mir wird doch Alles vergiftet . . . wer kann Erdbeeren essen, wenn eine Lawine über ihn zusammen zu stürzen droht?'[2] He ends the letter by an assurance that his feelings are unchanged: 'aber mir scheint, der Himmel fällt über mir ein und ich weiss nicht, wie ich meinen Kopf gegen die Zerschmetterung schützen soll!'[3] But the assertion of affection scarcely commands belief. The whole tone of the Roman letters contradicts it. Their comparative infrequency, it is true, was due to the high costs of transmission—and an enlightening glimpse of their two temperaments is afforded by the fact that Hebbel asks Elise five times in as many letters not to use an envelope and not to send any enclosure in the sheet, as he has had to make double payment on each of her letters for this reason. But the correspondence reveals other than surface irritations. A deep sense of grievance pervades it, issuing partly in reproaches, partly—when these are absent—in the increasing impersonality of the descriptions. Their letters must have made bitter reading for each other in these days. Elise, it is evident, replied to his despairing calculations by the reproach of hypochondria, and (alternatively) envied him his enjoyment of experience when, with a considerable effort, he had described some Roman festival. She had read out of the Paris letters definite confirmation of her hope, so long deferred, of marriage; and unwisely—though naturally enough—abandoning their previous precautions, had con-

[1] Letter to Elise Lensing, 21 Oct. 1844, *Briefe*, ed. cit., vol. iii, pp. 170–1.
[2] Ibid., p. 172. [3] Ibid., p. 173.

ducted business in Hamburg as his wife, and of her own motion had written as his betrothed to Copenhagen. To this pressure Hebbel reacted with some vehemence. Return to Hamburg had been precluded by her action, he declared, for marriage was doubly impossible in their present precarious position, and she had committed him irrevocably. In his displeasure he no longer concealed his real feelings about the second child: 'Wie kannst Du z.B. glauben, dass ich das eine Kind anders betrachten könne, als das andere? Ein Kind ist für mich ein Wechselbrief, den ich nicht bezahlen kann, weiter Nichts. Und eine Ehe, die kein reelles Fundament in einem Vermögen hat, das die Existenz sichert, ein Sprung in den Abgrund.'[1] And that this was no mere momentary reaction is plain from the close of the diary in 1844: 'Hier ist der Inhalt des Jahres. Was wird das neue mir bringen? Eine Frau zu dem Kinde, das schon wieder da ist? Kann ich, muss ich heirathen? Kann ich, muss ich einen Schritt thun, der mich auf jeden Fall unglücklich und Dich! nicht glücklich machen wird? . . . Elise ist das beste Weib der Erde, das edelste Herz, die reinste Seele, aber sie liebt, was sie nicht wieder lieben kann, die Liebe will besitzen, und wer nicht liebt, kann sich nicht hingeben, sondern sich höchstens opfern!'[2] It was of little comfort to end letters of naked veracity with the assurance of affection: 'Sey überzeugt, dass Du mir, wie auch meine Stimmungen und Verhältnisse seyn mögen, ewig theuer bleiben wirst, obgleich auf andere Weise, als Weiber den Männern gewöhnlich theuer sind.'[3] Nor was it surprising that Elise should have been reminded of the letters Hebbel wrote from Munich.[4] A similar apprehension now filled his mind—not only the fear of financial shipwreck, but the instinctive recoil from a claim upon his spirit: 'diess Dein Einbohren in mich, was ich bei der höchsten Freundschaft für Dich, bei den wärmsten Empfindungen nicht erwiedern konnte, denn ich

[1] Letter to Elise Lensing, 16 Dec. 1844, *Briefe*, ed. cit., vol. iii, p. 181.
[2] *Tagebücher*, ed. cit., vol. ii. 3277, 31 Dec. 1844.
[3] Letter to Elise Lensing, 23 Dec. 1844, *Briefe*, ed. cit., vol. iii, p. 184.
[4] Letter to Elise Lensing, 6 Feb. 1845, *Briefe*, ed. cit., vol. iii, p. 204.

ahnte, was daraus werden, zu welchen Verhältnissen es führen würde.'[1] Yet even now he evaded the final issue. 'Warum, könnte Einer fragen, nicht für immer einen festen Entschluss gefasst? Entschlüsse sind nicht für Schiffbrüchige; für den Fall, dass wir plötzlich festen Boden unter uns fühlen sollten, wissen wir, was wir thun werden.'[2] But he made it plain enough that her desperate state alone had prompted him to suggest the desperate remedy from Paris. Two significant entries in the journal occur in this same month. The first is a picture: '*Ein edles Mädchen*: so wie sie sieht, dass ihr Geliebter sich von ihr entfernt, in demselben Grade, um ihm Schmerz und Vorwürfe zu ersparen, entfernt sie sich von ihm, und als ihr das Herz bricht, sagt sie, ohne dass er ihr Opfer ahnt: wir taugen nicht für einander, widersteht seinen Bitten, scheint alle Schuld zu tragen und macht ihn frei.'[3] The second is a brief exhortation: 'Schüttle Alles ab, was Dich in Deiner Entwicklung hemmt, und wenn's auch ein Mensch wäre, der Dich liebt, denn was Dich vernichtet, kann keinen Anderen fördern.'[4] The thread is very near to breaking; nearly a year was to pass before the final painful severance, but the Roman letters and entries suggest that it might well have been cut earlier. Hebbel's feelings in the March of 1845 must have been plain:

'*Deine* Gefühle für mich kann ich nicht erwiedern, das hast Du immer wissen müssen und immer gewusst, und es ist doch wohl so wenig bei mir eine Sünde, wie bei Dir, dass ich über mein Herz nicht gebieten kann. Aber dessungeachtet bist Du mir das Theuerste auf der Welt.... Du bist eins der herrlichsten Weiber, die je über die Erde geschritten sind, und es ist mein höchster Schmerz, Dich nicht so lieben zu können, wie Du es verdienst. Alles diess solltest Du wissen, und wenn Du es weisst, wie kannst Du irre werden an Dir und mir?'[5]

Explain it as he might, his state of mind emerges clearly enough from the surface contradictions in terms. The tie with

[1] Letter to Elise Lensing, 6 Feb. 1845, *Briefe*, ed. cit., vol. iii, pp. 204.
[2] Ibid., pp. 206–7.
[3] *Tagebücher*, ed. cit., vol. iii. 3411, 21 Feb. 1845.
[4] Ibid. 3425, 21 Feb. 1845.
[5] Letter to Elise Lensing, 30 Mar. 1845, *Briefe*, ed. cit., vol. iii, pp. 221–2.

Elise had definitely become a fetter, her demands a terrifying addition to the general misery of his circumstances. Gratitude did not allow him to forget her qualities; but it could not make him overlook the clinging nature of her claims. While he experienced no other intimate relationship of understanding, he imagined that he could not live without her sympathy and friendship; yet his exasperation at her inability to grasp his state of mind, to read his letters as a whole instead of fastening upon separate statements in them, might have been an enlightenment to both of them. So, too, the significant fact that Hebbel grew less and less inclined to write to her. For the first time in nine years, the stream of outpoured confidence is checked; and this was the need which had been, for him, the heart of their relationship. The note of inequality, sounded at intervals throughout these years, now vibrates insistently. Its sombre warning could not long be disregarded; but panic does not bring forth wisdom, and Elise's letters—we seem to trace their faint writing beneath Hebbel's vehement characters—were fatally reproachful.

Affairs meanwhile were not prosperous. In December, Hebbel had sent a petition to Copenhagen asking for a renewal of his allowance for a third year, in order that he might spend a longer time in Italy. *Maria Magdalena* had been dedicated to the King (though an unfortunate oversight, due to Hebbel's absence, had somewhat marred the tribute) and in the petition he expresses the hope of completing several other works already planned. This document was handed to the Finance Chamber in Copenhagen, but their resolution, passed in March 1845, only granted 200 Taler to aid the expenses of return from Rome. It cost Hebbel some effort to accept this 'alms';[1] but he eventually decided that he could not afford the luxury of refusal. Gurlitt—an artist in Rome to whom he was drawn in genuine liking—offered with great delicacy a timely loan, part of which was to be made payable in Hamburg to Elise. This enabled Hebbel to carry out his plan of staying in Italy

[1] Letter to Elise Lensing, 29 May 1845, *Briefe*, ed. cit., vol. iii, p. 229.

until the autumn; and in mid-June he moved to Naples, hoping there to write another tragedy—'Giulietta', as it was then called, the later *Julia*.

Unproductive as he was even in a northern summer, Hebbel could hardly expect this hope to be fulfilled. He soon realized that work in Naples was impossible: the three men of Biblical story may have sung in the burning fiery furnace, he writes, but a modern poet can only sigh.[1] After an initial bout of fever, however, he became accustomed to the climate, and Naples in all its beauty caught at his spirit as Rome had never done. Apart from the regret at finding himself incapable of continuous work, he led a pleasant life there. One of two beautiful sisters from Messina, the balcony of whose apartment was adjacent to his own, evidently engaged his heart for the time being. Allusions to her are veiled and infrequent (save in lyric form); but when he left Naples, he wrote to Bamberg: 'Schon höre ich die wohllautendste Sprache der Welt nicht mehr von dem lieblichsten Munde. . . . Dennoch verbanne ich mich selbst, denn Nichts hindert mich, noch hier zu bleiben, aber mir däucht, der Silberblick ist vorüber. Auch den hätte ich festhalten können, doch das erlaubten meine Verhältnisse nicht, und ich glaube eine schwere Probe nicht gar zu schlecht bestanden zu haben.'[2] Pleasant intercourse with a family known to Gurlitt and the companionship of a young scholar—Hermann Hettner—with whom he could discuss theories of art and knowledge, provided the social contacts which he now found desirable: 'Jetzt bedarf ich der Berührung mit Menschen, auf die ich wirke, in denen ich meine Ideen Fleisch und Blut werden sehe.'[3] A hundred epigrams and some lyrics—including *Liebeszauber* and *Das Opfer des Frühlings*, which Hebbel was inclined to rank highest among his poems[4]—were the minor fruits of the Italian sojourn, and he hoped to publish them in a second volume of collected verse. But his letters from Italy to Campe on this and

[1] Letter to Elise Lensing, 7 July 1845, *Briefe*, ed. cit., vol. iii, p. 239.
[2] Letter to Felix Bamberg, 18 Oct. 1845, *Briefe*, ed. cit., vol. iii, p. 264.
[3] Letter to Ludwig Gurlitt, 10 July 1845, *Briefe*, ed. cit., vol. iii, p. 261.
[4] Letter to Felix Bamberg, 10 July 1845, *Briefe*, ed. cit., vol. iii, p. 257.

other proposals were unanswered, to his great indignation, so that by the time he left Italy the fate of the poems was still undecided.

From June till October, during Hebbel's stay in Naples, there is a perceptible hardening of tone in his letters to Elise. To a plan of going to Dresden which she had proposed he not only returns a negative reply but adds a definite refusal to contemplate marriage: 'Dem [Plan] müsste ja jedenfalls eine Heirath vorhergehen, von der ich nicht begreife, wie Du auch nur an die Möglichkeit denken kannst. Von dem unendlich Vielen abgesehen, das hier noch sonst zu berücksichtigen ist: ohne Geld, ohne Sicherheit für die Zukunft geht das nun und nimmermehr.'[1] To her reproach of contradictory statements he opposes the old argument that circumstances compelled him in Paris to suggest a plan that reason and reflection could not fail to disapprove. The constant reiteration of his resolve not to stay in Hamburg on his return to Germany, and not to fetter himself by an additional bond, weighs more heavily than the statement of his obligations to Elise and the child: 'Mich in eine Ecke hin zu hocken, Familien-Papa zu werden und mich daran zu ergötzen, wie der Junge wächs't, wird mir ewig unmöglich seyn. . . . Für Dich und das Kind werde ich thun, was in meinen Kräften steht. Das bedarf keiner Worte, es ist heilige Pflicht. Wenn ich zehn Jahre älter bin, kann auch ein Uebriges geschehen.'[2] This is followed by an entreaty—one of many—that she will consent to give up her apartment and lodge at less expense with her own family. As he felt the gradual development of power, as little by little his work seemed to be commanding admiration (even if it were that of a minority) his hopes and plans outgrew the mere struggle for existence which was all their calculations had envisaged: '. . . mehr und mehr wird es mir Bedürfniss, Wirkungen meiner Thätigkeit zu sehen. Wenn Du mir zuweilen von "Durchkommen" schreibst, überschleicht mich ein unsäglich peinliches Gefühl. Nein, damit bin ich jetzt nicht mehr

[1] Letter to Elise Lensing, 25 July 1845, *Briefe*, ed. cit., vol. iii, p. 252.

[2] Ibid., p. 253.

zufrieden. Lieber den Tod, als ein so enges Daseyn, wo man von Tag zu Tag, wie die Raupe von Blatt zu Blatt hinüber kriecht und selig ist, wenn man sich satt fühlt.'[1] And if it is a sin, he adds, to demand more than this of life, it is nevertheless a poet's doom—what else remains for a writer of tragedies than to be himself a tragic hero? Return to Elise and the return to Hamburg which she never ceased to urge, now woke the same aversion; moreover, Hebbel had grown to feel that she had no understanding for his work, because she had none for the conditions necessary to produce it. Nothing remained but a feeling of obligation, the determination to contract no further debt, and an immense aversion to any renewal of personal contact which would render this determination difficult to carry out.

We do not need the entry in the diary—'Das Weib und der Mann in ihrem reinen Verhältniss zu einander; jenes diesen vernichtend'[2]—to realize that decisive action would ensue. Hebbel left Rome in the last days of October, telling Elise that he was bound for Vienna, and possibly Berlin; she was not to expect news of him until he could give her an address.[3] On 4 November he arrived in Vienna; falling in by chance with an admirer of his work, he unexpectedly remained there, and met Christine Enghaus, of the Burgtheater, who was a passionate admirer of his *Judith*. At their fourth meeting, he became engaged to her.[4]

The swift reaction after the long period of preparation is characteristic both of the poet and the man. Confronted for the first time with the combination of artistic appreciation and a passionate sympathy, Hebbel was powerless to resist the sudden hope of salvation it held out;[5] while in him, admiration for Christine's interpretative genius doubled the response to her personal attraction. 'Sie kennen mein Verhältniss in Hamburg', he wrote early in 1846 to Bamberg, 'Sie kennen es ganz und wissen, dass ich dort verehrt, ja

[1] Letter to Elise Lensing, 26 July 1845, *Briefe*, ed. cit., vol. iii, p. 255.
[2] *Tagebücher*, ed. cit., vol. iii. 3475, 3 July 1845.
[3] Letter to Elise Lensing, 24 Oct. 1845, *Briefe*, ed. cit., vol. iii, p. 271.
[4] Letter to Charlotte Rousseau, 11 Apr. 1846, *Briefe*, ed. cit., vol. iii, p. 319.
[5] *Tagebücher*, ed. cit., vol. iii. 3874, 30–1 Dec. 1846.

angebetet habe, ohne zu lieben. Hier verehre ich, wie ich dort verehrte und liebe, wie ich noch niemals liebte.'[1] And every letter of this period to Bamberg and Gurlitt (who were both admitted to his confidence) draws the same distinction.

There is little contemporary evidence of the events of the winter and the conflict they involved. There are no entries in the diary—even the usual retrospect on New Year's Eve is lacking, for the journal, according to Hebbel's own account, was lying in a trunk not yet unpacked.[2] Letters to the few intimate friends all date from the early spring; and it is from these and from the survey in the diary of December 1846 that our information has to be derived. For Bamberg, in editing Hebbel's selected correspondence, thought fit to destroy all his letters to Elise during the crucial winter months.[3]

There was no escape, however, from the main issues of the situation. The latter was complicated by the fact that Christine had already an unfortunate love-affair behind her; and Hebbel asserts that Elise seized upon this as a ground for writing about her in unforgivably insulting fashion.[4] After all her protestations that he was free and that she was reconciled to an eventual separation, her behaviour in the event, he writes, was such that it lessened the feelings of compunction that must naturally assail him.[5] Repeatedly he emphasizes that she knew the facts about his feelings towards her, and that she should never have demanded, as she did, the sacrifice of his whole life. Emphatically he states that in Rome, long before his meeting with Christine, he had decided to put an end to all relations, save those of friendship, with Elise.[6] But his very insistence on the blame attaching to her reveals an unquiet mind. He could not,

[1] Letter to Felix Bamberg, 27 Feb. 1846, *Briefe*, ed. cit., vol. iii, p. 314.

[2] *Tagebücher*, ed. cit., vol. iii. 3874, 30–1 Dec. 1846.

[3] Cp. *Briefe*, ed. cit., vol. iii, p. 302 (Anmerkung). A brief sketch of the correspondence is given in E. Kuh, *Biographie Friedrich Hebbels*, ed. cit., vol. ii, p. 171.

[4] Letter to Felix Bamberg, 27 June 1846, *Briefe*, ed. cit., vol. iii, p. 341, and *Tagebücher*, ed. cit., vol. iii, 3874, 30–1 Dec. 1846.

[5] Letter to Felix Bamberg, 27 June 1846, *Briefe*, ed. cit., vol. iii, pp. 340, 342.

[6] Ibid., p. 338.

by any arguments, obliterate the moral obligation that he had contracted—and indeed, the constant reiteration that he had never returned Elise's love (though perhaps at best a half-truth) is in itself a grave indictment—nor could he, by recounting her failure in the higher mood, wipe out his own. Justification for his action lies elsewhere. Marriage with Elise, he was convinced, meant poetic sterility—a mere subsiding into the struggle for existence, sharpened by a certain antagonism of temperament and difference of standards. Marriage with Christine offered a sudden hope of an existence free from sordid care, with further scope for his creative powers and the promise of sympathetic interpretation. '*Der Dichter muss eine behagliche Existenz haben, ehe er arbeiten kann;* Andere arbeiten, um eine solche Existenz zu erlangen,'[1] he had written to Elise in the spring of 1845; in 1846 he writes to Gurlitt: 'Ueberhaupt, es giebt innere Nothwendigkeiten, wie äussere.'[2] This is the true rejoinder —nowhere more apparent than in Hebbel's later tragedies.

For Elise Lensing the problem was a very different one. Confronted with a situation which no woman—certainly no mother—could be expected to endure with calm, she recanted every theoretical view on Hebbel's freedom to contract other ties, and only hastened the catastrophe by attempts at discrediting her rival. There seems little doubt but that her natural resentment caused her to reveal the worst side of a disposition normally generous and warm-hearted (a disposition amply evidenced in her later correspondence with Christine). But she was sorely repaid for the single-minded devotion of ten years and for the trials it had brought her. In a lucid moment, when his happiness was assured, Hebbel recognized that the renunciation demanded of her was almost superhuman: 'ich will . . . darin Nichts, als den Beweis erblicken, dass der Mensch auf Alles, nur nicht auf die Grund-Bedingung seiner Existenz Verzicht zu leisten vermag, und mich der Hoffnung ergeben, dass sie einmal, früher oder später, zu einer klareren Einsicht in das

[1] Letter to Elise Lensing, 30 Mar. 1845, *Briefe*, ed. cit., vol. iii, pp. 222–3.
[2] Letter to Ludwig Gurlitt, 11 Apr. 1846, *Briefe*, ed. cit., vol. iii, p. 322.

Sach-Verhältniss gelangen wird.'[1] Thanks to Elise's innate magnanimity, and to Christine's generous heart, this hope was to be fulfilled later in a remarkable degree.

But in the meantime, while Elise suffered keenly and resentfully in Hamburg, Hebbel in Vienna conquered his prejudices against social convention—lightly enough, where Christine's feelings were concerned—and on 26 May 1846 the marriage took place. With it, the 'Wanderjahre' ended.

No observer of Hebbel and his temperament would expect the years of travel and new impressions to bear immediate fruit. It is an interesting fact, however, that the only completed product of this period, which for the first time yielded him the opportunity of wider experience, should be *Maria Magdalena*—a play of which the theme, in striking contrast to that of his earlier dramas, confines the action within the narrowest limits. Only with objectivity came mastery: the greater the element of actual experience (and in *Maria Magdalena* it was considerable) the more necessary to Hebbel was a different experience, producing the detachment needed for poetic fusion and a concentrated presentation. So his 'bürgerliches Trauerspiel', vaguely conceived in Munich, and begun in Copenhagen, flourished and was completed in Paris—a reversal of the conditions under which *Judith*, the drama of individuals in a larger world, came into being in the more restricted life of Hamburg.

Equally significant is the fact that in each of the three plays which were in Hebbel's mind during the years 1843 to 1846 (*Maria Magdalena*, *Julia*, and *Ein Trauerspiel in Sizilien*) the insistent question is one of 'Sittlichkeit', or social ethics in relation to the individual life—though it is only in *Maria Magdalena* that the dramatic solution is successfully achieved.

The most concise of Hebbel's dramas—

dies kleine Bild,
Vielleicht das Einfach-Schlichteste von allen,
Worin sich mir das Welt-Geschick enthüllt—

[1] *Tagebücher*, ed. cit., vol. iii. 3874, 30–1 Dec. 1846.

he calls it in the dedicatory verses—*Maria Magdalena* shows him to have attained complete control of the dramatic form. The actual events of the tragedy can be told in a few words, but their sequence is only intelligible when the characters in Hebbel's picture are seen as he sees them in their relations to each other. Each is essential to the balance of the whole; every moment of the drama adds a link to the tragic chain. There are, however, two figures of dominant interest: Klara, the passive victim, and Meister Anton, the active product, of their common environment. But while the passive figure of Klara becomes active through suffering, Meister Anton, rigidly maintaining his initial standpoint, suffers, passive and unchanged, the train of events that he himself has set in motion. Klara develops, but Meister Anton ends as he began: this is the tragic antithesis of the drama.

Economy of dramatic motive is matched by economy of structure. Even more than *Judith*, *Maria Magdalena* illustrates Hebbel's power of compression, and its very austerity of concentration emphasizes that narrow environment which is the first condition of the tragedy. The only change of scene is in the first half of the third (and final) act; for the rest, the action is confined to a room in the house of Meister Anton. All but one of the major characters enter this room in the course of the first act. The dialogue of Klara and her mother in the opening scene, the subsequent passage of Klara's brother Karl, with its immediate reactions on them both, and the appearance of Leonhard, heralded by Klara's previous conversation with her mother, prepare effectively for the entry of Meister Anton in Scene 5; and by the end of his first dialogue with Leonhard, the relevant facts of the situation are clear. We know that the house is ruled by Meister Anton's will, that Klara and her mother both subordinate their minds to his—save that the mother's partiality for Karl gently opposes her husband's belief that he has been burdened with a graceless son. At the slightest tinge of doubt in Klara's tone about her brother, the mother is indignant, and even to Meister Anton she defends her favourite and his pastimes. Between Klara and her father there is a tacit sympathy, betrayed by her tender, half-amused recollection of his gruffly hidden grief during the worst moment of her mother's illness. There is, too, something of his fierce integrity in her recoil from Leonhard's account of the successful tricks by which he has obtained a post that will ensure her father's consent to their early marriage. But the flash of spirit—'Unwürdiger! Mir aus den Augen!'—is lost at once in fear: 'O mein Gott, an diesen Menschen bin ich gekettet!' (I. 4). For the crucial condition of the tragedy has preceded the opening scene, and Klara's dialogue with Leonhard lays it bare. Shamed out of a girlish love for Friedrich, the 'Secretair', by his silence after his departure for the University, by the malicious comments of her contemporaries and by her mother's counsel to take the chance of marrying in her own sphere, she has drifted, half-reluctantly, into an engagement with Leonhard. The return of the Secretary, creating confusion in her own feelings and rousing Leonhard's jealousy, has produced a crisis: confronted with the choice of being jilted or yielding herself to Leonhard as proof of her real willingness to marry him, she has complied with his demand, feeling half-guilty because of her own interest in the Secretary's return: 'Du lästertest mein Herz und ich traute ihm selbst nicht mehr, Du stand'st vor mir, wie Einer, der eine Schuld einfordert . . .' (I. 4). Now, in the fuller realization of his character and the fetters she has bound upon herself, the confusion of her feelings is complete; she can endure neither the thought of marriage with Leonhard nor the picture of life without it. After the swift exposition of the vital situation in this scene, Meister Anton enters, and Leonhard has the opportunity of making his request for Klara. The character of the master-joiner emerges sharply defined from this interview. Imagination of a kind modifies his rigid limitations, unworldliness is combined with a shrewd realism. The mixture of gruff fear of sentiment with honourable sensibility is revealed in the tale of his lost savings, willingly sacrificed to a benefactor of his youth; his caustic comments on his only son betray the bitterness of a strong character in the face of an unstable one. In the beginning, he sees through Leonhard at once, and suspects the desire for information about Klara's dowry which underlies his questions; but when Leonhard with some adroitness changes his key, Meister Anton—half against his own judgement—thinks better of his prospective son-in-law. The following scene completes the exposition by showing Meister Anton's relations with his wife and their opposing views about their son; and by revealing the father's immediate suspicion of Karl's honesty when a jewel theft is said to have taken place at a house where he has worked, it carries the action a step farther. Swiftly on the mother's defence of her boy there follows the short scene which ends the act: two officers of the law enter to search the house, and one of them, who bears a grudge against the joiner, brutally announces that Karl has been arrested for the theft. His mother, scarcely recovered from her illness, is struck down by the news and dies; Leonhard, who slinks away, sends a letter to Klara renouncing their engagement; Meister Anton, mortally wounded by the accusation against Karl, which he does not for a moment disbelieve, turns on Klara, the only remaining member of his family, and in answer to her desperate cry that she cannot let Leonhard go, demands of her an oath that she at least is not bringing him dishonour. At her dead mother's side she swears that she will never give him cause for shame; and with Meister Anton's defiant exit the act closes.

In six scenes the second act moves rapidly towards the climax. Meister Anton, obsessed, almost to madness, by the thought of his damaged reputation, supplements Klara's vow by a solemn promise to cut his own throat if she is ever pointed at in scorn. The news of Karl's innocence, first brought by the owner of the jewels himself, does not relieve Klara's own despair, in which she prays for death as a deliverance; and when the tidings are repeated by the Secretary in person, her mingled feelings overwhelm her. To his tender recollections of their childhood she returns at first but little answer, suddenly realizing at the mention of Leonhard that she can now ask him to marry her, since her brother's good name has been restored: 'Zu Leonhard, wohin denn sonst? Nur den einen Weg hab' ich auf dieser Welt noch zu machen!' (II. 5). She replies to Friedrich's questions by a wild admission of her love for him, but his jubilant response elicits from her the facts of the situation, including Leonhard's letter and her own confession. The first moves him to frenzied anger, the second to an instinctive recoil, no less annihilating because it is involuntary and qualified in the next moment: 'Darüber kann kein Mann weg! Vor dem Kerl, dem man in's Gesicht spucken mögte, die Augen niederschlagen müssen? (*Er presst Klara wild an sich*) Aermste! Aermste!' (II. 5). His immediate hint of a different solution: 'Oder man müsste den Hund, der's weiss, aus der Welt wegschiessen!' passes over Klara's head. She has only heard the words which quench the slight hope in her heart; and left alone, she spurs herself to seek out Leonhard: 'Ja Vater, ich gehe, ich gehe! Deine Tochter wird Dich nicht zum Selbstmord treiben! Ich bin bald das Weib des Menschen, oder—Gott, nein! Ich bettle ja nicht um ein Glück, ich bettle um mein Elend, um mein tiefstes Elend—mein Elend wirst Du mir geben!' (II. 6).

The scene changes in the third act to Leonhard's apartment. Through his short soliloquy and the subsequent interlude of the nosegay brought him in Scene 3, we learn that he has lost no time in seeking a successor to Klara; there is thus an added incentive to the native shrewdness which makes him apprehend the weak point in her case: 'Liebst Du mich? Kommst Du, weil Dich Dein Herz treibt?' (III. 2). He grasps the opportunity of her high-strung response to refuse her plea, in words that are a variation on the Mephistophelian theme: 'Du sprichst, als ob Du die Erste und Letzte wärst! Tausende haben das vor Dir durchgemacht, und sie ergaben sich darein, Tausende werden nach Dir in den Fall kommen und sich in ihr Schicksal finden . . .' But when he adds that her father will forget his vow and resign himself to circumstance, as others have done before him, Klara finds for the first time a deadly answer: 'O, ich glaub's gern, dass Du nicht begreifst, wie irgend Einer in der Welt seinen Schwur halten sollte!' Again, when the announcement of her determination to save her father by seeking death for herself has shaken Leonhard for a moment into indecision, she rises to irony in her reply: 'Fort von hier! Der Mensch kann sprechen!' (III. 4).

Leonhard, left to his reflections, shows a hesitating mind. He is half persuaded that he must follow Klara, when the Secretary enters, and forces him at pistol point to follow him; Leonhard, in fear, immediately cedes what he imagines to be the main point in the argument: 'Wenn's des Mädchens wegen ist, ich kann sie ja heirathen! Dazu war ich schon halb und halb entschlossen, als sie selbst hier war!' And when this does not avail him: 'Noch heut' Abend verlobe ich mich mit ihr!' 'Das thu' ich, oder Keiner. Und wenn die Welt daran hinge, nicht den Saum ihres Kleides sollst Du wieder berühren!' is the Secretary's answer; and they go to fight a duel which, it is clear, must be a mortal one.

The remaining scenes are enacted in Meister Anton's house, on the same evening. Klara, returning, finds her brother there already, in a mood of reckless lightness which masks a certain bitterness. Their conversation hardly touches Klara's inner mind, which is engaged in a last struggle for decision, and their lack of comprehension for each other in this final dialogue completes with fitting irony the initial picture of their differing temperaments. Karl's request for a glass of water gives Klara her inspiration: an accident can so easily happen at the well. 'O Gott, ich komme nur, weil sonst mein Vater käme! Vergieb mir, wie ich—Sei mir gnädig—gnädig' (III. 8).

But her sacrifice is vain. The Secretary, arriving wounded at Meister Anton's house, betrays to the latter Klara's secret in a single word, prompted by his desire to win her father's forgiveness for her; and Karl, who has hastened out at the first hint of disaster, returns with tidings that confirm their dread: 'Vater, sie ist nicht hinein *gestürzt*, sie ist hinein *gesprungen*, eine Magd hat's gesehen!' Meister Anton's reaction to this news corresponds to all that the previous dialogue suggested: 'Die soll sich's überlegen, eh' sie spricht!

Es ist nicht hell genug, dass sie das mit Bestimmtheit hat unterscheiden können!' Of the Secretary's subsequent reproaches, he hears nothing but the word 'erspart'; and counters swiftly: 'Sie hat mir Nichts erspart—man hat's gesehen!'—to be met by the stern verdict: 'Er *war's nicht werth, dass ihre That gelang!*' True to himself, the father adds: 'Oder *sie* nicht!' and in the tumult which is heard outside as Klara's body is brought home he stands in sombre thought: 'Ich verstehe die Welt nicht mehr!'

As an example of what came to be entitled analytic technique—the gradual revelation through a drama of the essential factors in the dramatic situation—*Maria Magdalena* is remarkable. It plainly shows that this method originates, with Hebbel, in his absorbing interest in character. To reveal events is a mode of revealing character, which is apprehended through its reactions to the past as well as to the present; while this revelation of character in turn lays bare the necessity governing the sequence of events. The past conditions the present; and since it is the dramatist's aim to show the influence upon his characters of every factor in the dramatic situation, he is equally concerned with both. In *Maria Magdalena*, moreover, the characters are more than usually dependent upon their environment, more than usually powerless to free themselves from its control. The cumulative force of detailed circumstances is thus a governing factor in the situation; and it was natural to Hebbel, with his gift for allusion and compression, to suggest throughout the drama the interplay of past and present. A striking illustration of his mode of doing so is in the opening speech of Adam the bailiff in Meister Anton's house. It hints at the deep grudge the bailiff bears him, which is the cause of Karl's arrest and the tragic events that follow on it; but the allusion is only explained in the second act, when Karl's innocence has been discovered, and the owner of the jewels asks the reason for Adam's malice in hastening the action of the law. Similarly, the exposition of the situation between Klara and Leonhard, skilfully conducted in their initial dialogue, is completed by the conversation between Klara and the Secretary in Act II, Scene 5, and by Leonhard's rueful monologue at the beginning of Act III; not until then have we full knowledge of the fatal confusion in her feelings. Finally, every scene in which Meister Anton figures adds detail upon detail to his full-length portrait, only completed in his final words.

This predominant interest in character, and in environment conditioning character, makes *Maria Magdalena* an unusual 'bürgerliches Trauerspiel'. Hebbel was fully aware that it was different from the normal play of this description, still dominated by the interest in situation, and by the traditional opposition between one class and another. His play is dependent for its interest upon no such extraneous complications. The characters not only move in their own milieu, but this milieu itself constitutes the tragic necessity governing their actions. Tradition, in the narrow confines of a single class, assumes the proportions of necessity and law; it is a binding force on Meister Anton—and, in varying degree, on each of the other characters. Adherence to a rigid standard deprives the master-joiner of the freedom his strength of soul would otherwise attain; it makes of him a household tyrant, bound by fetters which he in turn lays on those he loves:

'Wie ein nichtswürdiger Banquerottirer steh' ich vor dem Angesicht der Welt, einen braven Mann, der in die Stelle dieses Invaliden treten könne, war ich ihr schuldig, mit einem Schelm hab' ich sie betrogen. Werde Du ein Weib, wie Deine Mutter war, dann wird man sprechen: an den Aeltern hat's nicht gelegen, dass der Bube abseits ging, denn die Tochter wandelt den rechten Weg, und ist allen Andern vorauf. . . . Ich kann's in einer Welt nicht aushalten, wo die Leute mitleidig sein müssten, wenn sie nicht vor mir ausspucken sollen' (II. 1).

Meister Anton never conquers the obsession of the finger of scorn. The whole motive of his life has been to bear his burdens 'in Züchten und Ehren' (II. 1), and at the first suspicion of dishonour, there is no room left in his heart for charity. The iron bonds of his own standards enchain him to the end, so that Klara's tragic sacrifice on his behalf only rouses him to comment on its fruitlessness. And though his final reflection—'Ich verstehe die Welt nicht mehr!'—betrays some apprehension of standards differing from his own, it still asserts his individual negation of such standards.

Klara is almost equally in bond to her environment. Her surrender to Leonhard's demand is in itself due partly to compliance with a practice common in her sphere of life—partly to an inability, fostered by her training, to resist his momentarily stronger purpose. She does not for an instant doubt her father's fulfilment of his vow, and consequently does not hesitate to invite misery for herself in asking Leonhard to rescue her good name. But there is a hint of recognition that the standards she is striving to uphold are not adequate to all demands:

> 'Wär's um mich allein—ich wollt's ja tragen, ich wollt's geduldig hinnehmen, als verdiente Strafe für, ich weiss nicht was, wenn die Welt mich in meinem Elend mit Füssen träte, statt mir beizustehen. . . . Aber ich bin's nicht allein, und leichter find' ich am jüngsten Tag noch eine Antwort auf des Richters Frage: warum hast Du Dich Selbst umgebracht? als auf die: warum hast Du Deinen Vater so weit getrieben?' (III. 2).[1]

The motive which at one and the same time governs Klara's decisive act by the force of traditional morality, and lifts that act into a higher sphere, is love for Meister Anton. Love brings her no comfort. Neither her father—for whom she reveals a devotion no less profound for being mixed with fear—nor Friedrich, whose own love for her is incapable at first of transcending his instinctive recoil from her confession, can match the quality of her emotion. Apart from her initial fault—so easily explained by the special situation—she too is an example of vicarious sacrifice.

Like Siegfried in *Genoveva*, Friedrich incurs a tragic guilt by his failure—short-lived though it be—to recognize Klara's true quality and to free himself from the bonds of a traditional creed. He sees it clearly at the end: 'Er hat sie auf den Weg des Todes hinaus gewiesen,' he says to Meister

[1] There is a close parallel here to Agnes Bernauer's cry: 'Bald weiss ich, ob's mit Recht geschah!' (*Agnes Bernauer*, V. 3).

Anton in the final scene, 'ich, ich bin Schuld, dass sie nicht umgekehrt ist'. Leonhard is an effective foil to Friedrich. A man of a mean temper, in a narrow sphere, he never for a moment rises above its limitations, or his own. His acts accord completely with his nature; even the small measure of compunction that assails him, when it is too late, is so mixed with calculations for his own advantage that it only reinforces the original impression of his character. 'Ich bin zufrieden,' Hebbel wrote when he had completed the fair copy, 'besonders damit, dass sie eigentlich Alle Recht haben, sogar Leonhard, wenn man nur nicht aus den Augen lässt, dass er von Haus aus eine gemeine Natur ist, die sich in höhere nicht finden und an sie nicht glauben kann. . . . Leonhard ist ein Lump, aber eben deswegen—ein Lump kann nichts Böses thun!'[1] It is the convincing picture of men and women bound by their situation, of 'die Gebundenheit des Lebens in der Einseitigkeit, aus der von vorn herein alles Unheil der Welt entspringt . . .'[2] that endows *Maria Magdalena* with its tragic force. By comparison with this, such an intrigue as that of *Kabale und Liebe* appears arbitrary—a caprice of fate which might conceivably have had a different issue. With Hebbel, the domestic tragedy takes a decisive turn; nineteenth-century thought, with its emphasis upon those factors in human life which are outside man's control, finds an interpreter in tragic art. *Maria Magdalena* is the first of a long line of domestic tragedies confined within the four narrow walls of a spiritual as well as a material habitation.

It was unfortunate that Hebbel thought it necessary—partly under the influence of Bamberg's interest in aesthetic theory—to accompany this play of convincing simplicity by a highly involved analysis of his dramatic aims. The *Preface to Maria Magdalena*, written in Paris and published with the play in 1844, is one of his least successful prose essays. In it he attempted to formulate the relation of drama to the life of the age, and the ultimate aim of all dramatic art. A considerable amount of incidental criticism increased the

[1] *Tagebücher*, ed. cit., vol. ii. 2926, 8 Dec. 1843. [2] Ibid.

controversial tone of the essay, which Campe shrewdly called a manifesto.[1] The intricate form in which Hebbel stated his main arguments certainly detracted from their value; it contrasts strongly with the plain, arresting phrases of his diaries or his letters, where similar ideas are frequently expressed.[2]

The major part of the Preface is concerned with general principles. The aim of drama in its highest form is to present the relation between human life and the governing idea, or ethical centre of the universe. Thus the highest drama is produced at crucial points in the world-process, such as the moments of transition from which Greek and Shakespearian tragedy emerged. Hebbel defines the process of transition to be observed in contemporary history as one of reconstruction: the social institutions are to be rebuilt on a securer basis of ethical law and of Necessity—two forces ultimately identical. It is therefore the task of modern drama to search for this ultimate unity—to show the relations of the fragment to the whole. In this sense—but in no other—drama must be dependent on contemporary life.

From the enunciation of these principles, which are substantially the same as those of his previous article, *Ein Wort über das Drama*, Hebbel passes to criticism of contemporary drama, which he denounces for subserving its age in an unworthy sense. After thus adding a further obstacle to the many difficulties in the way of recognition of his work, he concludes the Preface by a brief statement on the genre to which *Maria Magdalena* belongs. The decadence of the 'bürgerliche Trauerspiel' in Germany proceeds, he considers, from two causes. The speech of the people has been defaced, either by flowers of fine diction or by a lumpish woodenness, so that the characters in these tragedies of domestic life are entirely unlike those of our experience. Moreover—and this is the core of Hebbel's argument—not the inevitable inner restriction of life in a narrow sphere, but

[1] Letter to Elise Lensing, 30 July 1844, *Briefe*, ed. cit., vol. iii, p. 128.

[2] Cp. for example, *Tagebücher*, ed. cit., vol. ii. 2910, 4 Dec. 1843, and *Vorwort zur Maria Magdalene*. *Werke*, ed. cit., vol. xi, pp. 62–3.

external circumstances of an incidental character have formed the basis of such dramas. 'Daraus geht nun unläugbar viel Trauriges, aber nichts Tragisches, hervor, denn das Tragische muss als ein von vorn herein mit Nothwendigkeit Bedingtes . . . auftreten . . .'[1] The ring of tragic form, he concludes, must be complete. In this image we recognize the conception of Necessity which dominates *Maria Magdalena.*

The *Preface to Maria Magdalena* was to cast its shadow for some time on Hebbel's work. Since the play had been refused for performance in Berlin on grounds of delicacy—Hebbel's appeal to precedent in Gretchen fell unheeded—Preface and play became known at the same time, when they were published by Campe in the autumn of 1844. Critics did not fail to profit by this fact, which gave them opportunity for the now familiar argument that Hebbel's plays are dramatized ideas. To the unprejudiced, *Maria Magdalena* in its stark simplicity and power provides ample refutation of this charge; but if further proof were needed, biographical records would show that what first appealed to Hebbel was a dramatic situation. In the last year of his life, writing to Sigmund Engländer about *Gyges und sein Ring*, he declares that he came to the play 'wie der Knabe zum Vogel; er fängt ihn, weil er gerade da sitzt, und sieht sich ihn erst näher an, wenn er ihn in der Hand hat, um zu erfahren, was es für ein Kerl ist'.[2] This, he adds, has been the case with all his dramas. *Maria Magdalena* was founded on an occurrence which took place in Munich 'als ich bei einem Tischlermeister, der mit Vornamen sogar Anton hiess, wohnte. Ich sah, wie das ganze ehrbare Bürgerhaus sich verfinsterte, als die Gensd'armen den leichtsinnigen Sohn abführten, es erschütterte mich tief, als ich die Tochter, die mich bediente, ordentlich wieder aufathmen sah, wie ich mit ihr im alten Ton scherzte und Possen trieb.'[3]

If it is a little difficult to recognize Beppy in the 'Tochter,

[1] *Werke*, ed. cit., vol. xi, p. 62.

[2] Letter to Sigmund Engländer, 23 Feb. 1863, *Briefe*, ed. cit., vol. vii, p. 302.

[3] Ibid., pp. 302–3.

die mich bediente', the acute piece of observation in the anecdote rings true. And Beppy herself gave Hebbel another moment of experience vital to the drama. In January 1837, an entry in the diary records her confession of an unhappy love-affair;[1] two days later he reproaches himself with his reception of her story: 'Ja wohl, du armes Kind, bist Du zum Unglück geboren! Erst musst Du an den gerathen und nun an mich! An jenem Sonntag-Abend, wo Du mir die Geständnisse machtest, war es wohl menschlicher Kraft unmöglich, jedes bittre Gefühl auf einmal zu unterdrücken und Deine aus dem tiefsten Herzen kommende Bitte: "ach Gott, verzeih's mir" zu gewähren.'[2] And though Hebbel's failure in vision actually had no fatal consequences, Beppy did her best to invite them on that evening.[3]

Slowly, as was his way, he allowed these elements to fuse themselves into a whole. After a brief allusion to the theme in the spring of 1839, as he was leaving Munich, no specific mention of it occurs in the journal until the end of 1841, after the completion of *Der Diamant*. Even then, the time was not ripe—'obgleich sowohl Moloch, wie das bürgerliche Trauerspiel Klara stark in mir rumoren';[4] not until the March of 1843 did he begin to write the play, while he lay ill in Copenhagen. Memories and experiences from a much remoter period, figures and surroundings of his childhood, had by this time come to reinforce the picture of the joiner's house in Munich. Hebbel knew the environment of *Maria Magdalena* from experience as he knew no other in his dramas—the characters, in their truth to detail, recall a Dutch 'interior'; and it now seems hardly possible that their living speech should not have drowned the generalizations of the Preface.

Yet the effect of Hebbel's explanations on the one hand, and the scruples of theatrical managers on the other, sufficed for some little time to discredit this mature and vital drama. Christine Enghaus might, and did, recognize its power—

[1] *Tagebücher*, ed. cit., vol. i. 574, 7 Jan. 1837.
[2] Ibid. 582, 9 Jan. 1837.
[3] Ibid.
[4] *Tagebücher*, ed. cit., vol. ii. 2408, 28 Dec. 1841.

indeed, its aptness to her personal history added an element of torment to her artistic appreciation of the play—but it was not until the spring of 1846 that it was performed in Königsberg for the first time.[1]

[1] H. Wütschke, *Hebbel-Bibliographie* (Veröffentlichungen der Deutschen Bibliographischen Gesellschaft, vi), Berlin, 1910, p. 57.

VI

LIFE IN VIENNA—MINOR DRAMAS— 'HERODES UND MARIAMNE'— 'AGNES BERNAUER'

WITH his marriage to Christine Enghaus, a new mode of life began for Hebbel. A settled abode in Vienna replaced the varied lodgings of his travels, and through his wife's work he saw the theatre, both in light and shade, as he had never seen it. That the marriage brought him profound happiness there is no doubt: 'ich habe nicht mehr das Recht, mich über etwas zu beklagen', he wrote in an intimate letter to Gurlitt, 'der Himmel hat mir in ihr [Christine] im Voraus eine Entschädigung für Alles gegeben. Du glaubst nicht, wie gut sie ist, bloss ihretwegen musst Du einmal nach Wien kommen'.[1] To Christine's signature in the diary he appends the words: 'Da steht der Name eines Engels'[2]—an appreciation of her generous heart which persists through all their life together; and 'Eine Herzensreinheit und Engelgüte ohne Gleichen!' he exclaims in comparing her with other women.[3] For her artist's gift he had unbounded admiration, which only increased with the passing of the years. In 1847, when he saw her for the first time as Maria Stuart, he compared her favourably with Rachel, whom he had seen in Paris: 'eine Darstellung von meiner Frau, wie ich noch nie eine zweite sah, selbst in Paris nicht von der Rachel . . .';[4] her performance in *Judith* was 'eine vollendete Leistung. Jede Stellung ein antikes Bild';[5] and as Chriemhild in Raupach's *Nibelungenhort* she appeared to him as a flame of fire—a conception of profound significance for the later *Nibelungen* trilogy.[6] It is indeed in the Prologue to this drama that we find Hebbel's appreciation of Christine's art immortalized,

[1] Letter to Ludwig Gurlitt, 26 Nov. 1846; *Briefe*, ed. cit., vol. iii, p. 355.

[2] *Tagebücher*, ed. cit., vol. iii. 3644, 30 June 1846.

[3] Ibid. 4124, 28 Mar. 1847.

[4] Ibid. 4221, 1–8 July 1847.

[5] Ibid. 4526, 2 Feb. 1849.

[6] Ibid. 4244, 29 Aug. 1847.

after a long and intimate experience of her interpretative gift:

> D'rum nimm es hin, das Bild, das Du beseelt,
> Denn Dir gehört's, und wenn es dauern kann,
> So sei's allein zu Deinem Ruhm und lege
> Ein Zeugnis ab von Dir und Deiner Kunst!

But, as was to be expected, even a happy union of two artist natures had its problems; and Hebbel's own position in 1846 was not altogether easy. For some considerable time, Christine's was the stable income of their household, while his work brought only a highly irregular return. Yet it was Hebbel who tried to insist upon retrenchment and economy, and who resented in particular his wife's excessive generosity to relatives who showed little gratitude.[1] In October, the pair moved to a new home, which represented for Hebbel 'den Gipfel der Wünsche, der bei mir immer weit über den Gipfel der Hoffnungen hinaus geht';[2] and here, on 27 December, a son was born—Emil, or, as they called him, 'Ariel'. For this child Hebbel had the tenderest feelings: 'ich kann mir nicht helfen, aber ich empfinde für dieses Kind ganz anders . . . die Natur macht mehr von der Liebe, von dem unwillkürlichen Zug zweier Menschen zu einander abhängig, als man denkt, doch soll mich diess nie abhalten, meine Pflichten gegen mein Kind von Elise zu erfüllen,' he writes in the retrospect on New Year's Eve;[3] and later: 'Welch eine Freude mir mein kleines Kind macht, ist kaum zu sagen. Daran sehe ich, wie ich die Mutter liebe. Könnte ich der Welt zeigen, wie sehr sie es verdient!'[4] But neither joy nor good resolutions were to be of much avail. In February 1847 Ariel was seized by sudden illness and died in a few hours;

[1] Cp. *Tagebücher*, ed. cit., vol. iii. 4338, 31 Dec. 1847: 'Für die Verwandten, die sie ernähren muss, existirt sie nicht; ihre Mutter hat noch nicht ein einziges Mal nach ihrem Befinden fragen lassen, geschweige, dass sie selbst gekommen wäre.' And even in 1848, a familiar note recurs in the comment on their Christmas tree: 'Ein Tannenbaum für das kleine Titele, an dem mehr hing, als ich mein ganzes Lebelang bescheert erhalten habe; freilich Alles von aussen her in's Haus geschenkt, sonst wär' es sündlich gewesen.' Ibid. 4480, 25 Dec. 1848.

[2] Ibid. 3753, 10 Oct. 1846.

[3] Ibid. 3874, 30–1 Dec. 1846.

[4] Ibid. 3919, 20 Jan. 1847.

CHRISTINE HEBBEL

Portrait by KRIEHUBER, *1855*

three months later came news of the death of Ernst, Elise's second child, whom Hebbel never saw.

If it was inevitable that the father's sorrow should be keener for the child he knew and loved, there was little doubt as to which of the two women was the more sorely stricken. In her own grief, Christine realized that the loss of her child meant to Elise the loss of all she had; and her quick sympathy issued in immediate action. 'Was war das Erste, das meine Frau sagte, als sie die Todes-Botschaft wegen meines Kindes erfuhr? 'Lass' sie—die Mutter—zu uns kommen, lass' sie gleich kommen!' Und auf's Tödtlichste war sie von der gekränkt und beleidigt. Lebt noch eine Zweite auf Erden, die so spräche und gleich ein Zimmer einrichtete, Betten besorgte u.s.w.? Ich zweifle!'[1]

Three letters from Hebbel to Elise at this time have been (at least in part) allowed to escape destruction. A first proposal that the child should be transferred to Vienna if he should recover, since Elise herself had observed that the Hamburg climate did not suit him, is followed by a second letter, on the receipt of news that scarcely allowed room for hope. The hard tone of his reply to her reproaches is somewhat softened in face of the worse tidings; Hebbel entreats Elise in the event of the boy's death to go at once to Campe and draw money to enable her to travel to Berlin; then adds to this suggestion Christine's emendation: 'warum erst nach Berlin, warum nicht gleich zu uns?'[2] The third note, sent immediately after Elise's announcement of Ernst's death, repeats the pressing entreaty to her to come at once, and encloses a money order for the journey: 'Wir können Nichts sagen, als: je eher, je lieber! Ich darf hinzu setzen: Du wirst ein Wesen kennen lernen, vor dem wir Alle uns beugen müssen! Und auch ein Kind, ein liebes, gutes Kind wirst Du finden!'[3] The letter is mainly concerned with the practical details of her journey, but it ends with a peaceful, if a mournful

[1] *Tagebücher*, ed. cit., vol. iii. 4170, 16–20 May 1847.

[2] Letter to Elise Lensing, 9 May 1847, *Briefe*, ed. cit., vol. iv, pp. 22–3.

[3] Letter to Elise Lensing, 17 May 1847, *Briefe*, ed. cit., vol. iv, pp. 23–4. The reference is to Karl Hebbel, Christine's illegitimate son, whom Hebbel had adopted.

cadence: 'Ruhe den Todten, Friede den Lebendigen!' After Elise's visit to Vienna, it was Christine who became her correspondent.

At the end of May Elise Lensing arrived in Vienna, where she remained as the Hebbels' guest until 27 August 1848. On her departure, she took Christine's son Karl to Hamburg, and for the remainder of her life looked after him and his education—an arrangement which afforded her at least a stable, even if a scanty, income. It says much for both women that this solution to a critical situation could be found. The letters of Elise to Christine from 1847 to the former's death in 1854 show a warmth of affection and gratitude which bears clear witness to the magnanimity of each; they also show Elise's final attainment of serenity. The visit to Vienna convinced her that the marriage had justified itself, though the experience could not but be mixed with bitterness. In 1853, writing to Hebbel with news of some documents which had been missing when he asked for them, Elise looks back upon the situation; and for the only time in their relationship we can view it (even though in retrospect) directly through her eyes. 'Ich bin mit meiner Lage zufrieden, und erkenne dass es so kommen musste solltest *Du* glücklich werden und nicht untergehen; der Himmel hat für Dich doppelt gesorgt in dem er Dir die beste Seele zur Gefährtin gab und die zugleich in dem was Kunst und Bildung betrifft Dir würdig zur Seite steht', she writes in full acceptance;[1] but in a previous passage many of the bitter moments in Vienna stand revealed. Hebbel's vehement temper left her defenceless: '. . . Du stehst mir ja nicht gegenüber—also Deine Heftigkeit kann mich nicht Wehr und Wortlos oder stumm machen';[2] Christine's gentle intervention was frequently required, but sometimes drew down the storm upon her head.[3] In her state of frantic misery and physical distress, Elise was in no case to endure Hebbel's imposition of his own way of bearing sorrow: 'Ganz als wäre *Nichts vorgefallen* empfingst Du mich—

[1] *Elise Lensing, Briefe an Friedrich und Christine Hebbel*, herausgeg. im Auftrage des Hebbel-Museums in Wesselburen von Rudolf Kardel, Berlin und Leipzig, 1928, p. 146. Letter to Hebbel, 10 Apr. 1853.

[2] Op. cit., p. 144.

[3] Op. cit., p. 145.

ich musste statt mich auszusprechen, Alles verschliessen . . .';[1] 'Deine Heftigkeit wirst Du nie ablegen', she concludes, 'wenigstens nicht gegen Personen, gegen die Du wahr bist; . . . Nur dass Deine Heftigkeit *seidt ich in Wien war u jetzt hier die 2 mal gegen mich* stets mit einer *gehässigen Bitterkeit* gemischt war, u Du Dich immer bemühtest mich *herunter zu setzen*'.[2] The passage ends with an appeal: 'Tine ist mir eine treue Freundinn u Schwester so sei Du mir ein Gleiches . . .'[3] Elise was by then already feeling the approach of her last illness; it is comforting to read in a letter of the following August after their visit to Hamburg: '. . . ich denke doch gern zurück an die Tage wo wir miteinander gemüthlich lebten weil diesmal so Alles in *Frieden* abgegangen . . .'[4]

The healing process, it is clear, was only begun in Vienna—and chiefly through Christine Hebbel's delicate feelings and compassionate warmth. Not until after her return to Hamburg in 1848 did Elise fully find herself: 'In Wien war ich aufgelöst; zum Theil nicht ich selbst—ich habe mich wieder gefunden; und abgeschlossen.'[5] And she joyfully recognized Christine's part in this: 'Dass *unser* Verhältniss sich so rein gestaltete verdanke ich meinem Dortsein, Euren Ruf nach Wien zu kommen—Soviel Schmerzensstunden mir in jene unvergessliche Stadt auch bestimmt waren—nimmer würde es sich so gewendet haben hät ich nicht Dich, und Alles dort selbst kennen gelernt; jetzt ist unser Verhältniss gewiss eines von denen deren es Wenige giebt'.[6] Through all the multifarious details of Karl's life, education, and physical well-being, all the information about Hamburg and anxious queries about conditions in Vienna, there breathes in these later letters of Elise Lensing a warm affection for Christine, a devotion to Hebbel evident to the last for all her clearer vision of him, and a strangely moving love for their small daughter.

This child—Tinchen, or Titi as she is usually called in

[1] Op. cit., p. 145. [2] Op. cit., pp. 145–6. [3] Op. cit., p. 146.

[4] Op. cit., p. 152. Letter to Christine Hebbel, 25 Aug. 1853.

[5] Op. cit., p. 61. Letter to Christine Hebbel [Feb. 1850].

[6] Op. cit., p. 60.

Hebbel's diary—was born on Christmas Day 1847, while Elise (who acted as godmother) was still with them in Vienna; and although this time all went well, Hebbel's days and nights were passed in anxious foreboding, so that he vowed never to have another child.[1] By the summer, however, when Elise left them, Titi was flourishing; fortune seemed at length appeased, and the day of heavy care was past. The conciliatory close to the tragic relationship of Hebbel and Elise Lensing seemed to sound a truce with destiny—it was, at the least, a strange coincidence.

If marriage and new conditions of life brought Hebbel fresh experience, as usual this experience required time for its assimilation. There had been a pause in his dramatic work, long enough to cause him some uneasiness. In September 1846 he looked through the pages of his journal and discovered that nearly five years had elapsed since the completion of *Der Diamant*, nearly three since *Maria Magdalena*. 'Seitdem ist Nichts mehr entstanden'.[2] *Julia*, begun in Italy, had not progressed beyond the opening act. He now took it up again; by the end of November the third act was finished[3] and by the New Year only a few scenes were lacking.[4] Meanwhile the *Trauerspiel in Sizilien* was begun in mid-September, but an attack of influenza interrupted its progress: '[ich] konnte nicht fortschreiben, wie ich anfing, gerieth also in's Reflectiren hinein und werde nun schwerlich fortfahren können'.[5] By the end of the year, Hebbel felt that he would never finish it; but in February he wrote to Bamberg that it was completed, and had surpassed his expectations: it was 'ein höchst eigenartiges Product'.[6] The final scene of *Julia* was still lacking, and would, he adds, probably remain so, 'da das Stück wiederum gemissdeutet werden könnte und darum liegen bleiben soll, bis ein anderes ihm vorangegangen ist'.[7] This new drama, it is plain, was ab-

[1] *Tagebücher*, ed. cit., vol. iii. 4352, 18 Jan. 1848, and 4355, 20 Jan. 1848.
[2] Ibid. 3684, 21 Sept. 1846.
[3] Ibid. 3818, 29 Nov. 1846.
[4] Ibid. 3874, 30–1 Dec. 1846.
[5] Ibid. 3705, 26 Sept. 1846.
[6] Letter to Felix Bamberg, 26 Feb. 1847, *Briefe*, ed. cit., vol. iv, p. 12.
[7] Ibid.

sorbing Hebbel's mind; it was *Herodes und Mariamne*, heralded by a note in the journal in December 1846, but not actually begun until 23 February 1847, nine days after the death of Ariel. As ever, a state of heightened sensibility quickened his creative power, and though the actual world seemed sorrowfully empty, *Mariamne* sprang to life. The end of March saw the first act completed and the second begun, but by mid-April the customary reaction had set in:

'Diess werd' ich wohl nie los! Nach jeder schöpferischen Periode . . . stellt sich eine erbärmliche Pause elendester Ohnmacht ein, die aber nur in Bezug auf das Ausführen eine ist, nicht in Bezug auf das Erfinden und innerliche Fort-Bilden . . . eben darum aber, weil die Unthätigkeit, zu der ich mich verdammt sehe, keine absolute, sondern nur eine relative ist, erträgt sie sich um so schwerer'.[1]

The death of Ernst, Elise's arrival in Vienna, and the advent of summer were all inhibiting conditions, and the tragedy lay dormant till the autumn. On this occasion, however, Hebbel used the interval for minor tasks—aesthetic essays, revision of the Tales for publication, and the final preparations for a second volume of collected poems. In October, *Julia* was finished, at Engländer's instigation; soon he was at work on the second act of *Herodes und Mariamne*, which was completed in December. But the birth of their second child, his anxiety for the health of both mother and infant, and the lack of sleep entailed by their domestic situation, made the early months of 1848 quite unproductive. 'Die Tragödie geht darüber in die Brüche und wie viele Pläne mit ihr!'[2] he wrote in January. With March came the news of the French revolution and the declaration of a republic—news which he recognized at once as 'ein folgenschweres Ereigniss'.[3] In another fortnight the face of Austria had changed; a few days later came news of a rising in Berlin. Quick to appreciate the significance of social change, Hebbel realized the problems that would of necessity arise: '. . . man ist am Ziel. Was aber weiter werden wird, ist schwer zu sagen und jubeln kann ich

[1] *Tagebücher*, ed. cit., vol. iii. 4141, 11 Apr. 1847.
[2] Ibid. 4349, 15 Jan. 1848.
[3] Ibid. 4369, 1 Mar. 1848.

nur, wenn ich an eine spätere Generation denke, die jetzige ist wohl zu schweren Dingen bestimmt!'[1]

For a short time he played a public part. He was a member of the small deputation sent to seek out the Emperor in his retreat at Innsbruck at the end of May and to present a petition urging his return to Vienna; he also wrote a series of outspoken letters on events in Austria for the *Allgemeine Zeitung*. But, as might have been expected, he failed to secure election as a representative of Austria in the Frankfurt Parliament. In Vienna he was always a northern sojourner, and the difference of attitude grew plainer as the immediate fervour of the March upheaval passed. 'Man reisst jetzt das Pflaster des Staats und der Gesellschaft auf', he wrote in June. 'Mir ist, als ob dem Bau, der jetzt zerstört wird, uralte Erfahrungen zu Grunde lägen, aus Zuständen gewonnen, wie sie jetzt wieder im Anzug sind . . .'.[2] He recognized the dangers of the public mood: 'Hier in Wien sieht es schlimm aus, sehr schlimm, denn alles Maass ist verloren gegangen und was aus einem solchen Zustand hervorgehen muss, ermisst sich von selbst'.[3] October brought the counter-revolution. Vienna was besieged and surrendered to the imperial army; by November repressive measures were in full force, and the short reign of unfettered democracy was over.

In the perils and disorders of the October siege Hebbel found a measure of consolation. An unusually productive period in August had enabled him to write the third and fourth acts of *Herodes und Mariamne* 'in einem Zuge', as he wrote to Bamberg;[4] 'so strömte es in mir zur Zeit der Genoveva', he comments in the diary.[5] But the mood had passed, mainly through external irritations.[6] Danger, like illness, gave the needed stimulus, and now in the days of bombardment the main part of the fifth act was conceived and written. 'Ich schloss meine Mariamne in dieser Zeit,

[1] *Tagebücher*, ed. cit., vol. iii. 4372, 25 Mar. 1848.
[2] Ibid. 4411, 20 June 1848.
[3] Letter to Gustav Kühne, 16 June 1848, *Briefe*, ed. cit., vol. iv, p. 125.
[4] Letter to Felix Bamberg, 22 Aug. 1848, *Briefe*, ed. cit., vol. iv, p. 132.
[5] *Tagebücher*, ed. cit., vol. iii. 4431, 9 Aug. 1848.
[6] Ibid. 4435, 22 Aug. 1848.

sonst hätte mich das Element des Widerwärtigen vielleicht erstickt. Furchtbare, ekelhafte Tage; man erfuhr, was das Chaos eigentlich für ein Ding ist und lernte das *Pflaster* der Societät, von dem Niemand mehr weiss, wie schwer es zu legen war, gründlich schätzen'.[1] The play was finished in November 1848, nearly twenty-one months after he had begun work upon it.

The abolition of the censorship which was among the first consequences of the revolution had opened the doors of the Burgtheater to Hebbel. Till then, the Biblical titles of *Judith* and *Maria Magdalena* had been an effectual bar to their performance; but the acceptance of *Julia* at the end of March heralded the lifting of the ban. *Maria Magdalena* was performed in May, unaltered and uncurtailed, with Christine in the role of Klara. Although Hebbel had regretted the immediate cause—'Mir schmeckt das Ei nicht, das der Weltbrand geröstet hat',[2] he wrote when *Julia* was accepted—he could not but be gratified at the success which attended *Maria Magdalena* in Vienna, as elsewhere. The play was repeated on several occasions through the year; and at last the natural field for Hebbel's dramas seemed to be available. For the first time, and after a year of social and political upheaval, the survey in the diary records a hope of permanence: 'So steht's! Möge mir nur bleiben, was ich habe, mehr will ich vom neuen Jahr gar nicht fordern.'[3] It is a moment of significance for Hebbel's art.

In February 1849 *Judith*—in the Hamburg theatre version—was added to the Burgtheater repertory. This play also succeeded beyond expectation, and Hebbel's admiration for Christine's art grew as he watched her interpretation of his women characters. But when *Herodes und Mariamne* was performed in April, even her acting failed to save the drama from a cool reception,[4] and Hebbel came to the conclusion that it would be better if his plays were published before they were performed.[5] That he was profoundly affected by its

[1] *Tagebücher*, ed. cit., vol. iii. 4481, 31 Dec. 1848.
[2] Ibid. 4380, 28 Mar. 1848.
[3] Ibid. 4481, 31 Dec. 1848.
[4] Ibid. 4581, 19 Apr. 1849.
[5] Ibid. 4659, 31 Dec. 1849.

lack of success is plain: 'Ein schmerzenreicher, qualvoller Abend für mich als Mensch',[1] he records in the journal. The disappointment coincided with a period of illness for all three of them; but on their recovery he was able to complete the fairy-comedy *Der Rubin*, begun on 1 April. 'Nie arbeitete ich so rasch', he adds in comment.[2] In June he finished the first act of *Moloch*—a theme which had occupied him previously in Hamburg and in Naples—but the second act was not completed until October 1850, and when Hebbel took out the yellowing manuscript again in 1861 he decided that only total reconstruction would avail. 'Das ist aber ein Process, als ob man schon vorhandene Rosen, Bäume, Thiere u.s.w. durch chemische Zerstörung wieder in die Elemente zurück jagen sollte.'[3] The summer and the autumn of 1849 passed without creative achievement, as did the spring and summer of 1850. The diary no longer registers the period of inactivity resentfully; it seems as if with *Herodes und Mariamne* Hebbel attained a certainty hitherto unknown to him. We are content to believe his statement at the year's end: 'Ich selbst bin jetzt ruhiger, wie in den letzten zwei Jahren; ich weiss, dass es wieder Winter ist, aber auch, dass der Einzelne den Frühling nicht zurück rufen kann, darum lasse ich meinen Pflug im Stall stehen und thue, was sich hinter'm Ofen thun lässt'.[4] This mood was the more remarkable since both Hebbel and Christine had suffered under the hostility of Laube, the new Director of the Burgtheater, and Hebbel's own short-lived editorship of the artistic side of the Reichszeitung, which he accepted at the end of 1849, had still further embroiled him with his literary opponents. Meanwhile, the failure of *Der Rubin* at its first performance in November 1849 gave opportunity for malice to the new director, as to Hebbel's critics. Characteristically, Hebbel chose to accompany the publication of *Julia* in the spring of 1851 by a polemical essay against Julian Schmidt's criticism of his work. Abundantly justified as it was by his opponent's

[1] *Tagebücher*, ed. cit., vol. iii. 4581, 19 Apr. 1849. [2] Ibid. 4592, 19 May 1849.
[3] *Tagebücher*, ed. cit., vol. iv. 5940, 17 Dec. 1861.
[4] *Tagebücher*, ed. cit., vol. iii. 4774, 31 Dec. 1850.

methods, the *Abfertigung eines ästhetischen Kannegiessers* was not calculated to ease Hebbel's own position in Vienna or in Germany, where Julian Schmidt enjoyed considerable fame as critic and co-editor of the Leipzig *Grenzboten*. Nor does its mood seem appropriate to the poet who had just written *Herodes und Mariamne*. A more pleasing form of argument is to be found in the satirical comedy *Michel Angelo*, completed in December 1850. In this short play Hebbel used an anecdote of Buonarrotti's life to draw a picture of the struggle for recognition imposed on every artist, 'auf reiche eigene Erfahrungen gestützt', as he wrote in 1851,[1] it proved a safety-valve for his irritated consciousness of hostile criticism. 'Ich habe mir durch das kleine Stück Manches vom Halse geschafft, was mich quälte und was ich jetzt los bin. Denn so miserabel der Mensch auch ist: das ist löblich an ihm, dass er sich der Nothwendigkeit beugt, sobald er sie erkennt. Zu dieser Erkenntniss hat er's aber freilich erst dann gebracht, wenn er einsieht, dass für ihn selbst oder die Welt bei'm Spiessruthenlaufen etwas heraus kommt'.[2] He was satisfied with the solution offered by his drama, and his own irritation was appeased: 'Auf mich selbst hat noch nie eine eigene Production so segenreich, so besänftigend und beschwichtigend, zurück gewirkt, wie diese . . .'[3]

Michel Angelo is a comparatively unimportant work, but these comments have no small significance. Together with the New Year's Eve entries in the diary they offer evidence of change and growth. 'Wenn ich nur behalte, was ich habe, so will ich unendlich zufrieden seyn!', Hebbel writes at the end of 1850;[4] and henceforth there are no more plays like *Julia* or *Ein Trauerspiel in Sizilien*—uncertain products of the years of uncertainty. And although we know from Elise's letters after their summer visit to Hamburg that his temper was still vehement—as indeed it remained—new tones of a serener acceptance are heard in the diary now and then.

[1] Letter to Adolf Pichler, 11 May 1851, *Briefe*, ed. cit., vol. iv, p. 292.

[2] Letter to Karl von Holtei, 5 Feb. 1851, *Briefe*, ed. cit., vol. iv, p. 260.

[3] Letter to Franz Dingelstedt, 4 June 1851, *Briefe*, ed. cit., vol. iv, p. 303.

[4] *Tagebücher*, ed. cit., vol. iii. 4774, 31 Dec. 1850.

The *Epilogue to Genoveva* and *Agnes Bernauer* both suggest those harmonies which three years later were to sound in the full cadence of *Gyges und sein Ring*.

Five minor and two major dramatic works were thus completed during the first six years of Hebbel's life in Vienna. But a sharp line divides *Ein Trauerspiel in Sizilien* and *Julia* from *Michel Angelo*, *Der Rubin*, and the *Epilogue to Genoveva*. Whereas these three, though comparatively unimportant productions, visibly belong to the period of *Herodes und Mariamne* and *Agnes Bernauer*, *Julia* and the one-act *Trauerspiel* point backwards to a former mood—the mood of the *Preface to Maria Magdalena*.

For assert as Hebbel might that the theme of his domestic tragedy and of these two later plays alike was the contrast of morals and morality, the drama of *Maria Magdalena* vindicates the artist in Hebbel from the philosophic critic. Only the *Preface*, composed under the combined influence of Hegel's aesthetics and Bamberg's encouragement, forces this conception of the theme upon the reader; Klara herself is proof of her more spontaneous origin. *Ein Trauerspiel in Sizilien* and *Julia* provide interesting corroborative evidence of this. For they are indeed dramatic theses illustrating Hebbel's statements; and whereas the greater tragedies suggest to him ideas which he develops in his commentaries upon them (a process fruitful of misunderstanding), both *Julia* and the *Trauerspiel* seem to have been suggested by an already formulated contrast. Where Hebbel was not a great artist, inspired by a creative force too powerful for complete analysis, he yielded readily to the dominant reasoning process: thus his minor dramas illustrate, by force of contrast, the intuitive certainty of the greater plays.

Ein Trauerspiel in Sizilien in particular seems to issue from a calculated antithesis. Only in the figure of Angiolina (a pleasing memorial to her namesake of Messina) is there any warmth of feeling; the other characters are almost mathematically conceived. 'Das Tr[auerspiel] in Sic[ilien] veranschaulicht die schrecklichste Seite des Polizeistaats', Hebbel wrote, 'dass die Werkzeuge sich zuweilen umbiegen, und zugleich die Extreme der Besitzfrage'.[1] In this instance, the comment is almost a description. Yet the incident which Hebbel dramatized was an actual one, reported to him in Naples from Palermo.

Angiolina, promised by her father to the seventy-year-old Gregorio, mayor of Palermo, has been driven in despair to keep tryst and escape with her lover Sebastiano. Two ruffian soldiers of the military police observe her early arrival at the solitary meeting-place, and by skilful use of her innocent apprehensions and admissions learn her story. They murder her for the sake of the trinkets she is carrying, and then lie in wait for the advent of her lover. Seizing the moment of his abandoned grief at sight of her, they accuse him of the murder; and the accusation is repeated to Gregorio and Anselmo, Angiolina's father, who at that moment come in search of her. Sebastiano in his desperate grief does not dispute the charge; but all is revealed by an unseen witness of the crime. A peasant, having committed a small theft, had sought concealment in a tree to escape the officers of the law; and from this hiding-place he has been a horrified spectator. Proof is supplied by an involuntary exclamation from the weaker-minded of the two criminals, and they are taken for judgement to Palermo. Gregorio reiterates his threat to ruin Anselmo by claiming payment of the gambling debts for the redemption of which Angiolina's hand was to have served; but Sebastiano, learning for the first time the explanation of Anselmo's action, promises to earn enough to keep them both until the latter's death, when he himself will also put an end to life.

Writing to Emil Palleske in June 1847 Hebbel declared that he would have called the *Trauerspiel in Sizilien* a tragi-comedy, if the public were only capable of understanding such a title, instead of assigning to it the most trivial of meanings.[2] He added that the play was intimately connected with his comedy (i.e. *Der Diamant*), and that it would be his last production of this kind. The term 'tragi-comedy' was

[1] Letter to Gustav Kühne, 28 Jan. 1847, *Briefe*, ed. cit., vol. iv, pp. 7–8.
[2] Letter to Emil Palleske, 23 June 1847, *Briefe*, ed. cit., vol. iv, p. 40.

advised by Bamberg.[1] To Hebbel it denoted a situation of comedy subjected to a grim reversal—a conception similar to that of many of the Tales. But *Ein Trauerspiel in Sizilien* suffers even more than these from a constricted formula. Every situation implies a sharp antithesis. The father, whose function it is to protect his child, delivers her by his own action to disaster; the chief officer of justice, whose duty it is to maintain the moral standard, violates it by his unscrupulous lust for possession; the police, who exist to protect the community against evil-doing, commit a dastardly crime; finally the untrained, irresponsible peasant, himself answerable to the law for petty theft, is the instrument of justice for the revelation of the truth. But this mathematical certainty of retribution is not tempered by the warmth of sympathy: the characters of the little drama do not live.

Julia, also a picture of social morals, occupies a larger canvas. Hebbel called it 'ein zweiter Theil der *Maria Magdalena*, der eine, freilich gewagte, Lösung enthält'.[2] But there is little echo of the poignant tones of the earlier drama, though the situations, and the problems they present, bear some resemblance to each other.

Julia, at the opening of the play, faced with a choice similar to that of Klara, is shown one stage farther on her way: she has already left her father's house, in circumstances which afford him little room for doubt as to her cause of flight. Tobaldi, like Meister Anton, will not endure to have his daughter's good name questioned, and chooses a course that will leave him no alternative but to disown her, if she should return to him. With the reluctant aid of an old retainer and of Alberto, a doctor and devoted friend, he asserts her to have fallen a victim to a dangerous and infectious illness, and with bitter determination carries out the arrangements for her funeral. With the introduction of Graf Bertram in a forest scene, the opposite pole of the moral problem is presented. Shattered in health and spirits from the excesses of his earlier youth, wealthy, titled, and hopelessly

[1] *Tagebücher*, ed. cit., vol. iii. 3877, 2 Jan. 1847.

[2] Letter to Ludwig Gurlitt, 26 Nov. 1846, *Briefe*, ed. cit., vol. iii, p. 353.

aware of the failure of all material good fortune to redeem his spiritual bankruptcy, Bertram despairs of finding any valid reason for continuing to live. Only the devotion of an old servant prevents him from putting an end to his own life, now that he has realized his uselessness to himself and to society. But a chance encounter with Julia, threatened with death at the hands of a ruffianly guide through the forest, leads him to hear her story of betrayal by her lover; and gradually as he listens to her tale, an unexpected chance of redemption is revealed. He keeps her from further search for the death which she would welcome by a reminder of her duty to the child that she may bear, and by an offer of a formal marriage. The only promise he exacts is a full confession of her feelings should she ever meet again the man who has abandoned her. With Julia's acceptance of his terms and their resolve to seek her father's house with a suitable version of her story, the first act closes.

The appearance of Antonio in the second act supplies the missing facts of Julia's love-story, and establishes his innocence of any intention to desert her. His grief at the preparations in Tobaldi's house and his resolve to follow Julia's funeral before giving way to his despair only intensify the scruples of Tobaldi's servant Valentino; the succeeding dialogues however show the former immovably determined to bear the consequences of his action. The test of his resolution is immediately provided by the arrival of Graf Bertram, presenting himself as Julia's lover, and asking for his consent to their union. But unmoved even by the appearance of Julia herself and her grief at sight of a coffin she presumes to be her father's, Tobaldi reiterates the declaration that he is burying his only child. Only after his rejection of her, and Alberto's announcement that he at least will accompany the couple to the Count's home in Tyrol and see the marriage celebrated, does he melt for a moment into human feeling: 'Ich will sie nie wieder sehen! Aber—ich kann wieder anders von ihr denken!' (Act II, Sc. 11).

The third act brings Julia and Antonio face to face. His presence, his explanation of his outlawed state and of the past, his bitter anger at her marriage (betrayed to him, at the grave where he had been about to kill himself, by Valentino) rouse in Julia a momentary conflict. But it is solved for her by the recollection of Bertram's nobility of mind, and she is firm in her decision that Antonio must part from her for ever. Graf Bertram, entering with Alberto at this moment and quickly realizing the situation, reminds Julia of her promise; she in turn endeavours to conceal from him the fact of her renewed love for Antonio, since she divines it will cause him to seek death for himself in order to compass her release. As a last argument to move her from this position, Bertram reveals to them his past history and his own resolve to seek death before he met Julia. His magnanimity conquers Antonio, and the latter declares his determination to watch over Bertram's life and protect him from himself. Acquiescing in their refusal to profit wittingly by his intended sacrifice, Bertram demands in return a promise that should he die a natural death, they will not be deterred from seeking their happiness together. With Bertram's offer to Antonio to share their life, and his resolve (expressed in an aside) that his own death from misadventure shall not be long delayed, the drama closes.

Hebbel himself was only half satisfied with *Julia*. The play lay unfinished for some time; and though he might explain his reluctance to complete it by the likelihood that it would be misinterpreted, the explanation does not carry conviction. A more illuminating comment occurs in a letter to Bamberg; in enclosing a fair copy of *Julia*, he begs Bamberg not to show it to any German 'er sey auch, wer er sey. . . . Ich fühle mich sehr dadurch erleichtert, dass ich es endlich vom Halse los bin, es hat mich lange gedrückt und ist wohl meine letzte Production dieser Art'.[1] A few weeks later he wrote to Rötscher: 'Julia ist schon ganz Uebergangsproduct; ich trete nun in eine neue Sphäre ein . . . ja ich lebte eigentlich, während ich die letzten Acte der Julia ausführte, schon in der neuen und fühlte mich, als sie fertig war, von einer

[1] Letter to Felix Bamberg, 10 Nov. 1847, *Briefe*, ed. cit., vol. iv, p. 60.

wahren Last befreit'.[1] There is little suggestion here of the creative fervour plainly felt during the composition of *Judith*, *Genoveva*, or *Maria Magdalena*, and in the drama itself the lack of it is evident. This lack, however, is chiefly in the characters. *Julia*, no less than Hebbel's greater plays, is satisfying in its stage-craft: the skilful interweaving of past and present in the action, the gradual revelation of Antonio's situation and of Julia's love-story, the contrast of fact and fiction in the scene of Julia's arrival at her father's house, all reveal his wonted mastery of dramatic structure. But neither characters nor dialogue can bear comparison with those of Hebbel's other tragedies. Only the figure of Valentino, with his conflicting loyalties and simple fears, has life and warmth. Tobaldi's determination is but obstinacy compared with Meister Anton's tyranny of pride; Bertram and Antonio explain their motives and themselves at tedious length; Julia even, though she rouses our compassion, remains a pale figure round which the drama moves. Moreover, the solution of the problem, inconclusive as it is, leaves us dispirited. There is no tragic satisfaction either in Bertram's intended sacrifice or in the renunciation of Julia and Antonio. The postponement of the first gives it an abstract character, while the temporary nature of the second, so clearly indicated in the closing lines, detracts from its dramatic value.

Ein Trauerspiel in Sizilien and *Julia* represent a short phase of uncertainty in Hebbel's dramatic production. They were the result of his own unsolved ethical problems, his reflective travels, and his intercourse with Bamberg. With *Herodes und Mariamne* he transcended at a bound not only the unrealities of *Julia* but even the striking achievements of his earlier years, and placed himself once for all among the greater dramatists.

Hebbel was aware that in *Mariamne* (as the play is called in the diary and in his correspondence throughout the period of its composition) he was doing work of a very different quality. 'So, wie bei diesem Werk, stürmte es noch nie in meiner Brust; so fest hielt ich dem Sturm aber auch noch nie

[1] Letter to H. Th. Rötscher, 22 Dec. 1847, *Briefe*, ed. cit., vol. iv, p. 71.

die Stange! . . . diess wird ein höchstes oder ich werde nie so weit kommen'.[1] And 'Es ist ohne allen Zweifel mein Bestes' he wrote to Bamberg nearly three months after the drama was completed.[2]

Herodes und Mariamne is indeed a spacious and commanding tragedy. In it, Hebbel returned to Biblical legend for his theme; but as Herodes is a greater man than Holofernes, so too Mariamne is a more striking figure than was Judith. How far it was true to say, as Hebbel did in the first flush of creative energy: 'der Haupt-Character [ist] nicht bloss für meine Frau geschrieben, sondern [ist] meine Frau selbst'[3] is doubtful; but that marriage with Christine enlarged Hebbel's conception of woman as an independent being admits of no doubt—the characters of Mariamne and Rhodope bear witness to a broader view of feminine powers and qualities than do those of Judith, Genoveva, and Klara. Mariamne is a more important personality than any of Hebbel's previous heroines. It is true that the daughter of the Maccabees could not have been portrayed as purely passive; her heritage of war and passion, hate and sacrifice, must in any event have endowed her with significance and activity. But Mariamne is intensely individual. She is far more than the descendant of a proud and patriotic race. She is herself a forceful character, capable not only of great passion but of great restraint, and above all, possessor of a keen, logical, and penetrating mind. She sees through the intrigues of her mother as clearly as, piercing the processes of thought of Herodes, she apprehends to the full the implications of his actions and her own. Even Titus, in his Roman detachment, is moved to awe by her amazing logic; and that she should so move him is the supreme tribute to the power of her personality.

It was only by degrees that Hebbel came to realize the possibilities of the tale of Herodes and Mariamne. For some time he could not bring himself to deal with it because there

[1] Letter to Eduard Janinski, 14 Aug. 1848, *Briefe*, ed. cit., vol. iv, p. 129.
[2] Letter to Felix Bamberg, 3 Feb. 1849, *Briefe*, ed. cit., vol. iv, p. 144.
[3] Letter to Felix Bamberg, 22 Aug. 1848, *Briefe*, ed. cit., vol. iv, p. 132.

seemed too little scope for treatment, too little to be added to the material. But as usual, when he began to work at it, he saw the theme in a new light. 'Es ist doch Täuschung, wenn man glaubt, dass ein Stoff an sich schon etwas sey und dem gestaltenden Geist einen reinen Gehalt entgegen bringe; ich überzeuge mich bei dieser Arbeit zu meiner grossen Satisfaction vom Gegentheil'.[1] In his first reference to the subject, he visualized a full-length portrait: 'Herodes und Mariamne. Tragödie, aber natürlich das ganze Leben des Herodes umfassend.'[2] An entry a few weeks later indicates (without specific reference to the play) the ideal love that Mariamne would acknowledge, but that Herodes would compel: 'Einen Zauber sollte wahre Liebe ausüben, den, dass zwei Herzen, die in einander aufgehen, nicht getrennt werden, sondern nur zusammen sterben könnten; das sollte ihre Probe seyn und so sehr, dass auch der Entfernte stürbe in dem Moment, wo der oder die Andere gestorben wäre.'[3] It was clear to him that the tragedy depended on the action of Herodes: 'Diess Königsbild kann etwas werden, in den Character des Herodes hinein ist aber auch die ganze Bedeutung des Dramas zu legen.'[4] This statement does not of course imply that Mariamne plays a part subordinate to that played by the King. But it is he who by his act, and by the assumption underlying it, creates a situation which can only have a tragic issue. Mariamne's part in it is her inevitable reaction to Herodes' claim: his is the challenging, hers the challenged personality.

In order to make plain this tragic sequence of events and mental processes, Hebbel deemed it necessary to reconstruct the original tale, which he found in Josephus' *Antiquities of the Jews*. He was repelled by the lack of psychological coherence in the old narrative, and, stimulated by the defects he there observed, his mind re-conceived the story and saw in it a tragedy of 'unbedingtester Nothwendigkeit'.[5] It is therefore with a peculiar interest that we turn to the version

[1] *Tagebücher*, ed. cit., vol. iii. 4018, 10 Mar. 1847.
[2] Ibid. 3837, 7 Dec. 1846.
[3] Ibid. 3926, 22 Jan. 1847.
[4] Ibid. 4004, 4 Mar. 1847.
[5] Ibid. 4334, 22 Dec. 1847.

of Josephus and take the opportunity of comparing Hebbel's drama with its source.

The story somewhat incoherently related by Josephus is as follows:

Herod, after his marriage with Mariamne, causes her brother Aristobolus to be killed while bathing, in consequence of certain intrigues of their mother Alexandra. The latter appeals to Cleopatra, who persuades Antony to summon Herod, that he may defend himself against Alexandra's accusation. Herod leaves his uncle, Joseph, as procurator for public affairs, and charges him privately that if he himself should suffer death at the hands of Antony, Joseph should immediately kill Mariamne also, alleging as his reason for this order that since he loves his wife greatly, he is afraid lest after his death she should be engaged to another. Actually (the historian adds) he feared that through hearing accounts of her beauty Antony had fallen in love with her. Joseph, in frequent discourses with Mariamne, refers to Herod's affection for her, and in reply to Alexandra's scoffing, adduces the charge he has received from the king as showing that the latter could not endure separation from her even after death. But, as is natural, the women do not take this view, and regard the order as a proof rather of the king's tyranny than of his affection.

A report of Herod's death at Antony's hands now penetrates to the city, and the women are greatly disturbed—Alexandra, in particular, seeks to persuade Joseph to fly to the Roman camp and obtain security and favour. Almost immediately however the report is contradicted by letters from Herod himself; and on the latter's return, his mother and his sister Salome reveal to him Alexandra's plan; Salome, who bears ill-will to Mariamne, adds to this an accusation against Joseph of having held guilty intercourse with the queen. Herod, tormented by love and jealousy, questions Mariamne, who affirms her innocence on oath. But during the subsequent scene of reconciliation, Mariamne reproaches Herod with his command to Joseph, which, she says, is no sign of love towards her. Convinced that Joseph could only have uttered what was told to him in secret if he had in reality held guilty intercourse with Mariamne, Herod is dismayed at her knowledge; yet out of love for her he restrains his anger, 'though not without a lasting grief, and disquietude of mind'. He orders the death of Joseph and the imprisonment of Alexandra.[1]

After the battle of Actium and the defeat of Antony, Herod, conducting negotiations with Caesar, is again obliged to absent himself, and for fear of sedition in the kingdom, he commits Mariamne with her mother to the fortress of Alexandrium, under the guardianship of his treasurer Joseph and Sohemus of Iturea. These have orders to kill both should they hear that mischief has befallen Herod.

On his return at the conclusion of successful negotiations, the king finds his house in disorder and the women suspicious and uneasy. Mariamne, recalling his previous commands to Joseph, had endeavoured to please Sohemus. At first the latter had been faithful to his charge, but by 'kind words and liberal presents' the women had won him over. Believing that Herod would not return with the same authority as before, and wishing to gain the gratitude of Mariamne and her mother, he had finally revealed the instructions of the king. The queen, greatly displeased, had 'esteemed it an almost insupportable task to live with him [Herod] any longer. And this she afterwards openly declared, without concealing her resentments'. Herod, returning with good tidings, goes first to Mariamne to relate them, but she, unable to conceal her anger, shows open grief at his success. Disturbed at the signs of her dissatisfaction and troubled about their meaning, 'entangled between hatred and love', his mind is in continual agitation. His mother and sister excite him by calumnies about his wife, until he becomes worse disposed towards her, and she, in turn, feels increased aversion for him. While affairs thus hang in the balance, the king is obliged to leave once more to meet Caesar. Mariamne, before he goes, recommends Sohemus to him for a place in the government, and this Herod bestows on him.

[1] These events take place 'an. 34'. The next instalment of the story is found in Book XV, chaps. 6 ('an. 30') and 7 (an. 29').

Mariamne's quarrels with Herod's mother and sister become more frequent and acute, and last for a year after his return from this third expedition. One day she refuses to lie with the king, reproaching him with having caused her father and brother to be killed. Salome, seizing this occasion of Herod's anger to carry out with the king's cup-bearer a plot against Mariamne, pretends that the latter has caused poison to be prepared and given to Herod in the guise of a love-potion. Mariamne's eunuch, tortured to extract confession, declares that he knows nothing of the potion, but that Mariamne's anger against Herod has been caused by a saying of Sohemus. Persuaded that Sohemus must have been brought to betray his orders by the temptation of the queen's favours, Herod commands his death and the trial of Mariamne. The court, seeing the king resolved upon her execution, passes sentence upon her. Alexandra saves herself by playing traitor to her daughter, but Mariamne goes with unshaken firmness to her death. Afterwards, Herod's passion for her revives even more vehemently, and he is grievously afflicted. 'Mariamne', says the historian in summing up her character, 'wanted moderation, and had too much of contention in her nature'.[1]

Perhaps only in this last sentence does Josephus strike a kindred note; otherwise, Hebbel's version of the story differs freely both in facts and interpretation. 'Widersinnig', he says the play would be, if he used the material as he found it. 'So verzeiht Herodes nach dem Josephus der Mariamne den *ersten* Ehebruch und verurtheilt sie zum Tode wegen des *zweiten*; kann es etwas Abgeschmackteres geben und liegt nicht klar zu Tage, dass der Geschichtschreiber entweder über den Character seines Helden oder über die Begebenheit durchaus ununterrichtet war?'[2] Similarly he finds it impossible to believe—and we must agree with him—that Joseph could have informed Mariamne of Herodes' order as a proof of the king's love for her. Or, he adds, if he had been

[1] Account taken from Flavius Josephus, 'Of the Antiquities of the Jews' in *Works*, translated by K. Whiston, new ed., London, 1755, vol. ii, bk. xv, chaps. 3, 6, and 7.

[2] Letter to Felix Bamberg, 10 Nov. 1847, *Briefe*, ed. cit., vol. iv, p. 63.

so great a fool, would Herodes have confided to him a commission of such weight? An entry in the diary of 22 December 1847 shows him at the end of wrestling with the problem:

'Ich glaube, zufrieden seyn zu dürfen; ich habe es mir aber auch Schweiss kosten lassen, denn diess verrückte Motiv, dass Joseph der Mar. den erhaltenen Auftrag, sie zu tödten, verräth, um ihr zu zeigen, wie Herodes sie liebe, war fast nicht in Vernunft umzusetzen. Nun ist's gelungen. . . . Was es übrigens heisst, einen fast phantastischen Stoff auf die derbste Realität zurück zu führen, ahnt man nicht, wenn man's nicht selbst versucht hat'.[1]

What then is this 'actuality' to which Hebbel reduces the refractory material offered by Josephus?

The outward events of the story are reduced and simplified; their inward relationship is laid bare. The mind of Herodes is revealed as dominated by a single impulse—the desire to win from Mariamne an assurance of her unlimited devotion, her readiness to sacrifice her own life should he die. In the face of Mariamne's conviction of personal independence the effort of Herodes to compel her promise fails; and in the reaction from this failure he thinks to ensure his peace of mind by placing her life in the hands of an agent who will carry out his will. During his perilous journey, Joseph—husband of Herodes' sister Salome—is to hold supreme authority; and by playing on his fears, Herodes extracts a promise that he will put Mariamne to death if the king himself should fall.

By a succession of mistakes, Joseph unwittingly reveals this fact to Mariamne, and the queen, injured in her deepest feelings, receives Herodes coldly on his unexpected and triumphant return. When the king learns from her words that she is aware of the measures he had taken before going, he orders Joseph's death, but at the same time his suspicions of Mariamne are aroused. They are confirmed by Salome, who in her despair at her husband's sentence utters the wildest accusations against the queen. In this uncertainty, news comes to Herodes that he is summoned to battle in fulfilment of his agreement with Antony. Completely misinterpreting Mariamne's joyous relief at the chance of re-

[1] *Tagebücher*, ed. cit., vol. iii. 4334, 22 Dec. 1847.

demption that is being offered to him, the king grows more and more convinced that she does not return his love. With perverted logic he assures himself that having gone so far, he must go farther—and choosing Soemus, a man of integrity and loyalty, he repeats the command previously laid on Joseph.

On this occasion Mariamne shuns all intercourse with the King's deputy. But when Soemus is found to have contravened in one particular the orders of Herodes—now reported to have suffered a defeat—she insists that all the king's commands must be carried out as if he were expected to return. Soemus, who is only human and full of admiration for the queen, cannot refrain from disclosing Herodes' further order and asking her if that too must be fulfilled. From this moment Mariamne accepts the inevitable end. Her relations with the king are inwardly destroyed: she resolves upon an outward severance. Herodes shall see her as he believes her to be—and she gives orders for a festival to be held that night in celebration of the defeat at Actium. At the height of the feast the king returns in unexpected triumph. Disillusionment soon follows, and he learns from all sides the confirmation of his deepest fears—that the festival was ordered to celebrate, not his safety but his overthrow. The queen maintains a rigid silence; Herodes puts her under guard, and wrests from a hastily summoned council the death-sentence that in his anger he desires. Mariamne's only request is for an interview with the Roman general Titus; to him she confides the true motives for her action—but under vow of secrecy until her sentence has been carried out. Titus executes her trust, and reveals the facts to Herodes when she has been put to death. The king, though mortally stricken at the height of his passion, re-asserts himself in a few moments. Power is still his, and he will use it still: in response to the inquiry for a new-born Child from the Three Kings of Orient, he gives a final order for the destruction of the children in the neighbourhood of Bethlehem.

Thus the poet—in contrast to Josephus—sees the process of estrangement and tragic misunderstanding as a continuous, but not necessarily a long one. In the drama therefore, this process takes place in a short period of time, and with a tense causal connexion between each stage of its advance. Three journeys are reduced to two—the minimum necessary to permit of a possible atonement on Herodes' part. There is no chance interval of a year between the king's return and the queen's death; the climax of the action—the apparent proof of Mariamne's guilt—coincides with, indeed derives its meaning from, the triumphant return of Herodes. No petty occasion of anger or reproach provides opportunity for a conspiracy; the chain of evidence is forged by Mariamne herself, when she has learnt the basic fact of Herodes' second treachery. No easy plot to poison the king by an intermediary gives him ground for action: the subtle poison of a traitorous joy at his defeat is offered for his drinking by the queen in person, and she steadfastly refuses to defend herself against the charge of infidelity. The malice of Salome is sharpened to a jealous frenzy by the situation created when Joseph is no longer Herodes' uncle, but her husband; undying hatred of Mariamne must ensue when his death lies at her door. And finally, the crucial fact of Joseph's betrayal of Herodes' secret had to be intelligibly explained. This was the immense difficulty, 'diess verrückte Motiv'; as Hebbel saw it, only a flawlessly logical preparation could lead up to such a point. This preparation is in the drawing of Joseph's character, from his first appearance in Act I, Scene 5 to the disastrous moment in Act II, Scene 5, when Mariamne's quick intuition, keen intellect, and accurate memory combine in an irrefutable analysis of the evidence for Herodes' crime against her. Had Joseph been cleverer, he would not have let her guess the secret; but had Mariamne been a shade more stupid, she might not have surprised it out of him.

Thus every alteration that Hebbel makes in Josephus' story leads us to an analysis of the characters themselves: this was the 'unbedingteste Nothwendigkeit' that was his vision of the tragedy.

As *Judith* opened with the giant figure of Holofernes dominating the feeble priests who bowed before his will, so the tragedy of *Herodes und Mariamne* is ushered in with a picture of Herodes in his most imposing mood.

> Dich spreche ich nachher!
> Das Wichtigste zuerst!

are his first words, addressed to the messenger who has returned from Antony with tidings that may bode good or evil to the king. A fire in the city at midnight, which he observed and signalled to the watch—a woman standing at a window, dazed with fear—her sacrifice of life—her funeral —an argument with Sameas the Pharisee—the welcome of an adherent from Jerusalem—all these take precedence of the account from Alexandria which the messenger has brought. Omnipotent, all but omniscient, he holds the stage through the whole scene; quick decisions, keen retorts, shrewd judgements, mark the man of will and insight:

> Und—dieser Mensch bringt sicher schlechte Botschaft,
> Er war zu eilig, mir sie zu verkünden.

But on one point he is open to the lightest suggestion; when he hears of a woman who chooses death because her husband has been killed:

> Das will ich Mariamnen doch erzählen
> Und ihr dabei in's Auge schau'n! . . .

Herodes' position of power, dependent solely on his personal force, his antagonism and suspicion towards Alexandra, the obsession which governs his thoughts of Mariamne, his determination to assert his will against all obstacles, are all completely apparent after this opening scene and the short monologue which follows it. Mariamne's entry in Scene 3 finds us thus prepared for the full exposition of the complex situation between her and the king. That it is complex there is not a moment's doubt. The shadow of her brother's death lies between them—half convinced by Herodes' arguments she yet feels herself estranged. Beneath the irony of her speech, depth of feeling lies concealed; in her resentment, admiration finds unsought expression; through the studied coldness of her words indignation beats, and warmth belies her efforts at detachment. But these things speak to us, and not to Herodes. He sees only what he looks for, finds what he fears. To him one single fact emerges: Mariamne will not swear to follow him in the death which he may meet when he answers Antony's summons.

> Du hältst das Wort zurück,
> Das schlichte Wort, wo ich auf einen Schwur
> Von Dir gehofft; worauf noch soll ich bau'n?

And she, whose significant aside,

> Das kann man thun, erleiden kann man's nicht!

has already revealed her mind, answers him with words that would convince a heart less concentrated on itself:

> Und leistete ich den, was bürgte Dir,
> Dass ich ihn hielte? Immer nur ich selbst,
> Mein Wesen, wie Du's kennst. D'rum denke ich,
> Du fängst, da Du mit Hoffnung und Vertrau'n
> Doch enden musst, sogleich mit beiden an!
> Geh! Geh! Ich kann nicht anders! Heut' noch nicht!

The scene gives a magnificent picture of Mariamne's essential independence, as well as of Herodes' passionate dependence on her for a quality which would, in fact, be opposed to her whole nature. The conflict of will reflects a fundamental conflict of spirit.

It is characteristic of Hebbel's method that Herodes' subsequent monologue, in leading up to his resolve to suspend a sword over Mariamne's head while his own is in danger, also supplements our knowledge of her character, seen through Herodes' eyes:

> Zwar weiss ich's, dass sie oft,
> Wenn ich sie schön genannt, ihr Angesicht
> Verzog, bis sie es nicht mehr war.

The dramatist is confronted with the difficulty of making the monstrous resolve appear intelligible—in his own terms, inevitable. Only by presenting the extreme of proprietary passion, thwarted both in its possessive and its emotional impulse, spurred to a jealousy no less violent because it is entirely dependent on hypothesis, and flicked by the elusive spirit of Mariamne's independence, does he succeed in doing this. Every word of Herodes' monologue is meant to tell, and nothing can be slurred over if the effect is to be attained. It is a crucial moment in every interpretation of the part; the sequence of emotion through the successive scenes is coherent and convincing. There remains the vital interview with Joseph in Scene 5. The latter has to be convinced, and persuaded to undertake the hangman's task; Herodes handles him—as he handles all but Mariamne—with consummate skill, completing his answers in a different sense, playing on his fears, suggesting to the weakling points in which he may seem guilty to Mariamne and to Alexandra if he, the king, should no longer be alive to protect him. Skilfully he works upon Joseph's fears and self-interest:

> Ich lasse Dich nicht schwören, denn man liess
> Noch Keinen schwören, dass er eine Schlange
> Zertreten wolle, die den Tod ihm droht.

Herodes, left alone, reflects on his success:

> Nun lebt sie unter'm Schwert! Das wird mich spornen,
> Zu thun, was ich noch nie gethan; zu dulden,
> Was ich noch nie geduldet, und mich trösten,
> Wenn es umsonst geschieht! Nun fort!

As a commentary on the supremely egotistic nature of a passion, this is perhaps unequalled.

The second act takes place in the apartments of Alexandra, and at once, in her interview with Sameas, the fanatical Pharisee, she is revealed as the active conspirator we have been led to expect. No less skilful than Herodes in seizing upon the vulnerable points of others, she plays at once upon the rigid morality and the immense self-confidence of Sameas, until he regards himself as the divinely appointed instrument of Herodes' fall, and goes forth to proclaim a 'holy war', an organized revolt that shall serve to discredit the latter's rule in the eyes of Antony. The streak of mystic fervour in Sameas is quite foreign to Alexandra's calculating mind. With all her ferocity and determination, she does not mistake the possible dangers of Mariamne's strength of will;

she realizes that if Herodes falls at the hands of Antony, the queen's loyalty to his memory may only be the firmer. She is completely aware of Mariamne's state of mind:

> . . . Doch, sie hasst und liebt ihn jetzt zugleich!

The third scene of this act shows the two women together and contrasted. Mariamne's repressed, at first almost monosyllabic replies stand out sharply against Alexandra's passionate flow of words, her matter-of-fact simplicity against her mother's theatrical appeal, until at last she is goaded to protest against the constant schemes and plots:

> O, ich weiss!
> Ich hätte mir von ihm für jeden Kuss
> Im Voraus einen Kopf, der Dir missfiel,
> Bedingen und zuletzt, wenn keiner Dir
> Mehr trotzte, als sein eig'ner, ihn zum Selbstmord
> Bewegen, oder auch, wenn das nicht ging,
> An ihm in stiller Nacht die Katzenthat
> Der Judith wiederholen sollen,
> Dann hätt'st Du mich mit Stolz Dein Kind genannt!

Mariamne's fundamental trait of ruthless honesty shows itself clearly in this scene. When Alexandra recalls to her mind the anger she showed against Herodes on the death of Aristobolus, she explains that it proceeded from a mind in fever at the sudden horror overwhelming her, and adds, aside:

> Auch hätt' ich's nicht gethan,
> Wär' er in Trauerkleidern nicht gekommen!
> Roth, dunkelroth hätt' ich ihn sehen können. . . .

And the same quality of honesty compels her to the recognition that nothing can now be as it was before, since Alexandra by her plots has given them a shadowy third for company—the ghost of Aristobolus. In passionate repudiation of any part in Alexandra's scheming for revenge, she registers a vow of loyalty: the oath which she held back when Herodes demanded it, she now swears of her own free will:

> Ich sterbe
> Wenn er stirbt.

The splendid irony of this becomes apparent in Scene 5,

where Joseph, convinced that Herodes' safe return is now impossible, and that the revolt which has broken out among the populace will gain in strength and overwhelm him unless he carries out his charge, betrays the latter unwittingly to Mariamne. She is first startled by his apparently pointless repetition of her oath, but her suspicions are only roused in earnest by the thought of Salome; and when Joseph, in answer to her disdain, eagerly seizes on the hypothesis and completes the argument in the very words Herodes had used to her to make out his case, suspicion is converted into certainty:

> Von jetzt erst fängt mein Leben an,
> Bis heute träumt' ich!

The frenzied jealousy of Salome clears her finally in Mariamne's mind of the graver charge:

> Die ist es sicher nicht. So ist er's selbst! . . .
> Ich war ihm nur ein Ding und weiter Nichts.

And swiftly on the realization of this blinding fact comes the breathless announcement that the king is in the palace.

The opening scene of Act III forms a parallel to that of Act I. Herodes is again in the centre of the stage, and is again (we know) to be confronted with adverse tidings. He is in the first triumph of his negotiations with Antony—but in ironic contrast to the situation in the first act, he is, although more tangibly successful, in a less favourable relationship to Mariamne. His contemptuous treatment of Alexandra, his angry boasts in answer to Salome's charge against the queen, acquire by this fact a poignantly ironic flavour, and the advent of Mariamne in answer to his summons is the more anxiously awaited.

The queen's greeting does not tend to lessen the tensity of the situation; cold and contained, she lets it fall from her lips, as if without participation of her feelings, so that Alexandra marvels in a swift aside:

> Ist diess das Weib, das schwur, sich selbst zu tödten,
> Wenn er nicht wiederkehrte?

Herodes, goaded by her coldness into protest, ends an impassioned speech by asking

> So ist Dir meine Wiederkunft verhasst?

to which Mariamne returns the short, revealing answer:

> Wie sollte sie? Sie gibt mir ja das *Leben*
> Zurück!

The king, realizing the effect her knowledge of his secret orders must have upon her mind, is completely absorbed in speculation on the problem of how the discovery can have taken place. Thus her reproaches, which might have led to a better understanding of her point of view, pass over his head. Could he have appreciated them, the course of events would have been different—but, we may also add, the tragedy would not have arisen. For the fundamental deficiency in Herodes' character is made wholly plain when, after Mariamne's bitter

> Er lässt
> Zum Opfertod ihr nicht einmal die Zeit:

—(a revealing statement to a dispassionate hearer)—he hurls at her the most damning of all queries:

> Um welchen Preis erfuhrst
> Du dies Geheimniss? Wohlfeil war es nicht!
> Mir stand ein Kopf zum Pfand!

In answer to the queen's contemptuous recoil, he gives the order for the delivery of the letter sealing Joseph's fate.

The attempt at explanation on Herodes' part which follows fails, as it was bound to fail. A half-truth is opposed to Mariamne's absolute conviction. Herodes' excuse—that like a soldier on the field of battle he hurled from him the precious standard into the midst of the foe, to spur himself in desperation to efforts otherwise impossible—does not lack an element of truth. But the queen disregards the specious analogy. She goes straight to the heart of the matter—she is a human being, with life and soul that are her own, no inanimate possession, no banner to symbolize a victory.

> Du sprichst umsonst! Du hast in mir die Menschheit
> Geschändet, meinen Schmerz muss Jeder theilen,
> Der Mensch ist, wie ich selbst. . . .

And if, she adds, her human feelings are so outraged by his act, what of her feelings as a wife?

> Wie steh' ich jetzt zu Dir und Du zu mir?

No answer is given to this vital question, for Salome rushes in to plead for her husband's life. Misunderstanding the whole situation, she believes that Joseph's death is the consequence of her own accusation against him and Mariamne. Not all Herodes' denials will convince her of the contrary, and her initial appeal for the queen's intercession changes swiftly to a passionately repeated condemnation of her infidelity. At her exit, both Herodes and Mariamne suffer some confusion of feeling—the queen, though struck with horror, hardly condemns Herodes for his summary vengeance, but the king himself half repents his haste. At this moment of suspense, a messenger from Antony arrives to summon Herodes to his aid against Caesar Octavian. The whole tragic misconception of this scene—where the king interprets Mariamne's joy in accordance with his frenzied jealousy, while she is almost breathless with relief that there is to be 'another time', a second chance—rests immediately on the preceding scenes, and on the king's failure to appreciate in the least what she has felt and suffered. So full is Herodes' mind of the suspicion aroused by the queen's expression of relief that—memorably, for it is utterly unlike his wonted mastery—he can scarcely give instructions to the messenger. The effect and meaning of this scene are entirely dependent upon action and asides: Mariamne's joyful relief and Herodes' consequent suspicions are separate actions which do not mingle, until the king in bitter irony recalls her to the present:

> Dein Angesicht
> Hat sich erheitert! Aber hoffe nicht
> Zu viel! Man stirbt nicht stets in einem Krieg,
> Aus manchem kehrt' ich schon zurück.

Then her restraint becomes deliberate—she is resolved the second chance shall be a real test. The stage direction is important here: Mariamne (*will reden, unterbricht sich aber*)

> Nein! Nein!

and later

Die Probe
Ist keine, wenn er ahnt, was Dich bewegt.
Besteht er die, wie wirst Du selbst belohnt,
Wie kannst Du ihn belohnen! . . .

Herodes' misunderstanding is complete:

Ich danke Dir! Du hast mir jetzt das Herz
Erleichtert! Mag ich auch an Deiner Menschheit
Gefrevelt haben, das erkenn' ich klar,
An Deiner Liebe frevelte ich nicht!

The queen's tacit refusal to enlighten him on her own attitude of mind proceeds from the deepest feeling of her nature—her sense of injury that can only be obliterated by the one atonement; but her subsequent refusal, in answer to his direct appeal, to explain how Joseph came to betray his trust, is due in part at least to injured pride. Stirred to frenzy by this refusal, Herodes allows his rage to master him, until the queen utters solemn words of warning—words which seem to embody the deepest meaning of the drama:

Herodes, mäss'ge Dich! Du hast vielleicht
Gerade jetzt Dein Schicksal in den Händen
Und kannst es wenden, wie es Dir gefällt!
Für jeden Menschen kommt der Augenblick,
In dem der Lenker seines Sterns ihm selbst
Die Zügel übergiebt. Nur das ist schlimm,
Dass er den Augenblick nicht kennt, dass jeder
Es sein kann, der vorüberrollt! Mir ahnt,
Für Dich ist's dieser! Darum halte ein!

The figure of Mariamne gains enormously in weight and majesty by these lines. They suspend the rapid thrust and parry of the interview with the solemnity of reflection: the fleeting moments of the dialogue are suddenly arrested by a suggestion of eternal values, which yet is intimately related to the personal situation. The words are in no sense a general moral reflection. They are the burning expression of a profound and personal conviction of human fate, and they fall on the action as a roll of thunder steadies the mind in the rapid play of lightning.

Few things in the drama are more damaging to Herodes than the commonplace words with which he replies to this appeal:

> Ich fürchte sehr, Du ahnst nur halb das Rechte,
> Der Wendepunkt ist da, allein für Dich!
> Denn ich, was will ich denn? Doch nur ein Mittel,
> Womit ich böse Träume scheuchen kann!

Yet even after this, Mariamne clings to her hope:

> (*gen Himmel*) Lenk', Ewiger, sein Herz! . . .
>
> . . . .
>
> Du thatest, was Du nie noch thatst, Du wälztest
> Das Rad der Zeit zurück; es steht noch einmal,
> Wie es vorher stand; lass ihn anders denn
> Jetzt handeln, so vergess' ich, was gescheh'n;
> Vergess' es so, als hätte er im Fieber
> Mit seinem Schwert mir einen Todesstreich
> Versetzt und mich genesend selbst verbunden.

But after a final outburst of Herodes' anger, the interview ends on a note of gloom, which the king confirms, in words that seem to spring unbidden, with a funereal cadence:

> Wahr ist's, ich ging zu weit.

But swiftly recovering himself, he returns to his obsessing thought:

> Doch wahr nicht minder,
> Wenn sie mich liebte, würde sie's verzeih'n!

This monologue, which closes the third act, shows Herodes passing through conflicting states of mind—now catching a glimpse of truth, now conquered again by passion and desire, and finally yielding to the fatal logic:

> Hätt' ich geahnt,
> Dass sie's erfahren könnte, nimmer wär' ich
> So weit gegangen. Jetzt, da sie es weiss,
> Jetzt muss ich weiter geh'n! Denn nun sie's weiss,
> Nun muss ich das von ihrer Rache fürchten,
> Was ich von ihrer Wankelmüthigkeit
> Vielleicht mit Unrecht fürchtete, muss fürchten,
> Dass sie auf meinem Grabe Hochzeit hält!

And so he too institutes a second 'test'—if Soemus betrays him, after receiving the order Joseph had, then indeed Salome must have spoken truly and Mariamne be unfaithful. The road now lies open to the end.

The scene of Act IV is set in the apartments of Mariamne. The queen is the central figure, and once more she is shown in contrast with Alexandra. Although no less aloof from intrigue than formerly, her bitterness escapes with every word. Herodes, she observes, will not be able to say on this occasion that she has tempted his lieutenant with favours and soft words to reveal a secret, if he has one to conceal. Yet in the sharp antithesis between Mariamne's view and that of Sameas the influence of her feeling for the king is still plainly to be seen. Similarly she makes excuse for his ruthless words to the Pharisee:

Er war gereizt!
Er fand den Aufruhr vor!

—a sufficiently ironical foreshadowing of the coming situation between herself and Herodes.

The third scene brings the crucial revelation of Herodes' order to Soemus—a difficult moment, triumphantly achieved. By a profound irony, it is Mariamne's absolute loyalty to the king—reported to have been defeated, and considered by Soemus to be in great danger from the vengeance of Caesar —which brings about the second, and catastrophic revelation. Not *one* command of Herodes shall be unfulfilled as long as she is queen, she tells Soemus, with the order to re-imprison Sameas. Convinced as he is that the king cannot return, Soemus makes the obvious reply:

Soll ich auch Dich, damit das Todtenopfer,
Das Du zu bringen denkst, vollkommen sei,
Soll ich auch Dich mit meinem Schwert durchstossen?
Ich hab' auch dazu den Befehl von ihm!

Despite her detestation of Herodes, Alexandra is incredulous at this; but Mariamne's answer, in words of a poignant simplicity, shows that she completely accepts the tragedy:

So ist das Ende da!
Und welch' ein Ende! . . .

> Die Vergangenheit
> Lös't, wie die Zukunft, sich in Nichts mir auf.
> Ich hatte Nichts, ich habe Nichts, ich werde
> Nichts haben. War denn je ein Mensch so arm!

The last emphasis, like the first, is on her 'Menschheit'. The last—because these are the last words that Mariamne utters, until after her sentence, that contain a suggestion of any emotion except that of bitter anger. It is Alexandra who prevents her from taking the easy way of escape—her immediate impulse is to turn her dagger against herself. But Alexandra plays no part in the subsequent events. With a suddenness of decision and a precision of detail only possible to a contained but passionate anger, Mariamne gives her orders for the feast that is to celebrate Herodes' defeat. In cold condemnation she spurns Soemus' sympathy, until touched by his explanation that he refuses any longer to be the king's tool:

> Ich bitt' Dir ab. Du stehst zu ihm, wie ich,
> Du bist, wie ich, in Deinem Heiligsten
> Gekränkt, wie ich, zum Ding herabgesetzt!
>
> . . . .
>
> Komm' auf mein Fest! (*ab*).

Preparations for the feast occupy the fourth scene, which is a retarding moment in the action; three following scenes heighten the suspense by showing Mariamne in contact successively with Alexandra, Salome, and the Roman Titus—proclaiming to each more emphatically her intention to celebrate Herodes' death. Her final speech in Scene 7 at the mirror shows how far she has been driven in despair—almost beyond herself—and her feverish vision leads immediately to the great climax of the entry of Herodes. Converted, by his fearlessness as well as by his fortune, into Caesar's friend, the king arrives at a feast which he supposes to be in honour of his safe return—to learn from Salome and Titus that the messenger announcing it has not arrived, and that Mariamne is celebrating the report of the defeat at Actium. After his first word to Mariamne—whom he seeks before all else—Herodes turns to others, and from the silence of Soemus, coupled with the facts to which Titus bears witness, deduces that she is guilty. The queen's sole question is

Ich bin Gefang'ne?—

her only answer

So führt mich ab!
Der Tod kann mein Gemahl nicht länger sein!

The scene changes in Act V to the great hall of audience in which the first act was played. Herodes appears once more in the character of king and judge; but there is a tragic contrast between then and now. His inner mind is obsessed, no longer by doubt but by certainty, which violently conflicts with his emotions. Salome intensifies his passionate condemnation; yet her vehemence might conceivably have a contrary effect, were the facts not vouched for by the dispassionate evidence of Titus. In vain does the latter in Scene 3 repeat Soemus' denial of any guilty relations with the queen. The character of Soemus himself damns him in Herodes' eyes, since it seems to demand a temptation of irresistible force in order to make credible his betrayal of a trust.

The account in the following scene of Sameas' triumphant resistance to torture has a twofold object. The prophecy of the birth of a child who shall rule the world is to recur later to the mind of Herodes. But at the moment, he is only concerned with the resemblance to Mariamne's stiff-necked pride:

So sind sie! Ja!—Und wird sie anders sein?

The scene leads immediately to the trial of Mariamne, which does indeed prove her likeness to those great ancestors to whom she appeals, passing over the tribunal Herodes has set up. By her own will she is condemned; for she refuses to allow Alexandra to give evidence, and Herodes alone understands her veiled references to his sinister command. Nor will she acquiesce in Titus' protest against Herodes' arbitrary dictatorship over the tribunal; and it is she herself who pronounces the ultimate judgement:

> Wohlan denn! Da Du's selbst so tief empfindest,
> Was sich für mich geziemt, da Deine Furcht
> Mich über meine Pflicht belehrt, so will
> Ich endlich diese heil'ge Pflicht erfüllen,
> D'rum scheid' ich mich auf ewig von Dir ab!

After this, her sole request is for a final interview with Titus. For the rest, she meets Herodes' long scrutiny with silence—and Joab is entrusted with the preparations for her death. With the words of Aaron, the spokesman of the tribunal, we feel the solemn summary of a chorus:

> Es ist die letzte Maccabäerin!

The final scene of Mariamne's life is enacted with Titus, to whom she entrusts the history and explanation of her actions, so that *one* human being may keep her portrait unsullied in his heart, and may raise the veil if hatred and calumny should go too far. But before she tells her story, she exacts a vow of silence until after her own death. Herodes would have made himself her slayer had he died—she is resolved that he shall become so while he lives. Her picture in his mind has been that of a woman without loyalty or love: she has vowed in her own heart:

> Du sollst das Weib, das Du erblicktest, tödten
> Und erst im Tod mich sehen, wie ich bin!

Titus, appalled at her resolution, begs her to reconsider it, and to permit him to explain her actions. But Mariamne is utterly resolved. She no longer feels pain, for pain implies life:

> und das Leben ist
> In mir erloschen, ich bin längst nur noch
> Ein Mittelding vom Menschen und vom Schatten. . . .

She does not doubt that Herodes would revoke his sentence if he knew the truth:

> Und folgte ich, so würde mir der Lohn,
> Dass ich vor einem Jeden, der mir nahte,
> Von jetzt an schaudern und mir sagen müsste:
> Hab' Acht, das kann Dein dritter Henker sein!

Nothing shows more clearly how deeply Herodes has

wounded her personality. She asks Titus whether—if there were a way of escape—she would not have thought of it in bidding farewell to her children. (But it is noteworthy that this motif is not really used—it is only here alluded to. It is as woman and as wife, and not as mother, that Mariamne is a tragic figure.) The only solution to the problem cannot offer itself, for it is fundamentally impossible to the nature of Herodes:

Titus. O fühlt' er das, und käm' von selbst, und würfe
Sich Dir zu Füssen!

Mariamne. Ja! Dann hätte er
Den Dämon überwunden, und ich könnte
Ihm Alles sagen!

But as Titus breathes

Ahnst Du Nichts,
Herodes?

Joab enters to lead Mariamne to her death. And when, in answer to a last appeal from Titus, she repeats her passionate refusal to live on in such conditions, even he must give a verdict more convincing than any other she could seek:

Sie hat recht!

Her stoic courage is unbroken to the end;

Du, Aristobolus, sei mir gegrüsst!
Gleich bin ich bei Dir in der ew'gen Nacht!

A short monologue of Salome's, showing that the appeal made by Aaron to the king might have succeeded but for her, brings us back to actuality after the majestic tones of Mariamne's passing, and immediately upon it follows the pageant-like entry of the three Kings of Orient, come to Herodes' court on a mistaken errand—to greet the Child who shall be King. The query and its answer have a bitter irony:

Ward Dir nicht ein Sohn
Geboren?

Herodes. Mir? O nein! Mir starb mein Weib!

There is a mystical note in the speeches of the Kings which

contrasts strangely and effectively with the grim reality of the subsequent announcement that the queen is dead, and with Titus' proclamation of her innocence. Herodes' reply to this is characteristic:

> Ihr Zauber war ihr selbst im Tode treu!

It is Alexandra who dissipates his unbelief by telling him of Mariamne's vow to die a voluntary death, should he not return from his first journey. Herodes is at last convinced by this, the most cruel stroke, suppressed by Titus out of pity. For a moment, he succumbs to the bitterness of regret; but at Alexandra's expression of triumph he summons pride and resolution: he is still king, and the world shall feel his power. And he rouses himself to measures against the Pharisees, and against the child whose coming has been foretold. His last order to Joab is for the massacre of the children in Bethlehem; but the shadow falls again, and his final words are 'Mariamne', and an appeal to 'Titus!' The star of Herodes declines as the new era opens. With the death of Mariamne, the good dies in him; distrustful love, thwarted passion, and a too successful vengeance have opened the door to his evil genius.

Of all Hebbel's tragedies, perhaps *Herodes und Mariamne* is the most modern in its problem. The opposition which he conceives to be fundamental between man and woman is here presented at its highest power, in a profound analysis of a woman's mind and heart. With none of Rhodope's gentle charm, so magically combined with unswerving determination, Mariamne, no less than Rhodope, represents the relentless logic of the more steadfast of her sex. She is a being made for deep and understanding passion; tragically she meets a passion which, though of profound intensity, is incapable of realizing the force and independence of her character, its possibilities of heroism and sacrifice. Matched with a mind of equal generosity, Mariamne would have risen of her own will to the height of passionate sympathy demanded by Herodes; met by intense and subtle jealousy, her personality feels itself first injured, then destroyed, by the distrust of her love which in his heart he does not attempt to conquer. Passion in him is not counterbalanced by respect for personality; and two noble natures—for Herodes himself is not wanting in greatness—are thus destroyed by the wanton assertion of possessive rights. It is a tragedy of distrust. But we need only compare Herodes with Othello to realize that Hebbel presents that distrust as a fundamental difficulty in the relations between two passionate natures. There is a jealousy which, though it is inherent, may at least be fanned by circumstance; machinations, such as those of Iago, may play upon the weakness of a character and bring about a situation where tragedy perforce ensues. But Herodes' jealous demand for complete and lasting possession, even to the possible sacrifice of Mariamne's life, should his be forfeited, is more than this. It implies an unmoderated assertion of the individual, who thereby infringes the rights of another individual, even of one passionately beloved. The tragic guilt is once more that of 'Unmässigkeit'—both Herodes and Mariamne are guilty in this sense, but the first, and greater, crime must be charged to Herodes. The magnitude of his passion cannot be denied; when he declares, after her death:

> Wäre meine Krone
> Mit allen Sternen, die am Himmel flammen,
> Besetzt: für Mariamne gäbe ich
> Sie hin und, hätt' ich ihn, den Erdball mit.
> Ja, könnte ich sie dadurch, dass ich selbst,
> Lebendig, wie ich bin, in's Grab mich legte,
> Erlösen aus dem ihrigen: ich thät's,
> Ich grübe mich mit eig'nen Händen ein!

it does not occur to us to call his speech exaggerated. But passion is not to be measured by magnitude alone; and when he shows that the disaster has in no wise illuminated the dark places of his mind, that possession still to him means the inalienable right to a complete surrender, then only do we fully realize how inevitable has been the tragedy:

> Allein ich kann's nicht! Darum bleib' ich noch
> Und halte fest, was ich noch hab'!

It is perhaps the unchanging character of Herodes which

makes this the most relentlessly tragic of all Hebbel's dramas. The vista of a new world, it is true, is suggested in the final scene to balance the terror of the old; but the vision of dread Necessity remains unchallenged. Titus, pronouncing like a Chorus an impartial judgement, puts it into words:

> Mich hielt mein Wort zurück und mehr, als das:
> Die unerbittliche Nothwendigkeit.

He alone bows to this supremacy; neither Herodes nor Mariamne acquiesces in it—as do Kandaules and Rhodope in the next great tragedy that Hebbel wrote. But while the characters themselves end in the darkness of night, the whole action of *Herodes und Mariamne* evokes that satisfaction which emerges from the contemplation of a flawless sequence—or in Hebbel's words, the 'ring of form'.[1] It creates a sense of completeness and finality characteristic of great tragedy; unresolved though the individual discords be, to watch the inevitable process, when each character is driven by an inner compulsion to act in accordance with his deepest nature, is to feel convinced of an ordered universe, and so to divine in it a harmony inclusive of such discords.

Between *Herodes und Mariamne* and Hebbel's next tragedy the early tale of *Der Rubin* was dramatized into a fairy-comedy. Although the actual material was little altered, tale and comedy are very different from each other; they are separated by the formative years of Hebbel's development as a dramatic artist. The shadowy characters of the prose version are endowed with life, and the events are concentrated into a swift dramatic sequence. Nevertheless, it is doubtful whether Hebbel was justified in considering the material suited to the stage. The Princess Fatime's enchantment in the ruby, her appearance out of the precious stone and her disappearance into it, are elements essential to the tale, but they do not lend themselves easily to dramatic treatment. To create the fairy-tale atmosphere which alone can produce such an illusion needs a special aptitude, and

[1] Letter to Gustav Kühne, 28 Jan. 1847, *Briefe*, ed. cit., vol. iv, p. 8.

Hebbel's genius did not lie in this direction. As in *Der Diamant*, he suggested two worlds, sharply divided from each other: and only one—the world of the rogue Hakam, the stern Kadi, and the despotic Caliph—conveys any impression of reality. The figures of the enchanted princess and the enigmatic sage, on the other hand, lessen the vitality of the remaining characters, and the alternate sway of good and evil magicians—the fairy-tale explanation of an insistent dualism—lends a further element of unreality. A wholly symbolic treatment was required if such premises and such conclusions were to be accepted; Hebbel's picture of a two-fold world precludes belief in either. Moreover, there is a certain inconsistency in the implications of the story. To find the true nature of the ruby, Assad must first renounce it. Neither the mysterious sage who rescues him from the consequences of his seizure of the jewel, nor Fatime herself, can reveal to him the means for her release; of his own accord he must abandon that which is most precious to him. But it is precious because of its peculiar character; the instant appeal it makes to Assad is deepened a hundredfold when the princess has made her single appearance from her prison. Assad himself is well aware of the logical deduction:

Fatime. Warfst Du den Stein nicht weg?
Assad (*bitter*). Das that ich! O, das that ich! Weisst Du's schon,
Und gönnst mir doch noch einen Blick und lächelst
Mich freundlich an? Das habe ich verdient!
Von Raserei der Eifersucht erfüllt—
Ja, ja, der Eifersucht, ich!—schleuderte
Ich ihn hinunter in den Fluss und wusste
Doch längst, dass er Dein holdes Selbst umschloss.
Pfui über mich! Nie werd' ich's mir verzeih'n.

The sage announces, however, that the will of Allah has prevailed:

Der böse Geist hat, ohne es zu ahnen,
Für seinen Plan gewirkt!

But Assad's simple resolve to earn the gratitude of thousands by releasing them from the prisons of his kingdom is followed by a subtle indication from the sage that good will not of necessity prevail:

> Der böse Geist erwacht,
> Ich fühl' es schon, und ich muss schlafen geh'n!

The fairy-comedy ends thus on a note of irony. The metamorphosis of the princess, unwittingly accomplished by the simple fisherman's son, is succeeded by his own, which is equally remote from actuality. Allah has guided all things to good. Assad's determination to possess the ruby, which is not his to take, calls to his side the good magician, who saves him from the human penalty he has incurred; the access of jealousy which causes him to throw away the jewel, rather than give it into the hands of others, directly serves the ends of good and frustrates the evil enchanter's calculations. It was not altogether surprising that the audience at the first performance of the comedy should have failed to understand it. Hebbel had insisted that the new chief of the Burgtheater should fulfil his predecessor's undertaking to perform *Der Rubin*, though he was warned that the play was unsuitable. The result was the anticipated failure. At the time, Hebbel attributed this to the exotic nature of the subject matter and the number of his enemies; but later he struck a truer note: 'Ob ich nicht doch im Rubin eine Granate in einen Rosenkelch hinein gelegt habe?'[1]

Three years elapsed between the completion of *Herodes und Mariamne* and the second major drama of this middle period. The fruit of three months' labour, *Agnes Bernauer* was finished in December 1851; and the entry in Hebbel's journal that records this fact records also a sense of security: 'Den 5ten Act der Agn: B. geschlossen. Zufrieden.'[2]

No other of the greater plays, except *Gyges und sein Ring*, gives occasion for so few entries in the diary; and of no other did Hebbel make the prediction that he made of this drama: 'Von [Agnes Bernauer] . . . wage ich zu prophezeien, dass sie mich populair machen wird'.[3] He had wrestled with the

[1] *Tagebücher*, ed. cit., vol. iii. 4777, 1 Jan. 1851.
[2] Ibid. 4966, 17 Dec. 1851.
[3] Letter to Felix Bamberg, 11 May 1852, *Briefe*, ed. cit., vol. v, p. 15.

theme of *Herodes und Mariamne*; here, in striking contrast, there is an apparently effortless mastery, both of the subject and the form. *Agnes Bernauer*, indeed, stands apart in more than one respect from Hebbel's other plays. The sex conflict, with all its complexity of psychological reactions, which formed the main theme of *Judith*, *Genoveva*, or *Herodes und Mariamne*, is absent; the tragic situation arises, in fact, from the complete simplicity of emotion governing the actions of Agnes and Albrecht, and there is perhaps no relation in all Hebbel's dramas so uncomplicated in its personal aspects. Was it a realization of this fact that prompted Hebbel's conviction that the drama would make a wide appeal? Or did this conviction rest on the belief that—for the first time—he had offered a tragic solution within the play itself? It may at least be surmised that the absence of such a conflict and the presence of such a close form a significant coincidence.

Yet it would seem that the complex conflict of man and woman underlying Hebbel's other great dramas was of the very substance of life to the dramatist. It is in virtue of it that in these plays we are held, lifted, and released in a dramatic experience; whereas the splendid conception of duty and law in *Agnes Bernauer* compels our admiration, but does not command our hearts. It is an admirably written play; its structure is faultless, its form a model of vivid dramatic prose; Herzog Ernst is one of Hebbel's finest male characters. Yet the drama is the most intellectual of all his greater plays; and even the emotional quality in the 'Angel of Augsburg', with her simple beauty and her simple sacrifice of love, hardly outweighs the dominant impression of logic in the whole.

The story of the Augsburg barber's daughter whose beauty, captivating the heart of Albrecht, heir to the Bavarian throne, endangered the safety of the state and the welfare of the dynasty, had been a popular theme among the dramas of chivalry current at the end of the eighteenth century. The contrast between Agnes Bernauer's innocence and the complex situation created by her love-story afforded opportunity for external contrasts of simplicity and pageantry that were well suited to this type of play. Hebbel read von Törring's *Agnes Bernauerinn* (written in 1782), and was partly stimulated to creative work by the defects he criticized in the older drama: '[ich] konnte mich aber mit der Auffassung so wenig befreunden, dass gerade sie mich vorzugsweise mit zu meiner Arbeit antrieb', he wrote in 1853.[1] He found in it 'fertiges Verhältniss gleich zu Anfang und Donner und Blitz folgt unmittelbar hinterdrein';[2] whereas in his own treatment he notes, on beginning the fourth act, the gradual intensification of the dramatic interest, though by the simplest means.[3] Both criticism and claim are justified. In von Törring's play the marriage of Agnes and Albrecht has just taken place as the action begins, and their love and courtship are only seen in retrospect. Hebbel presents the whole of this tempestuous wooing, and in so doing reveals both the character of Agnes and her environment, in a series of vivid pictures. Theobald the unlucky suitor, whose devotion to her forms an effective foil to the conquering passion of Albrecht, the simple, honest father who has Meister Anton's rectitude without his ruthlessness, the Augsburg maids, who already hate Agnes for her beauty because she steals their triumphs, though involuntarily—all throw light upon the tragic heroine. Albrecht's position, too, is made clear. It is of the essence of the story that he should be hot-headed and irresponsible; but the touch of self-importance which is combined with his impetuosity in the older play is absent from Hebbel's picture. Here he possesses the virtues of his defects; his loyalty to Agnes is more unquestioning, and the love-scenes are drawn with convincing sincerity. But the most important difference between the two dramas is in the catastrophe. Whereas in von Törring's play, Duke Ernst arrives too late to prevent his lieutenant from going beyond his orders and putting Agnes to death, Hebbel will admit no such accidental solution: the Duke orders her death, when every effort to avert the necessity for it has proved of no avail. Thus it is through the figure of Herzog

[1] *Tagebücher*, ed. cit., vol. iii. 5159 [an Gutzkow, 20 Aug. 1853].
[2] Ibid.
[3] Ibid. 4963, 1 Nov. 1851.

Ernst that the play acquires its intellectual character. Acts I and II are entirely devoted to the swift sequence of courtship and marriage; in Act III the Duke appears, and henceforth embodies the forces of law and order that oppose the union of Agnes and Albrecht. This act falls into three parts. The opening scenes, laid in Munich, show Herzog Ernst and his Chancellor Preising, preparing a counter-stroke to Albrecht's reported infatuation; the next scenes, in Vohburg, oppose to this the consummated marriage and the secluded happiness of the two lovers, but sound a note of warning as Albrecht's interview with Preising ends in a promise to attend a tourney at his father's orders; the final scene at the Regensburg tournament shows the two parties at issue. Herzog Ernst's accusation against his son for unknightly conduct is refuted by Albrecht's public proclamation of his marriage; to this the Duke replies by declaring Adolph, his young nephew, as his heir. With a threatened clash of forces between Herzog Ernst, backed by the weight of the Empire, and Albrecht, insurgent against the knights by the aid of peasants and burghers, the act ends.

From this point onwards, the tempestuous lover and rebellious son recedes in interest as the figure of Herzog Ernst grows dominant. The sickly child adopted as the heir to the throne of Bavaria dies, leaving the Duke no alternative but the sacrifice of Agnes, if the state is to be preserved from civil war or dismemberment. The first half of the fourth act shows him arriving at this decision and finally signing the warrant for her death; in the second half, the arrest of Agnes takes place in Albrecht's castle after he has left her. Act V opens with the efforts of Preising to save Agnes from death by inducing her to forswear her marriage. But in steadfast refusal she accepts her doom. The scene changes to the field of battle. There Albrecht and Herzog Ernst meet (after two years and a half) in the clash of arms, but on the capture of the Duke, Albrecht's lust for vengeance suffers its first check, and with his refusal to take advantage of the capture, Herzog Ernst's opportunity arrives. He warns his son in solemn terms of his responsibilities, and at the decisive moment his plea is reinforced by the arrival of an imperial messenger to proclaim a ban on Albrecht as a rebel against divine and human ordinance. Against his impulse and his will, Albrecht is convinced by the Duke's arguments; and the drama ends with Herzog Ernst's promise to honour Agnes by solemn obsequies and his abdication in favour of his son. Albrecht is to test the responsibilities of sovereignty; the arguments of reason are to be supported by experience.

Thus the death of Agnes Bernauer, first seen as the fatal issue of a tragic conflict, acquires in the last act a new significance. The death of Mariamne, by intensifying those characteristics of Herodes' mind which had conditioned its necessity, clearly revealed the unavoidable nature of the tragedy. That of Agnes, on the other hand, forms at once the inevitable close of a tragic sequence and the bridge to a recognition of cause and effect on Albrecht's part—a recognition that would have averted the very action from which it springs. To the tragic theme of beauty and goodness entailing their own downfall a new issue is related: the human revolt against such downfall is converted, by Duke Ernst and Albrecht, into acquiescence. Necessity not only governs the action but is, in the end, specifically acknowledged as the victor. Like disputants upon a controversial theme, father and son in the final scene meet in the clash of argument; and to the question posed in the cry of Agnes: 'Bald weiss ich, ob's mit Recht geschah!' the Duke in measured terms gives answer. Albrecht the lover is silenced; the heir to the throne is convinced. In fact, that which is normally implicit in a tragic sequence becomes explicit; the reconciliation of disharmony, which elsewhere Hebbel deemed to be above and beyond the individual case, here becomes an integral part of the dramatic action. It is true that at the close of *Herodes und Mariamne* the passing pageant suggests a larger harmony, but Herodes himself remains a figure of tragic dissonance; in *Agnes Bernauer*, on the contrary, the resolution of the conflict occurs within the mind of Albrecht, through whose action that conflict has arisen. A solution of the tragic discord is also to be found in Hebbel's next drama, *Gyges und sein Ring*. But here, as will be seen, each of the individual characters attains a clearer vision: the sacrifice has become a conscious one, the recognition of necessity does not follow but precede it. Thus the solution in *Gyges* has an emotional quality absent in that of *Agnes Bernauer*, where sacrifice and solution do not coincide. All Rhodope's charm makes her choice of atonement the more certain; but the charm and beauty of Agnes move others to force death upon her, and whereas her sacrifice stirs our emotions in a high degree, it is by our reason that we are called to acquiesce in the subsequent justification of her death.

That Hebbel deliberately chose to offer a specific reconciliation of the tragic problem in *Agnes Bernauer* is a fact which demands consideration, for in this choice he was abandoning previous theory and practice alike. Writing of Oehlenschläger in 1843, he had commented: 'er will die Versöhnung des Individuums, als ob das Tragische im Kreise der individuellen Ausgleichung möglich wäre!'[1] and in 1844, more generally: 'Dass in der dramatischen Kunst die Versöhnung immer über den Kreis des speciellen Dramas hinaus fällt, werden Wenige begreifen.'[2] And in *Judith*, *Genoveva*, *Maria Magdalena*, and *Herodes und Mariamne*, it is only the remote suggestion of a far-off harmony that issues from the individual discords. But it is interesting to note that in the same year which saw the completion of *Agnes Bernauer* Hebbel wrote the *Epilogue to Genoveva*.

The impression that on this one occasion the poet in Hebbel yielded to a dominantly intellectual interest is supported by the contrast with his other dramas. After the moment of tragic emphasis at the death of Mariamne, the portrait of Herodes is amplified: the impression of his character that has already been created is intensified by his reaction to the crisis. After the death of Agnes, it is the impression of Herzog Ernst that is intensified; Albrecht's reaction to events is a change of mind. The opposing forces in this play are thus represented by Agnes herself and Herzog Ernst; and the antagonism between this pair is one in which

[1] *Tagebücher*, ed. cit., vol. ii. 2634, 5 Jan. 1843.
[2] Ibid. 3168, 25 June 1844.

reason, not emotion, plays the major part. Hebbel's own statement about *Agnes Bernauer*—that 'der Verfasser selbst auf der Seite des alten Herzogs steht und zwar so entschieden, dass nur dieser ihn für den ganzen Gegenstand entzündet hat'[1]—has been widely accepted as a measure of his philosophy. That he saw in Herzog Ernst the embodiment of Necessity, or law, is clear; but it may well be doubted whether this was his original vision. In the diary for 1851 he wrote: 'Mir ist bei der Arbeit unendlich wohl zu Muthe gewesen und abermals hat sich's mir bestätigt, was ich freilich schon oft an mir selbst erfuhr, dass in der Kunst das Kind den Vater, das Werk den Meister, belehrt. Nie habe ich das Verhältniss, worin das Individuum zum Staat steht, so deutlich erkannt, wie jetzt, und das ist doch ein grosser Gewinn.'[2] It would appear from this that Hebbel did not consciously begin with the problem of the individual and the state, sometimes proclaimed as the basic problem of this play. Fresh ideas would often come to him as he worked out a theme, and the entry clearly suggests that recognition here was gradual. It is not so clear, however, that he did not begin with a different and perhaps more interesting idea. It is true that too much weight cannot be attached to the clear-cut entry in September, when he had written the first act: 'Längst hatte ich die Idee, auch die Schönheit einmal von der tragischen, den Untergang durch sich selbst bedingenden Seite darzustellen und die Agnes Bernauerin ist dazu, wie gefunden.'[3] It was Hebbel's way to describe his dramas in terms of an idea, but such descriptions are not of necessity complete, nor do they take account of that initial process of visualization which he describes elsewhere. Nevertheless, the tragic fate of beauty and virtue is a theme implicit, at least, in *Genoveva*, though here the heroine's passivity is balanced by the passion of Golo, who gradually comes to dominate the drama. And as early as 1841—while *Genoveva* still occupied his mind—an entry in the diary suggests the tragic interest of Abraham

[1] Letter to Friedrich von Uechtritz, 14 Dec. 1854, *Briefe*, ed. cit., vol. v, p. 205.

[2] *Tagebücher*, ed. cit., vol. iii. 4982, 24 Dec. 1851.

[3] Ibid. 4941, 30 Sept. 1851.

sacrificing his child: '*Abrahams Opfer* wäre ein sehr bedeutender Stoff für ein Drama. Die Idee des Opferns müsste aus ihm selbst kommen und je schwerer ihm die Ausführung fiele, um so mehr müsste er an dem furchtbaren Pflichtgedanken fest halten. Dann die Stimme des Herrn'.[1] Such a conflict is presented in the fourth act of *Agnes Bernauer*:

Preising. Aber es ist doch auch entsetzlich, dass sie sterben soll, bloss weil sie schön und sittsam war!

Ernst. Das ist es auch! Ja! Darum stellt' ich's Gott anheim. Er hat gesprochen. Ich warf mein eignes Junges aus dem Nest und legte ein fremdes hinein. Es ist todt! (IV. 4)

Agnes is, in the Duke's own words, 'das reinste Opfer, das der Nothwendigkeit im Lauf aller Jahrhunderte gefallen ist' (V. 10); and she herself, in choosing death rather than betrayal of her love, stresses the consciousness of innocence: 'Nein, nein, Ihr bringt Euer Opfer nicht so weit, dass es sich selbst befleckt. Rein war mein erster Hauch, rein soll auch mein letzter sein! Thut mir, wie Ihr müsst und dürft, ich will's leiden! Bald weiss ich, ob's mit Recht geschah!' (V. 3).

Sacrifice and purity are fundamental conceptions in *Agnes Bernauer*. The problem of vicarious suffering, of the pure victim, is presented in its stark contrast of innocence and tragic fate. Deeper far than his belief that the individual must yield to the welfare of the state lay Hebbel's conviction that 'what's come to perfection perishes'. The time-setting of his drama governed his presentation of the state's necessity, but no historical conditions could alter, for him, this deep law of being. The tragic fate of perfection—rather than the 'Tragödie der Schönheit'—was his theme; and in the figure of Agnes he was not only showing the fate of the beautiful 'Bernauerin', but was illustrating an idea of profound significance in the mid-nineteenth century: the value of sacrifice in the evolutionary process. In terms of the later theory of evolution, the tragic individual is the individual who must, for one reason or another, be sacrificed to the welfare of the race, or of the type, which can only evolve by the balance

[1] *Tagebücher*, ed. cit., vol. ii. 2315, 25 Mar. 1841.

of extremes. Excess, of whatever kind, endangers the cosmic process; the whole depends upon the balance of its parts. Thus by her excess of beauty and virtue Agnes Bernauer sins against the survival factor of society, and by her mere existence, in its perfect individual form, she incurs a tragic guilt. The single life is of necessity sacrificed to the type, so carefully conserved in the forward movement of the whole. Thus tragic guilt and ethical guilt need not—and in the figure of Agnes do not—coincide. She does not violate the distinctions of right and wrong which men have laid down for the guidance of their conduct; but though she is guiltless in this sense, her excess of quality itself constitutes a tragic flaw.

Such a tragic theme could have been treated apart from the historical conditions which involved Agnes Bernauer in the problem of the Bavarian dynasty. But in the time-setting of the story, it was evident that her sacrifice was conditioned by political circumstance. In rejecting the accidental catastrophe, Hebbel accented the fundamental necessity for that sacrifice, but he also came to stress the motives governing the Duke's decision. Thus the opposition between the interests of the lovers and the interests of the state was more sharply stated as the play progressed; and gradually Hebbel emphasized the historical connotations of his theme. Some critics have found it difficult to recognize the logical connexion between the 'tragedy of beauty' and the 'tragedy of the individual and the state'. It seems clear, however, that the fundamental conception is that of the tragic individual, conditioning its own destruction by its inherent excess of quality; the circumstances in which this tragic fate occurs are those of an opposition between the interests of the one and the many. If this be so, Hebbel's own statement is explained. He did not begin with the idea of the individual and the state; this idea, as he asserts, became clearer as the work progressed. But the reason why it became clearer, why it emerged from the individual love-story of Agnes and Albrecht, was that it formed a corollary to the conception which—consciously or no—he was embodying in the figure of Agnes. The 'conservation of the type' became merged in the 'well-being of the state'; Herzog Ernst became more interesting to Hebbel as this equation emerged, until at last he dominated the poet's mind. (It is worth noting that the Duke does not actually appear until the first two acts have been devoted to the love-story.) Hence the logical reconciliation of the two opposing points of view—so contrary to Hebbel's wonted manner: hence the Duke's occupation of the centre of the stage in the last scene. Hence too the gradual *decrescendo* in the part of Agnes (originally the bearer of the tragic message) and the ensuing feeling of a division between sympathy and reason. In no other of Hebbel's major dramas is such a division felt. Judith and Holofernes, Herodes and Mariamne, Siegfried and Brunhild, for example, may evoke their tragic destiny by their individual conflicts, and our sympathy may be claimed by each antagonist; but interest is concentrated on the furthering of the conflict by every act of the individual opponents, while the recognition of its necessity proceeds equally from intellectual and emotional sympathy. And in *Gyges und sein Ring* Hebbel was to bring forth a new vision of harmony in sacrifice. Thus *Agnes Bernauer* stands alone among his greater dramas; and if in itself it lends colour to the belief that his tragedies are primarily intellectual in character, yet the contrast between this and the other plays indicates that such a generalization cannot be maintained.

Hebbel turned again in *Agnes Bernauer* to the prose medium of *Maria Magdalena*. Compared with the impressive rhythm of the verse in *Herodes und Mariamne* and with the serene beauty of that in *Gyges und sein Ring*, the language at first seems ordinary. But closer examination reveals the amazing mastery of prose rhythms (differing completely, as they should, from those of verse) which characterizes his best prose work.

'Mich graus't! Manch ähnliches Blatt hielt ich schon in der Hand, aber da ging dem strengen Spruch jedesmal eine Reihe schnöder Gewaltthaten voran, man las viel von Raub, Mord, Brand und Friedensbruch, ehe man an die Strafe kam. Hier könnte höchstens stehen: sie trug keinen Schleier und schnitt sich die Haare nicht ab!' (IV. 3).

And in contrast to the restraint of the language, there is a striking richness of colour in the setting. Nowhere hitherto has Hebbel put so much historical detail on to his canvas—though he is always a master in the art of suggesting it. 'Das alte Deutsche Reich', he wrote after beginning the play, 'wird in voller Kraft und Herrlichkeit den Hintergrund bilden und ein rein menschliches Problem, das sich durchaus im Kreise des Schönen hält, das Centrum';[1] and two months later: 'Ich habe eine einfach rührende, menschlich schöne Handlung . . . in die Mitte gestellt und das Reich mit allen seinen Elementen steht dahinter, wie ein ungeheurer Berg mit Donner und Blitz . . .'[2] Indeed, the glaring contrasts of medieval life are skilfully suggested. The dance in Augsburg, the tourney at Regensburg, the battle array of the final act, evoke with vivid clarity the picture of the Empire in its days of pageantry and war, while the scenes in the Augsburg house and in the castles of Vohburg and Straubing point the essential contrast of the drama. This fulness of colour and actuality of detail remain a unique achievement in Hebbel's work, where in general the relation of his themes to the 'moment' of history is symbolically treated; but even the admirable stage-craft of the play does not counterbalance that duality of interest which lessens its tragic force.

[1] Letter to H. Th. Rötscher, 6 Oct. 1851, *Briefe*, ed. cit., vol. iv, p. 328.

[2] Letter to Franz Dingelstedt, 12 Dec. 1851, *Briefe*, ed. cit., vol. iv, p. 337.

VII

LAST YEARS. 'GYGES UND SEIN RING'—'MUTTER UND KIND'—'DIE NIBELUNGEN'—'DEMETRIUS'

THE years from 1851 to 1863 in Hebbel's life recall the image of the mountain torrent, transformed into a broad river and traversing the fruitful plain. The diary's records, while they may gain in wisdom, lose something of their dramatic interest as documents of change and growth; the rapidly increasing volume of correspondence is more general, less intimately personal in its tone—save on Hebbel's occasional absences from home without Christine. The note of harmony, suggested more than once in the years 1850 and 1851, recurs in different combinations, with a growing strength. In face of trying political conditions, Hebbel makes only a mild comment in the annual retrospect for 1852. The journal had been locked away during the year because of the frequent inquisitions that took place in Vienna, even in the homes of harmless citizens: 'und lieber wollte ich meine Gedanken einbüssen, als mich in meiner aphoristischen Unterhaltung mit mir selbst belauschen lassen'.[1] This year had brought Hebbel little, save the successful performances of *Agnes Bernauer* in Munich (which he revisited for the first time on this occasion), in Weimar, and in Stuttgart, and a summer holiday with Christine in Milan and Venice. The accustomed pause in achievement had lasted, except for some lyric poems, through the year; yet with only an exclamation of regret Hebbel passes on to comment in the journal on a slight improvement in Christine's position at the theatre. The possibility of migration to Munich, suggested during Hebbel's visit by his friendship with Dingelstedt and his successful audiences with the reigning sovereign, had been rejected after the evidences of journalistic and literary intrigue that followed his return to Vienna. 'Bleibe es im nächsten Jahre, wie es ist!'[2] he ends his survey of the year 1852.

[1] *Tagebücher*, ed. cit., vol. iii. 5047, 31 Dec. 1852. [2] Ibid.

The following year was almost equally barren of dramatic production. Political conditions were not improved by the attempt of a Hungarian early in the spring to assassinate the Emperor; Hebbel's record of this event in his journal ends with words which reveal the strength of his belief in German unity: 'Italien schickt abermals die Revolution, Ungarn nun gar den Kaisermord: sollte das nicht ein Wink seyn, nirgends das Fundament des Throns zu suchen, als in Deutschland und also Deutschland und Deutsches Element zu kräftigen? Mein altes Lied! Soll ichs noch länger allein singen?'[1] His fortieth birthday passed in pleasant harmony, accompanied by the reflection in the diary that already he had exceeded by two years his father's span of life; but strength of mind and body was still evident: 'da ist die Zeit denn gleichgültig'.[2] A visit to Hamburg in the summer, and thence to Heligoland, is only recorded in the diary by an allusion at the end of the year; but we know from Elise's subsequent letters to Christine that this—their last visit to her—passed in harmony.[3] On their return, interminable negotiations ended in Laube's rejection of *Agnes Bernauer*, Christine was ill, and by the end of December Hebbel himself had fallen a victim to jaundice. Nevertheless, he wrote in hopeful mood on New Year's Eve: 'freudigen Muths der Zukunft entgegensehend. Titi blüht. Bleibe Alles, wie es ist!'[4] Immediately before this attack of illness, he had completed the first act of a new tragedy: on 14 December he wrote: 'Heute den 1sten Act der Rhodope geendigt. . . . Freilich wird die Motivirung der Königin schwer seyn'.[5] His mind absorbed in this new subject, he could face the new year with hope.

Gyges und sein Ring occupied Hebbel until November 1854. It was half finished when he and Christine left for Marienbad in July; the latter part was written in the autumn, after their return to Vienna.[6] He had no thought of offering it to the

[1] *Tagebücher*, ed. cit., vol. iii. 5077, 19 Feb. 1853.
[2] Ibid. 5090, 18 Mar. 1853.
[3] *Elise Lensing, Briefe*, ed. cit., p. 152.
[4] *Tagebücher*, ed. cit., vol. iii. 5218, 31 Dec. 1853.
[5] Ibid. 5213, 14 Dec. 1853.
[6] *Tagebücher*, ed. cit., vol. iv. 5348, 14 Nov. 1854.

Burgtheater: Laube's hostility against them both was too apparent. Hebbel had written to Sigmund Engländer earlier in 1854: 'Es ist nun einmal, wie es ist, und wäre ich nicht mit auf den Erwerb angewiesen, so würde ich die Welt schon jetzt nicht mehr incommodiren, als ob ich schon im Sarge läge; ich würde in aller Stille ausführen, was mir noch am Herzen liegt, aber so wenig etwas drucken, als spielen lassen'.[1] His plays had disappeared, for one reason or another, from the Burgtheater. *Agnes Bernauer* had been refused; *Genoveva*, in the mutilated form of *Magellona* (to avoid the clerical objection which years before had banned it from the stage) was successfully played early in 1854 six times and then dropped out of the repertory. Hebbel's wife also had to suffer for his literary sins; her roles were diminished, wherever possible, in number and importance. It was not surprising that Hebbel locked the manuscript of *Gyges und sein Ring* away, with the sole comment: 'das erste Stück, das ich in den Kasten lege'.[2]

Four days after the entry recording its completion, Elise Lensing died in Hamburg. The news had not been unexpected: for some time she had been confined to bed, and her last letters show the feebleness of mortal illness, together with a moving affection for them all.[3] Hebbel's survey of the year is very brief, but it contains the only allusion in the diary to her death.

'Elise ist nicht mehr; am 18ten November 1854 gegen Morgen ist sie verschieden. Lange vorher schon war für sie Nichts mehr zu hoffen, und also nur der Tod noch zu wünschen; so erschütterte mich die Schmerzens-Kunde denn im Moment des Eintreffens nicht so sehr, als sie in mir nachzitterte und nachzittern wird! Welch ein verworrenes Leben; wie tief mit dem meinigen verflochten, und doch gegen den Willen der Natur und ohne den rechten inneren Bezug! Dennoch werde ich Niemand lieber, als ihr, in den reineren Regionen begegnen, wenn sie sich mir dereinst erschliessen'.[4]

To the end, it seems, there was an element in this relationship

[1] Letter to Sigmund Engländer, 6 May 1854, *Briefe*, ed. cit., vol. v, p. 159.

[2] *Tagebücher*, ed. cit., vol. iv. 5363, 31 Dec. 1854.

[3] *Elise Lensing*, *Briefe*, ed. cit., pp. 188–9, 190–1, 192.

[4] *Tagebücher*, ed. cit., vol. iv. 5363, 31 Dec. 1854.

that eluded Hebbel's self-analysis: a slight, involuntary sigh of relief complicates his feelings of regret and resignation. Elise's last message is of a simpler character: 'Ich schliesse Euch Alle an mein Herz Bis in die Ewigkeit Euch ich lieb—'.[1] But then Hebbel had found new life and happiness—she, in her solitude, had reached serenity. The impress of their relations stamped itself plainly on Hebbel's tragic art. In Elise's life their mark was equally indelible; but with her, it was self-conquest, painfully attained, that opened the way to a new means of self-expression in her devotion to them all. The solution for Elise lay in the affectionate care she lavished, after her return from Vienna, on Karl Hebbel and (whenever occasion offered) on the Hebbel household; these relations, it is plain, became the mainstay of her life. Hebbel, the poet, had a more arduous task. Only by slow degrees for him did the tragic dissonance resolve itself, under the influence of new experience and a deeper insight. It is perhaps the strangest synchronization of events in Hebbel's life—which is not lacking in coincidence—that the same month which brought news of Elise Lensing's death should have seen the completion of that drama which creates a fuller sense of harmony than any other of his tragedies.

'Ich will das Ueble um des Guten willen gern ertragen' is the last word of the diary for 1854.

The opening entry for 1855 reflects the subject that was now occupying the poet's mind—it contains a quotation from Frederick the Great disparaging the newly reprinted *Nibelungenlied*. 'A worthy parallel to the views of George III on Shakespeare!' is Hebbel's comment. The 'Nibelungenmotiv' thus first begins to sound; for five years it forms a major and recurrent theme, until in March, 1860, Hebbel notes in his diary that he has written the last lines of *Kriemhilds Rache*, and that the work is 'Beendet, wenn nicht vollendet'.[2]

But at first, through the spring and summer of 1855, there is no mention of work upon *Die Nibelungen*. During the summer—in no circumstances a creative time for Hebbel—

[1] *Elise Lensing, Briefe*, ed. cit., p. 192.

[2] *Tagebücher*, ed. cit., vol. iv. 5798, 22 Mar. 1860.

his mind was fully occupied by the unfamiliar pleasure of proprietorship; in August he acquired a cottage and a piece of land at Orth, on Lake Gmunden, which was henceforth their summer home. A delightful entry records the occasion of this purchase:

'Ich habe Shakespeare immer für unerreichbar gehalten und mir nie eingebildet, ihm in irgend Etwas nachzukommen. Dennoch hätte ich in früheren Jahren immer noch eher gehofft, einmal irgend einen Character zu zeichnen, wie er, oder irgend eine Situation zu malen, als mir, wie er, ein Grundstück zu kaufen. Nichtsdestoweniger habe ich heute Mittag 10 Uhr einen Contract unterzeichnet, durch den ich Besitzer eines Hauses am Gmundner See geworden bin!'[1]

Hebbel's real love of nature and his powers of observation found great satisfaction in the surroundings of their new summer residence. An added pleasure in stability is evident—the contrast with the conditions of his youth was often present in his mind. 'Wie glücklich [wäre] mein armer Vater gewesen, wenn er es jemals zu einem so bescheidenen kleinen Besitz gebracht hätte!'[2] It was not until the autumn that the Nibelungen plan was seriously considered. By 18 October the first act of ten that were planned was well begun: Hagen and Siegfried had been introduced, Kriemhild was about to make her entry, Hebbel writes.[3] A fortnight later, the first act of 'Kriemhildens Leid' was finished.[4] At the end of the year he could report the completion of two acts—but also the illness of Christine and a general mood of uncertainty. 'Zufrieden mit dem Fertigen, jedoch ohne Vertrauen zu dem Ganzen und zweifelnd, ob ich fortfahren werde.'[5] This mood yielded in the New Year to the soothing influence of a new work—the idyllic epic *Mutter und Kind*, which was begun on Christine's birthday and progressed rapidly for the first three cantos. The fourth was written in April, almost entirely while Hebbel was gathering violets in the Prater: 'es waren himmlische Tage. So wie ich einen Strauss beisammen hatte, waren auch

[1] *Tagebücher*, ed. cit., vol. iv. 5388, 14 Aug. 1855.
[2] Ibid. 5389, 21 Aug. 1855.
[3] Ibid. 5396, 18 Oct. 1855.
[4] Ibid. 5397, 2 Nov. 1855.
[5] Ibid. 5411, 31 Dec. 1855.

dreizig oder vierzig Hexameter fertig.'[1] The fallow period of summer then set in; July and most of August were spent in Gmunden; and by the beginning of October *Die Nibelungen* had been taken up again. The projected plan of ten short acts had now been abandoned in favour of five long ones. The reason for the change was practical: Hebbel felt convinced that a long drama (offering the possibility of cutting) would be more readily accepted for performance than two plays linked into a whole. 'Und das Theater', he writes—perhaps remembering *Gyges*—'ist hier doch Hauptsache, denn es kann sich absolut nur um die dramatische Vermittlung des Gedichts mit der Nation handeln.'[2] This is a statement of some importance for a just appreciation of Hebbel's *Nibelungen*. In this work he never forgot his original object—the transformation into drama of an epic which he felt to be essentially dramatic; and the treatment of material in *Die Nibelungen* thus differs from that in other plays.

By the year's end two of the new long acts were written: in the second of them Hebbel thought he could discern 'etwas Zaubergold des versunkenen Horts'.[3] He had also revised his lyrics for a new collected edition, and was so mastered by the lyric impulse that he found difficulty in returning to the drama.[4] In reflecting on the productivity of the whole year, Hebbel cites an epigram that he added to the earlier ones, which had expressed a spirit of discontent. It reveals the major mood of his last years—thanksgiving for attainment and a prayer for permanence:

Götter, öffnet die Hände nicht mehr, ich würde erschrecken,
Denn Ihr gabt mir genug: hebt sie nur schirmend empor![5]

Composing (as he frequently did) while walking in the streets, Hebbel completed on 18 February 1857 the third act of the Nibelungen tragedy—this, he writes, formed the end of the first part: *Siegfrieds Tod*.[6] Almost immediately he took up *Mutter und Kind* again, and by 20 March the seventh,

[1] *Tagebücher*, ed. cit., vol. iv. 5428, 15 Apr. 1856.
[2] Ibid. 5477, 3 Oct. 1856.
[3] Ibid. 5537, 31 Dec. 1856.
[4] Ibid.
[5] Ibid.
[6] Ibid. 5555, 18 Feb. 1857.

and last, canto was finished. 'Ich glaube', he adds, 'das Thema hat gehalten, was es versprach und sogar noch etwas mehr.'[1] The poem gained the prize awarded by the Tiedge-Stiftung in Dresden, but was not published until 1859. Meanwhile the lyric poems appeared in a new collected edition, which Hebbel (as mindful of good as he was of ill) dedicated to Uhland.

After two years of unusual productivity, he wrote little during the year 1858. An opera text which he composed in three weeks for Anton Rubinstein, entitled *Der Steinwurf* oder *Opfer um Opfer*, brought him in more than he had received for *Judith*, *Genoveva*, *Maria Magdalena*, *Der Diamant*, and the collected lyrics all together; with a pleasant satisfaction he observes that it was not only 'ein gutes Geschäft', but also an interesting opportunity for new insight into the relations of music and drama—even into the nature of drama itself.[2] At the end of the previous year, he had been undecided whether to engage upon the second part of the Nibelungen or to try and complete Schiller's *Demetrius*. In the course of 1858 he wrote two acts of *Demetrius*, but in reviewing them felt some uncertainty.[3] The subject had occupied his mind, he recalls, at a very early age—it was to persist until the end.

Cordial relations with Weimar were established during a visit paid by Hebbel in June at the invitation of Dingelstedt, who had been appointed Director of the Court Theatre. Many distinctions were showered upon the poet of *Genoveva*, the performance of which was the original reason for his visit. Success and honour were his, as they had never been in Austria; he returned home with an order given by the Grand Duke, and with the memory of delightful intercourse, alike with court and theatre. From now onwards Weimar was to play an important part in his thoughts and plans, and though the migration seriously contemplated in 1861 did not take place, Hebbel's relations with the theatre and the court persisted. In the year of his death he was made Honorary Court

[1] *Tagebücher*, ed. cit., vol. iv. 5575, 20 Mar. 1857.
[2] Ibid. 5627, 16 Mar. 1858.
[3] Ibid. 5642, 31 Dec. 1858.

Librarian—a sinecure, merely conferring distinction on the holder.

In spite of the external stimulus to *Demetrius* offered by the Weimar connexion and the plans for a Schiller celebration there in 1859, *Die Nibelungen* was still dominant in Hebbel's mind. The autumn of 1859—till then an unproductive year—saw the rapid completion of three acts of *Kriemhilds Rache*. 'So giebt's am Ende wirklich noch eine Trilogie', Hebbel comments at the end of October, when the first act had been written in three weeks.[1] On 17 December Act III was finished: 'Nie arbeitete ich mehr in Einem Zuge, nie hat mich ein Werk aber auch so angegriffen, ich habe Abends ordentlich Fieber.'[2] In addition, a third act was added to *Demetrius*.[3] And yet this year had been broken by a crippling attack of rheumatism which lasted for two months, and the effects of which had not wholly disappeared by the time the new year opened.

With this new year an event occurred which affected Hebbel deeply—the complete break in his intimate friendship with Emil Kuh, his subsequent biographer. Hebbel alludes briefly to the episode; Emil Kuh relates it—if elliptically; but a just evaluation of it demands consideration of the previous history of their relationship. Among the admiring young men of talent who had begun to gather round Hebbel a short time after he had settled in Vienna, Emil Kuh and Karl Debrois van Bruyck had been the most devoted and most promising. Emil Kuh, in particular, grew into a confidential companion, at the same time as he was becoming a competent and a perceptive critic; the relation between them—though less warm on Hebbel's side—had a flavour of the old friendship with Emil Rousseau. But to those admitted to the freedom of his inner mind, Hebbel, throughout his life, was singularly exacting. Uncompromising in the extreme, he demanded of them an absolute surrender. (Indeed, perhaps only Christine, among the people whom he loved, was able fully to preserve her individuality: and she grew, he confides

[1] *Tagebücher*, ed. cit., vol. iv. 5754, 26 Oct. 1859.

[2] Ibid. 5774, 17 Dec. 1859.

[3] Ibid. 5777, 31 Dec. 1859.

to the diary, 'von Jahr zu Jahr, von Tag zu Tag theurer'[1]—no insignificant coincidence.) As Emil Kuh grew into manhood and independence, as he contracted other ties, the difficulties of the relationship became more evident. Hebbel, conscious of all that he had given his disciple (and which he was accustomed to withhold) was apt to regard independence and differences of outlook as ingratitude; Kuh, perhaps forgetful of the fact that his relations with Hebbel were due to his own choice and that without the advantage of this intercourse he might have been less adequately equipped as a literary critic, grew increasingly impatient of the restraint thereby imposed upon his own convictions. It is plain from their correspondence that the younger man became more susceptible as time went on; his letters indicate a hypersensitiveness which was ill-matched with Hebbel's temperament. But the first editor of Hebbel's diaries has rendered illegible the poet's own view of the break; Kuh's allusive account of it at the end of his *Life of Hebbel* is thus left without a counterpart, save for the one entry in the diary referring to their first meeting after the quarrel:

'Bei der letzten Vorstellung des Leare war ich mit Emil Kuh im Theater; es sind keine drei Wochen. Die Vorstellung regte uns Beide an zu lebhaftem Gespräch. Gestern Abend sah ich Lessings Emilia Galotti; Emil Kuh kam auch, sass dicht vor mir und grüsste mich nicht. Es war für mich die Reprise des Leare, nur dass er diess Mal nicht auf der Bühne, sondern im Parterre spielte. Ich habe durch diesen Menschen . . . schweres Unrecht erlitten und gründlich erfahren, wie bitter der Undank ist. Aber ich habe es mir, obgleich ich vierzehn Tage lang keine Nacht schlief und dem Typhus nahe war, doch dadurch zu versüssen gewusst, dass ich es als eine Art von Compensation für das Unrecht betrachtete, das ich selbst begangen haben mag und dadurch wirkliche Erleichterung gefühlt. So liegt der Gedanke der Busse in der Menschenseele.'[2]

Against this is to be placed Kuh's statement of Hebbel's unwarrantable refusal to acknowledge his personal liberty and

[1] *Tagebücher*, ed. cit., vol. iv. 5620, 31 Dec. 1857.
[2] Ibid. 5785, 1 Feb. 1860.

independence[1]—which he couples, however, with appreciation of his real kindliness and friendship. It may well be thought that the provocation should have been great to induce so violent and obvious a rupture as the entry in Hebbel's diary indicates—only explicable as the sudden culmination of a process that must have been long preparing in the spirit of the younger man. Hebbel's subsequent letter to Karl Debrois van Bruyck, at once concluding their intercourse and pronouncing judgement on it, puts the position as he saw it, when some months had passed:

'Nun die magern [Jahre] vor der Thür stehen, nun Alter, Krankheit, Lebensüberdruss u.s.w. sich melden, wenden Sie mir den Rücken und beziehen Sich dabei auf eine Character-Eigenschaft, die Sie am ersten Tage entdecken mussten und die mich, je nachdem man den hohen oder den niedern Styl liebt, den unschädlichen Dämonen oder den gutmüthigen Polterern anreiht, da ich in meinen nordischen Berserker-Anfällen, die ich keineswegs zu läugnen oder zu beschönigen gedenke, noch nie zum letzten Wort gekommen bin, ohne, wie Sie Beide recht gut wissen, mir selbst zu sagen: Das ist ja Alles nicht wahr! und jede mögliche Genugthuung zu geben. . . .'[2]

And if part of this letter shows the bitterness of disillusion, the end has a moving dignity:

'Ihren Dank gebe ich Ihnen aber von Herzen zurück, denn auch ich habe die Anregungen, die mir der um mich versammelte jugendliche Kreis so oft gewährte, nicht vergessen, und ich werde sie nicht ohne Schmerz entbehren'.[3]

The defection of Kuh—for whom, there is little doubt, Hebbel with all his domineering ways had a warm affection—was a deep wound. Only on the poet's death-bed was this discord resolved: Emil Kuh, of whom he had spoken to a common friend in regretful and affectionate terms a few days earlier, paid him a visit shortly before the end, and without word of explanation the old intimacy was restored for a short hour.[4]

Echoes of the unhappy quarrel occur at intervals through

[1] Emil Kuh, *Biographie Friedrich Hebbels*, ed. cit., vol. ii, p. 485.

[2] *Tagebücher*, ed. cit., vol. iv. 5825, 7 June 1860, and *Briefe*, ed. cit., vol. vi, pp. 322–3.

[3] Ibid.

[4] v. Emil Kuh, *Biographie Friedrich Hebbels*, ed. cit., vol. ii, pp. 521–2.

Hebbel's diary. No other took the place of this younger friend, in whom a deep admiration and a critical mind had been united. But with his wonted determination Hebbel turned (after a short period of nervous prostration) to strenuous activity. By 7 March 1860 the fourth act of *Kriemhilds Rache* was written, and a fortnight later the drama was completed. Four and a half years had passed since he had begun to write *Die Nibelungen*; it was to be his last entirely finished work.

Early in the following year, a performance of the first and second parts of the trilogy took place in Weimar, and Hebbel, invited by the Grand Duke to attend, was overwhelmed with favours and success. When the whole drama was performed in May, Christine played the part of Brunhild in *Siegfrieds Tod*, and of Kriemhild in *Kriemhilds Rache*. 'Die Wirkung [war] ausserordentlich', Hebbel wrote in his year's survey 'und die Leistung meiner Frau gewaltig.'[1] But this successful event was accompanied by disagreeable experiences. The permission for Frau Hebbel's engagement in Weimar and for her absence from the Burgtheater had been obtained direct by the Grand Duke from the Emperor; but this did not prevent private and public comments of an unpleasant character. Dingelstedt, when informed of the fact, immediately suggested that they should move to Weimar; both the Grand Duke and the Grand Duchess approved the scheme and were prepared to help in its execution. But as the plan matured, Dingelstedt grew less enthusiastic; after their return to Vienna, and when Laube had already been approached, he wrote advising them against it. A series of complicated negotiations then took place; their outcome was a decision to remain in Vienna which did nothing to better the position of the Hebbels in either quarter.

The next years, however, brought compensation in more unalloyed success. *Die Nibelungen* was printed early in 1862; performances in Berlin and Schwerin were given 'mit Pauken und Trompeten', Hebbel states;[2] Mannheim and Vienna

[1] *Tagebücher*, ed. cit., vol. iv. 5947, 31 Dec. 1861.

[2] Ibid. 6052, 31 Dec. 1862.

followed suit in 1863. For the first time, he had the experience of widespread and unqualified success; he had struck, in this trilogy, a note to which the heart of Germany responded. With a strange prescience, he drew the conclusion in his diary: 'Aufhören, den Dudelsack an den Nagel hängen wäre jetzt vielleicht das Beste!'[1] When in February 1863 at long last he had celebrated a signal success in the Burgtheater—where conditions for so many years had been a formidable obstacle—he wrote in his delightful vein of naïve wonder: 'Heute gratulirten mir zu dem Erfolg zwei Damen, deren Namen ich schon oft las, als ich mich noch in Wesselburen befand, nämlich Charlotte von Hagn . . . und Fanny Elsler . . . Märchenhaft; man schläft ein auf Stroh und erwacht in einem Palast'.[2] 'Ich bin einmal wieder am Leben für die Wiener', he writes in humorous astonishment after the fifth crowded performance of the trilogy;[3] the royalties which he received in April for the first eight performances amounted to 860 florins.[4]

But with this outward climax of achievement came the first indications of physical disaster. In 1861 Hebbel had visited Rendsburg and Hamburg, arranging with Campe for the publication of *Die Nibelungen*; in June of the following year he had made a journey to London, on the occasion of the industrial exhibition, and to his great pleasure had revived the former friendship with Sigmund Engländer, now settled there; in August he had spent some time in Wilhelmsthal as the guest of the Grand Duchess of Weimar. But from the autumn of 1862 onwards, the pleasure of travel was denied him. A neglected chill, contracted in Wilhelmsthal, caused him trouble through the winter; and in the spring, when some improvement had taken place, a further chill made his condition worse. In the middle of June he was ordered to Gmunden for treatment, and for the first time he went there alone. But the so-called rheumatism—which had attacked him recurrently throughout his life—seized him

[1] *Tagebücher,* ed. cit., vol. iv. 6052, 31 Dec. 1862.
[2] Ibid. 6084, 21 Feb. 1863.
[3] Ibid. 6100, 6 Mar. 1863.
[4] Ibid. 6122, 10 Apr. 1863.

more firmly in its grip, till he was crippled by it. An improvement took place in the autumn, bringing with it an access of cheerfulness, but was of short duration. Soon he was almost completely paralysed, and confined to bed. But strangely, as through all his life, illness brought its compensating visitant, and the creative spirit stirred in him for the last time. *Demetrius*—which had lain 'still as a stone' at the end of 1862,[1] when he was well and vigorous—sprang to life again; and the poet who had been wont to compose while he was walking, who had cried in 1859: 'wer mir die Beine nimmt, der nimmt mir auch den Kopf',[2] now wrote the third, fourth, and the main part of the fifth act of his last tragedy while he lay crippled in his bed. The last entry of the diary dates from the beginning of this creative period:

'Eine grosse Leidens-Periode, die noch nicht vorüber ist, so dass ich sie erst später fixiren kann. Aber seltsam genug, hat seit 14 Tagen der poetische Geist angefangen, sich in mir zu regen, es entstanden anderthalb Acte des Demetrius, obgleich ich, durch Rheumatismen verhindert, kaum im Stande war, sie nieder zu schreiben, und wenn es so fort geht, darf ich hoffen, das Stück im Winter unter Dach und Fach zu bringen. Wunderlich-eigensinnige Kraft, die sich Jahre lang so tief verbirgt, wie eine zurückgetretene Quelle unter der Erde, und die dann, wie diese, plötzlich und oft zur unbequemsten Stunde, wieder hervor bricht!'[3]

Early in November the Berlin Schiller prize was awarded to him for *Die Nibelungen*. His reception of the news was characteristic for this time of stress, when mortal illness seemed to endow him with a serenity his spirit had not known in vigorous days: 'Das ist Menschenlos', he is recorded to have said, and smiled: 'bald fehlt uns der Wein, bald fehlt uns der Becher'.[4] He died little more than a month afterwards, on 13 December 1863.

With *Gyges und sein Ring*—one is tempted to believe—Hebbel reached the summit of his inner development, while

[1] *Tagebücher*, ed. cit., vol. iv. 6052, 31 Dec. 1862.
[2] Ibid. 5777, 31 Dec. 1859.
[3] Ibid. 6176, 25 Oct. 1863.
[4] Emil Kuh, *Biographie Friedrich Hebbels*, ed. cit., vol. ii, p. 521.

Die Nibelungen represents the outward climax of achievement. Whereas the trilogy was performed and acclaimed in the major theatres of Germany, the former drama was silently laid away. But as *Torquato Tasso* and *Libussa* stand apart from the other works of Goethe and of Grillparzer, making a more intimate appeal to those who seek the subtler distillation of experience, so *Gyges und sein Ring*, among all Hebbel's tragedies, offers the most delicately balanced interpretation of spiritual reactions.

Once again the poet of *Herodes und Mariamne* portrays the relations of two widely divergent and unusual natures. Kandaules, like Herodes, has a wife who forms the most precious jewel in his crown. But the situation here is a very different one. Herodes' passion for Mariamne makes him tremble, in the pride of his possession, lest any other should inherit what he owns; Kandaules, filled with equal conviction that he has a peerless wife, cannot be fully satisfied until he has proved her transcendent quality to others. So Herodes—had he his way—would willingly keep even the sight of Mariamne's picture from any other man; but Kandaules, who is deprived by her determined seclusion of the opportunity of displaying the beauty of Rhodope to the world, would fain show his possession to his closest friend. Two opposite desires are portrayed in these two tragedies—yet they have a common root in the possessive claims of passion.

Mariamne and Rhodope differ no less widely. In contrast to Mariamne's active vengeance, the retribution exacted by the Lydian queen is almost an impersonal process. Unswerving in her determination, the gentle Rhodope appears as the priestess of a higher ethic, to which, in the end, Kandaules and Gyges pay a late allegiance. Yet both the active and the passive nature are moved by a deep impulse—the revolt of the spirit against the violation of its freedom. But while Mariamne's protest (though none the less a just one) is mixed with vehement pride, Rhodope acts so completely in obedience to an inner law that her logic loses the quality of personal argument. There is no element of vengeance in it—save on behalf of an offended deity; she convinces both those who have sinned against her, and by her means, atonement is offered to the higher law.

The fable of Herodotus which provided Hebbel with the main outline of his story suggests little of such a solution. According to this narrative, Kandaules, King of Lydia, who is deeply in love with his beautiful wife, considers her to be the fairest woman in the world. Wishing to prove this to his favourite lance-bearer Gyges, the king proposes that the latter should behold her in her naked beauty. In spite of his protests, Kandaules arranges to hide him behind the open door of their sleeping-chamber; he is to escape while the queen's back is turned. But Rhodope sees Gyges as he steals away. Realizing that her husband must have brought this shame upon her, she restrains herself, and resolves on vengeance. Calling Gyges to her on the following day, she offers him the choice of killing Kandaules or accepting death himself. Gyges pleads in vain; the queen is relentless, and to save himself, he chooses the alternative of avenging her upon her husband. The queen assigns to him the same hiding-place in their chamber, and gives him a dagger, with which he stabs Kandaules as he lies asleep. Gyges then succeeds to Kandaules' kingdom and his wife; his sovereignty is confirmed by the oracle at Delphi, though an adverse fate is predicted for his descendants.[1]

This story was casually mentioned to Hebbel by Braun von Braunthal in the Library of the Police head-quarters: 'ich las sie nach', he writes in the diary 'und fand, dass allerdings eine Tragödie darin stecke'. But he realized at once the crucial difficulty: 'Freilich wird die Motivirung der Königin schwer seyn'.[2] Indeed, the story of Rhodope is as radically changed as was that of Mariamne. Not only the mind of Rhodope, but the actions of Gyges and Kandaules had to be made comprehensible, and Hebbel could admit neither the crude vengeance of the queen nor the primitive morality of

[1] v. *Die Geschichten des Herodotos* übersetzt von Friedrich Lange, i. 8–13. 2te verbesserte Auflage, Breslau, 1824, Erster Theil, pp. 6–9. According to Emil Kuh (*Biographie Friedrich Hebbels*, ed. cit., vol. ii, p. 385) this was the translation used by Hebbel.

[2] *Tagebücher*, ed. cit., vol. iii. 5213, 14 Dec. 1853.

Gyges. The motive for Kandaules' action, on the other hand, was essential to the tragedy, and remained. But it was modified—the possession of the magic ring provides at once an additional temptation to Kandaules and the means for carrying out his plan. This motive of the ring was drawn from a different source—a story used by Plato as an illustration in the course of an argument on justice.[1] The assumption there expressed—that the temptation offered by the power to become invisible at will would assail just and unjust alike—finds an echo in Hebbel's use of the magic ring to betray the sensitive Gyges into an action that is opposed to his own standards and involves him in a conflict whose only possible issue is a tragic one.

In treating the story of Herodotus, Hebbel was faced with psychological difficulties similar to those offered by the narrative of Josephus concerning Herod and his wife. The state of mind of Kandaules had first to be portrayed, before his action in displaying Rhodope's charms could have value as a dramatic motive. This revelation forms a large part of the exposition in Act I. Through the arguments of Kandaules, first with his old servant Thoas, then with Gyges, the picture of the Lydian king emerges in broad outline. He will not yield to the wishes of Thoas, who clings, in common with the majority of the people, to the ancient customs and the ancient symbols. It is only with great reluctance that he retracts his first refusal to allow the Grecian Gyges to risk participation in the arduous Lydian games. He is wont to have his way; and neither respect for the devotion of Thoas nor consideration for the pride of Gyges as an athlete restrains him from forceful expression of his will. But Gyges, by virtue of his own determination, wrests consent from the reluctant king, and in return bestows upon him a ring from a ruined tomb in Thessaly, which he has gained by a strange chance, and to which he already owes the preservation of his life. By turning this ring upon his finger a man can suddenly become invisible; but Gyges—after his initial discovery of the

[1] v. Plato, *Republic*, ii. 359–60 (trans. by A. D. Lindsay, London, 1907, p. 43).

secret when he was in danger—has not worn it, and he gives it to Kandaules with the words:

> Es ist ein Königsring. . . .
> Du bist der Einz'ge, der ihn tragen darf!

The king, at first unwilling, gradually becomes more eager, and finally accepts the gift, intending to put it to the test. The ensuing scene in the apartments of Rhodope reveals the widely differing reactions of Kandaules and his queen towards the magic ring. Rhodope, already characterized in a conversation with her maids, stands in the sharpest contrast to the king when he relates to her the secret powers with which the ring endows him.

Rhodope. Wie fürchterlich!
Kandaules. Für jeden Bösen, meinst Du.
Rhodope. Nein doch, nein!
Für jeden Guten noch viel mehr! . . .
. . . Herr, wirf ihn fort,
Hinunter in den tiefsten Fluss! Wem mehr
Als Menschenkraft beschieden ist, der wird
Als Halbgott gleich geboren! Gib ihn mir!
Man sagt bei uns, dass Dinge, die die Welt
Zertrümmern können, hie und da auf Erden
Verborgen sind . . .
. . . .
Mich schaudert, wenn ich ihn nur seh'! So gib! (I. 2.)

But Kandaules, who has already proved its magic powers, will only give up the ring on one condition: that the queen should withdraw her refusal to appear in public, and should attend the festival of the Lydian games that day. But this she will not do. It is against her nature and the custom of her people, and she steadfastly refuses:

> Du holtest Dir von weit entleg'ner Gränze
> Die stille Braut und wusstest, wie sie war.
> Auch hat's Dich einst beglückt, dass vor dem Deinen
> Nur noch das Vaterauge auf mir ruhte,
> Und dass nach Dir mich Keiner mehr erblickt.

The king's answer, matching all that we already know of him, softly suggests the leading theme:

Vergib! Ich denke nur, der Edelstein,
Den man nicht zeigt—

but Rhodope completes his sentence in a different way:

Lockt keine Räuber an!—

an image recalling *Genoveva.*

Kandaules accepts the decision, as he has done before—and keeps the ring. Rhodope, giving permission to Hero and Lesbia to attend the festival, sighs as they go: not even those nearest to her understand her love of reflection and seclusion. After this scene, we are prepared for the King's determination to use the ring in order to prove his possession of the unseen and fairest jewel in his treasury. The occasion for his resolve is provided at the games, when Gyges, covered with glory, and conqueror at every turn, is for the first time confused by the sight of Hero and Lesbia who are watching from a balcony. Their charms—half revealed by the fluttering veils—are praised by Kandaules, who is thereby led to speak of the incomparable beauty of Rhodope, whom Gyges has not seen. But, he adds, there is little use in vaunting a treasure that cannot be displayed. And though Gyges assures him of belief, the king will not be satisfied, but demands of Gyges' friendship that he, a chosen witness, should satisfy himself that the praise of Rhodope's beauty is no idle boast. To Gyges' remonstrances he opposes the reminder of the ring, with its powers:

Sie kann's ja nie erfahren!
Hast Du den Ring vergessen? Und ich bin
Erst glücklich, wenn Dein Mund mir sagt, ich sei's.
Ei, frag' Dich selbst, ob Du die Krone möchtest,
Wenn Du sie nur im Dunkeln tragen solltest!

Thus arguing, the king carries off Gyges, silent and unconvinced.

This first act clearly shows the possibilities of tragedy. In the interval of one night which separates it from the second act, a tragic development has been assured. The first problem presented by the narrative of Herodotus has been solved by the characterization of the king; his act has been shown to be the result of temperament combined with circumstance. The second problem lies in the character of Gyges. The opportunist of the Greek story—saving his own life by sacrificing that of Kandaules—diverts such sympathy as the story arouses away from himself and towards the murdered king. Hebbel's Gyges, on the contrary, stands between Rhodope and Kandaules—entering into the feelings of the one, but still loyal to his friendship with the other; and the second act is mainly devoted to the revelation of his state of mind.

With a delicate touch the impression of Gyges as he enters the palace hall is conveyed by Thoas, who is disturbed by talk of a new king that he has overheard during the past night:

> Still, still! Sind das nicht Schritte? Ja! Wer steht
> Denn mit den Greisen schon vor Morgen auf?
> Der junge Gyges! Ei, wenn Du das wüsstest,
> Was ich jetzt weiss, Du gingest nicht gebückt. (II. 1.)

From his replies to Thoas, it is plain that Gyges is troubled; his confusion of feeling is fully revealed in the subsequent dialogue with Kandaules. Through this conversation the story of the night's events emerges; and gradually the king divines that here is a trouble deeper than that caused by the recognition of Rhodope's peerless beauty. Gyges, on his part, is at the mercy of conflicting feelings. At one moment in the night, we learn, he turned the ring about, so that discovery might follow and Kandaules be compelled to slay him where he stood. To the king—who thought it a mere chance due to the powerful impression made by Rhodope's beauty, and who hastily interposed to cover Gyges—this revelation is disturbing; and when Gyges adds to it an entreaty to accept his life as a sacrifice, offered to the gods for Kandaules' welfare, he feels a moment of remorse:

> Fast reut mich, was ich that! Hier Raserei
> Und drinnen Argwohn—

Thus we know that Rhodope is not as unconscious of events as the king would fain believe. With a parting word of confidence that the fresh breezes of the morning will restore Gyges to serenity, Kandaules leaves him; and Gyges falls immediately into an opposite frame of mind, wishing that he had kept the ring, in order that he might be ever in the presence of Rhodope, undiscovered. This passionate soliloquy is interrupted by the arrival of Thoas with the veiled Lesbia—the gift of Kandaules to his favourite. Regardless of the maiden's feelings, Gyges gives expression to his own:

> Der König will mich höhnen und das habe
> Ich nicht um ihn verdient, auch duld' ich's nicht!

And through the cross-currents of his talk with her, the dominant preoccupation of his mind is evident. On the king's arrival, Gyges presents Lesbia with her freedom—an unwelcome gift—and refuses his proffered gifts of treasure:

> Ich kann Nichts weiter brauchen, als mein Schwert,
> Doch, wenn Du Dich mir gnädig zeigen willst,
> So schenke mir die Köpfe Deiner Feinde,
> Ich sammle sie bis auf den letzten ein.

The change in Gyges strikes even the king, who has not hitherto been notably perceptive:

> Du bist ein Andrer, Gyges, als Du warst.

But to his definite assertion:

> Du liebst Rhodopen!

Gyges only answers that he can no longer serve him. Kandaules cannot reply to this, and offers to restore the ring. Gyges refuses it, but as a parting gift he returns to the king a diamond taken from Rhodope in the night:

> Ich nahm ihn mit,
> Weil er an ihrem Hals—Erlass' es mir,
> Es ist gebüsst!

This rouses Kandaules at last to a sense of what he may have brought about:

> Erynnien, seid Ihr's?
> O, es ist wahr, Ihr habt den leicht'sten Schlaf!
> *Gyges.* Du grollst mir?
> *Kandaules.* Nein! Nicht Dir! Leb' wohl, leb' wohl!
> Doch niemals dürfen wir uns wiederseh'n.

Thus both Gyges and the king have come to realize the

gravity of that which they have done. This needs no further exposition. It remains, however, for Rhodope to point its full significance; the third act shows her discovery of the facts, and the effect of this discovery on her mind.

Warum sind diese Spiegel nicht verhüllt?

are her first words on entering her apartment; and she orders doors to be closed and mirrors turned towards the wall. Thus we know her to suspect the truth; and so the king finds her, as one who mourns a loss. Convinced at first that he comes as an avenger, she assures him that she is prepared to die; when he protests against her words, she asks in wonder if all who were alive the previous day still live. Gradually however Kandaules soothes her suspicions, finally conquering them by producing the diamond, whose loss had seemed a proof that they were justified.

But the king's exclamation of relief:

Erynnien, hinab!

is premature. Filled with a joy that is deepened by Rhodope's unwonted words of praise, he tells her that Gyges is departing. Just this one excessive touch rouses once more the suspicions of the queen. Memory is wakened; the name of Gyges recalls the figure in the night that she has dimly seen—all the king's efforts at evasion when she questions him concerning the ring, and the reason for Gyges' sudden departure, are of no avail:

Du weisst es nicht? So will ich Dir es sagen:
Er hat an Dir gefrevelt, wie noch Keiner,
Und Du musst strafen, wie Du nie gestraft!

In face of his remonstrances, she begs him to leave her, and when alone, forges her chain of logic:

Kein And'rer ist's, als Gyges—das ist klar!
Er hat den Ring gehabt—das ist noch klarer!
Kandaules ahnt's, er muss—das ist am klarsten!
Und statt das Ungeheure ungeheuer
An ihm zu ahnden, lässt er ihn entfliehn.
So wird ein Räthsel durch ein and'res Räthsel
Gelöst, das mich von Sinnen bringen kann,
Wenn es mir dunkel bleibt! . . .

Resolved to attain both clarity and vengeance, she sends a faithful servant to summon Gyges to her presence. Lesbia meanwhile has returned; her innocent attempt to vindicate Gyges from a supposed offence by telling Rhodope her discovery that he loves the queen, only emphasizes certainty:

Rhodope. Er liebt mich!
So ist's gewiss!
Lesbia. Wie?
Rhodope. Thörin, sage mir,
Kann man das lieben, was man niemals sah?
Und wenn mich Gyges sah: wann sah er mich?
Lesbia (*legt sich die Hand vor die Augen*).
Rhodope. Nun sprich als Mädchen, ob er sterben muss!

On this climax the act closes.

The decisive interview between Gyges and Rhodope occupies the whole of the fourth act. The third problem offered by the story of Herodotus still remained: the motivation of the queen's action, and its effect on Gyges. Rhodope's first thought is to take vengeance on one who, as she believes, has basely deceived Kandaules and dishonoured her by using the power of the magic ring to hide his unlawful presence. She gives orders to her own servant that Gyges is to die, after she has seen him to pronounce the sentence. But the interview has an unexpected issue. Gyges, who at first supposed the queen to have full knowledge of the facts, gradually realizes her vital ignorance of the part played by Kandaules, and skilfully adapting his answers to the situation, assumes entire responsibility. But the king, who enters at the decisive moment of the conversation, refuses to be shielded in this way:

Kandaules. Gyges, ich bin kein Schurke.
Gyges. Herr, Du bist
Rhodopens Gatte, bist ihr Schutz und Schirm
Und musst ihr Rächer sein.
Kandaules. Ich bin vor Allem
Ein Mann, der für den Frevel, den er selbst
Beging, nicht einen Andern sterben lässt.

And to the despairing cry of Gyges:

König, was rettest Du?

he returns the unassailable reply:

> Mich selbst!

Then bidding Gyges tell the queen the true course of events, he leaves them together.

The efforts made by Gyges to explain and palliate the act of Kandaules only cause Rhodope to realize his own nobility of mind. She can no longer accept the death of Gyges as sufficient atonement for the sin that has been committed; Kandaules, the nearer to her person, is the more guilty of the two, and it is impossible for her to contemplate a continuance of their relationship. 'Du musst ihn tödten!' she returns to Gyges' announcement that he himself will now seek death to expiate his crime. And, she adds, when he has done this, she will marry him. Gyges at first refuses, but on Rhodope's warning that she herself will in that case make the due atonement, he consents—not to kill the king, but to challenge him to mortal combat. The queen is now fully aware of Gyges' quality of soul:

> Leb' wohl!—
> Und wenn's Dich freuen kann, vernimm noch Eins:
> Du hättest mich der Heimat nicht entführt,
> Um so an mir zu thun!

She is equally resolved in her own mind:

> Nun, Brautgewand und Todtenhemd, herbei!

The events of the fifth act are fully anticipated here.

But these events, foreseen and inescapable, are not the main contribution of the final act. Its true import lies deeper, in the meeting of Gyges and Kandaules. Opposed, as they have never been before, in bodily combat, their spirits meet in a unity which they have not known since the fatal experiment urged by Kandaules in Act I. Their meeting is preceded by a dialogue between Thoas and the king, in which the old servant—wrapping his advice in many words—warns Kandaules to beware of Gyges, whose popularity and prowess render him a dangerous rival, even against his will. Although the irony of this warning touches him nearly, the king does not listen with impatience, as in the opening scene; the change that has come over him is visible even in this fact. And when, through the self-reproachful speech of Gyges, Rhodope's purpose becomes clear to him, he greets it with grave acquiescence:

> Wer frevelte,
> Muss Busse thun, und wer nicht lächelnd opfert,
> Der opfert nicht!—Kennst Du mich denn so schlecht
> Und hältst mich so gering, dass Du darob
> Erstaunen, ja erschrecken kannst? Ich werde
> Doch sie nicht zwingen, mit den Rosenfingern,
> Die noch zu zart für's Blumenpflücken sind,
> Nach einem Dolch zu greifen und zu prüfen,
> Ob sie das Herz zu finden weiss?

He has realized the significance of her convictions:

> Auch fühl' ich's wohl, ich habe schwer gefehlt,
> Und was mich trifft, das trifft mich nur mit Recht.
> . . . Man soll nicht immer fragen:
> Was ist ein Ding? Zuweilen auch: was gilt's?

And when Gyges reveals Rhodope's whole purpose and the intended marriage, Kandaules' last words are:

> Ha! Nun versteh' ich sie!

The scene changes to the temple, where a pyre has already been erected. The queen's maids—blind until now—suddenly realize the significance of the funeral preparations. Gyges, entering, is greeted by Thoas with the Lydian crown —bestowed upon him by the people, who acclaim him as their leader against a suddenly invading enemy. Rhodope confirms the gift, and against the plea of Gyges to postpone their union until he has at least fought this one fight in Kandaules' memory, she insists on the immediate fulfilment of her vow. Then turning to the figure of Hestia—'the austere goddess, at whose glance the greenest garland fades and dies', the guardian of the sacred flame which, where it cannot purify, consumes—she offers thanks that she may once more appear unsullied in her eyes:

Ich bin entsühnt,
Denn Keiner sah mich mehr, als dem es ziemte.
Jetzt aber scheide ich mich
(*sie durchsticht sich*)
so von Dir!

So with the last words of the drama, the final problem offered by the source is solved: Rhodope's exaction of atonement from Gyges and Kandaules is completed, and justified, by the offering of herself.

Thus the tragic knot in *Gyges und sein Ring* is loosened by the decisive action of Rhodope, which is supported by the voluntary acquiescence of both the other actors in the drama. The queen maintains her individual right, but in a way which deprives her action of any hint of personal vengeance. She is akin in this respect to Agnes, Klara, or Genoveva, rather than to Mariamne; but unlike them, she is able to enforce her will, to restore a balance that has been disturbed, and thus to guide her destiny. Rhodope, in fact, is the bearer of the ethical values in the drama; in defending herself, she maintains them also.

'Nun das Stück fertig ist', Hebbel wrote in 1854 to Friedrich von Uechtritz, 'steigt plötzlich zu meiner eigenen Ueberraschung wie eine Insel aus dem Ocean die Idee der Sitte als die Alles bedingende und bindende daraus hervor. Ich gestehe, dass ich diess kaum begreifen kann, es bestärkt mich aber nur um so mehr in meiner freilich längst gehegten Ueberzeugung, dass der Künstler, wenn er von einem Gegenstand mächtig ergriffen wird, sich um den Gehalt desselben gar nicht ängstlich zu kümmern braucht, sondern dass dieser ganz von selbst hinzutritt, wie der Saft in die Bäume, vorausgesetzt allerdings, dass er ihn in der Brust trägt'.[1]

The word 'Sitte' bore for Hebbel a full meaning. Rhodope's offended deity and her own injured feeling together stand for a force of stability which (irrespective of its form of expression at any given moment of history) safeguards the right of human beings to their own inner citadel. In an

[1] Letter to Friedrich von Uechtritz, 14 Dec. 1854, *Briefe*, ed. cit., vol. v, p. 204.

antique form, the content of *Gyges und sein Ring* is of universal application; while Rhodope's special problem could only shape itself thus in an age remote from ours, the underlying problem of the individual's freedom to protect his spirit from invasion is one which recurs, in differing form, in every age. So, too, does the situation of Kandaules. Disregarding traditions, he also disregards the force that underlies them; but it is this very force that defeats him, when he assails its stronghold:

> Auch darf's nicht anders sein!
> Die Welt braucht ihren Schlaf, wie Du und ich
> Den uns'rigen, sie wächst, wie wir, und stärkt sich,
> Wenn sie dem Tod verfallen scheint und Thoren
> Zum Spotte reizt . . .
> D'rum, Gyges, wie Dich auch die Lebenswoge
> Noch heben mag, sie thut es ganz gewiss
> Und höher, als Du denkst: vertraue ihr
> Und schaudre selbst vor Kronen nicht zurück,
> Nur rühre nimmer an den Schlaf der Welt!

But had Kandaules not ignored the profound feeling of Rhodope for her seclusion, and her dedication to himself alone, his disregard of other traditions would have had small importance. Herein lies the significance of Hebbel's portrait of the king. He cannot enter into the heart and mind of her whom he loves best; he catches at her veil, in spite of her deep belief in it. Had his love for Rhodope been great enough to overcome his intellectual convictions, he would have been saved from the decisive step which invites his downfall. But, free of prejudice as he believes himself to be, Kandaules is fast bound by his own nature; contemning the blind beliefs of others, he himself disregards a freedom more vital than that which is invaded by such beliefs, and—yielding to an elemental impulse to display his treasure—he not only disturbs the world-sleep, but destroys Rhodope's peace of mind. This failure in love and comprehension directly brings about the tragedy. Kandaules has aroused a resistance whose strength he had not gauged. And though even in the end he measures the catastrophe in general terms—

Herakles war der Mann, ich bin es nicht;
Zu stolz, um ihn in Demuth zu beerben,
Und viel zu schwach, um ihm es gleich zu thun,
Hab' ich den Grund gelockert, der mich trug,
Und dieser knirscht nun rächend mich hinab—

yet it is by virtue of his love for Rhodope that he finally reaches comprehension. He grows to a man's height before our eyes—as Gyges also grows from youth to manhood through his insight into Rhodope's heart.

The attainment of harmony through sacrifice, thus presented by Hebbel for the first time in a tragic close, is reflected in the measured beauty of the verse of *Gyges und sein Ring*. With all its simplicity and stately flow, it can express both intensity of feeling and variety of mood. Its flexibility may be illustrated by the subtle variations in the following dialogue between Gyges and Rhodope:

Gyges. Was er empfand, das kann ich nachempfinden
Und ganz so voll und glühend, wie er selbst.
Doch, wie er warb und wie er Dich gewann,
Ist sein Geheimniss; Einer nur kann's haben,
Und dieser Einzige ist er, nicht ich.
Nun weisst Du denn, warum ich zitterte:
Ein Wonneschauer war's, der mich ergriff,
Ein heil'ges Grausen, das mich schüttelte,
Als ich so plötzlich vor Dir stand und sah,
Dass Aphrodite eine Schwester hat;
So sag' mir jetzt, wozu beriefst Du mich!
Rhodope. Zum Tode!—

The delicacy of the characterization is matched by the delicate changes of the verse; within its smooth rhythm there are innumerable gradations. It is of interest to note that Hebbel was aware of its unfamiliar quality. He seriously considered the possibility of having *Gyges* translated into French and performed at the Théâtre Français, and in writing to Bamberg observed: 'Aeusserlich steht es nach meiner Meinung dem Racine so nah, wie innerlich fern.'[1]

The symbolic use of the magic ring emphasizes the sug-

[1] Letter to Felix Bamberg, 13 Jan. 1856, *Briefe*, ed. cit., vol. v, p. 298.

gestion of remoteness conveyed by the serenity of form. As Rhodope's veil is a symbol of her inmost being, so the ring that Gyges finds embodies unseen forces too strong for its possessors. Only Rhodope, by nature mystically endowed, apprehends immediately its hidden might:

> Wer weiss, an welche Hand
> Ihn eine Göttin steckte, welchen Bund
> Er einst besiegeln musste! Graus't Dich nicht,
> Dir ihre dunkle Gabe anzueignen
> Und ihre Rache auf Dein Haupt zu zieh'n?

But by the end, Kandaules also realizes its true significance:

> Rhodopens Ahnung hat sie nicht betrogen
> Und Dich Dein Schauder nicht umsonst gewarnt.
> Denn nicht zum Spiel und nicht zu eitlen Possen
> Ist er geschmiedet worden, und es hängt
> Vielleicht an ihm das ganze Weltgeschick.

There is no question, however, of endowing the symbol with activity. To Gyges' self-reproach at having bestowed the ring upon Kandaules, the king at once replies:

> Du thatest recht und wäre ich
> Dir gleich, so hätte er mich nicht verlockt,
> Ich hätt' ihn still der Nacht zurückgegeben
> Und Alles würde stehen, wie zuvor.
> Drum dinge mir des Werkzeugs wegen Nichts
> Vom Frevel ab, die ganze Schuld ist mein!

And when Kandaules falls, the ring is left upon his finger, that it may return to the earth from which it came—the circle is completed. In no other tragedy did Hebbel unite the impression of completion with such a sense of peace—of

> Sleepe after toyle, port after stormie seas,
> Ease after warre . . . .

for in no other do the central characters make their fate their own by a free recognition of Necessity.

The theme of *Die Nibelungen*, to which he next turned, did not admit of this. Hebbel was determined to dramatize the

Middle High German epic with the least possible alteration, and the medieval tale of love and guilt and vengeance offered a spectacle of violent retribution. It took him five years to complete the tragedy; but his preoccupation with the epic source bore earlier fruit in the idyllic epic which was written in the intervals of work on that portion of the drama which now forms the Prologue and Second Part.

Mutter und Kind is Hebbel's only long narrative poem, and in it he combines to a remarkable degree the qualities of dramatist and lyrist. Structure and characterization are concise and logical, while at the same time there is an epic breadth in the description of events and scenes. The two couples—Christian and Magdalena, and the rich merchant and his wife—are strongly contrasted, both in character and circumstance; but the maternal instinct fundamentally connects the two women, while the actions of the two men are governed by more conscious principles. The two-fold position of a woman as a wife and mother was a problem which had presented itself to Hebbel with singular force in the crucial period of his relations with Elise Lensing; the death of their first child had discovered to him—it is plain from the Paris correspondence—a complex psychological situation. His own comment in the journal on his feelings towards the first child born to Christine and himself shows an increased comprehension of the interdependence of the two sets of instincts; it was perhaps Christine Hebbel herself who revealed to him the possibility of uniting them to the full. In their differing situations, Magdalena and the merchant's wife both show the development of the maternal instinct, and the obstacle that may thereby be presented to the happiness of marriage. The childless woman frets her life and her husband's peace of mind away; in spite of her resolutions, she is unable to rise above the sorrow of her unfulfilled desire. But riches, while they cannot remedy the evil, may be used to mitigate it; and at the suggestion of their friend the doctor, the couple offer to the servant Magdalena the means of preventing her lover from emigrating to seek his fortune in America. Magdalena and Christian can marry as soon as they wish, and the latter will be appointed steward of a distant farm if they will sacrifice their first infant to be brought up as the merchant's child. In deep distress at Christian's intended departure, Magdalena consents to any means of providing for their marriage; her lover, though more dubiously, agrees. The first four cantos complete the exposition of the situation. Its immediate consequences are unfolded in the fifth. The expectation of their first child reminds Magdalena of that which in her rejoicing at their union and the new home she had forgotten; its arrival, while filling her with joy, confirms her secret apprehensions. She realizes that she cannot bear to part with it. Gradually, through the sixth canto, she reaches her decision. When the expected letter arrives from Italy, where the merchant and his wife have been awaiting the news, Christian insists that she shall wean the child; and realizing that his honour is involved in the keeping of their promise, she takes flight secretly into the forest with the boy. But her husband follows and overtakes her; unable to resist the strength of her resolve thus amply proved, he consents that they shall all fly from their home before the merchant's arrival to claim the child. Leaving all things in order, with a faithful account of his stewardship, Christian conducts his wife and child by solitary ways to Bremen, where they hope to carry out the original plan and take ship for America.

The problem is solved in the final canto. Learning from a chance meeting with an old acquaintance that the merchant and his wife have been searching widely for them during their flight, and realizing that their good name is involved, Christian resolves to confront the couple and justify their determination to keep the child. But the merchant and his wife have meanwhile learnt, from the circumstance of their flight, the harshness of the condition imposed upon the parents—all their efforts to trace the couple have been inspired by the wish to reassure them, and to release them from their promise. As they are anxiously awaiting news, the fugitives present themselves, and all doubts are removed when the two women meet:

Aber die Gattin faltet die Hände und hebt sie zum Himmel,
Presst dann Mutter und Kind an's Herz und schluchzt: Ich geniesse
Jetzt die seligste Stunde des Lebens durch reichste Erfüllung
Meines heiligsten Wunsches und opf're mit Freuden die andern.
Ja, nun sag' ich mit Dir—sie wendet sich innig zum Gatten—
Unsere Kinder sind die Armen, doch bleibt mir von Allen
Dieser Knabe der Nächste, denn ihm verdank' ich den Frieden,
Den ich nie noch gekannt, und den die Erde nicht mindert,
Wenn man ihn einmal errang, und selbst der Himmel nicht steigert. (VII, ll. 2061–9.)

The serenity of the idyll is finally attained, though the emotional intensity of experience through the last cantos belongs rather to the larger genre of epic, and the delicate shading of the characters recalls the fact that the poet was before all a dramatist. The gold rush in California forms the remoter background to the individual destinies of Christian and Magdalena, while the environment of two other couples—the poverty-stricken home of Wilhelm and Anna, and the richly furnished house of Magdalena's employers—forms a more immediate contrast. Changes in the face of nature are reflected in conjunction with the changing situation of the central characters; it is winter in Holstein and Hamburg when they accept their chance of marriage; the first joyful work in their own home in the Harz country coincides with spring and summer; autumn sees the birth of the child, and the next Easter-tide Magdalena's revolt and flight for freedom. Hebbel indicates the natural background to the human action—nowhere perhaps more delicately than in the opening lines of the fifth canto which describe a favourite theme, the coming of spring:

O, wie schön ist die Zeit, wenn schalkhaft hinter dem Winter
Schon der Lenz sich versteckt, wenn früh am Morgen die Lerche
Wirbelt, als hätte sie längst das Veilchen gesehen, und dennoch
Abends gern mit dem Spatz sich unter dem Balken verkröche,
Wo er im Neste kauert, und wenn die erste der Primeln
Durch den nämlichen Tropfen, an dem sie sich Mittags erquickte,

Während die so Sonne brannte, vor Nacht ihr Ende noch findet,
Weil er gefriert und sie knickt! Wie ist sie in Ahnung und Hoff-
nung
Jener später'n voraus, wo schleichend hinter dem Sommer
So der Herbst sich verbirgt! (V, ll. 1049–58.)

The lyric qualities that distinguish such a poem as *Das Opfer des Frühlings* also characterize *Mutter und Kind*, and to them it largely owes its rank as idyll. Hebbel's delight in his Gmunden surroundings had heightened his sensitiveness to natural beauty, and even the less familiar form of the hexameter shows a lyric flexibility in reproducing scenes and feelings connected with the world of Nature. *Mutter und Kind*, though his only experiment in the epic-idyll, illuminates both by its mood and by its art the period of serene maturity that begins with *Gyges und sein Ring*.

Die Nibelungen has often been hailed as Hebbel's masterpiece—his one achievement of indubitable fame. Its popularity exceeded that of his other dramas during the poet's lifetime; it has continued to do so since his death, and perhaps only *Herodes und Mariamne* shares with the *Nibelungen* trilogy some immunity from the present comparative neglect of Hebbel's dramas on the German stage (a neglect which contrasts strikingly enough with the output of critical literature dealing with his position as a dramatist). Yet it may be doubted whether the intrinsic dramatic value of *Die Nibelungen* is as supreme as such indications would suggest. It was a great and difficult achievement 'den dramatischen Schatz des Nibelungen-Liedes für die reale Bühne flüssig zu machen';[1] but in that respect for the medieval poet's treatment which he determined to observe Hebbel laid unaccustomed fetters on his own dramatic powers, and the characterization of Kriemhild in particular taxed those powers to the uttermost. But it was the figure of Kriemhild, there is little doubt, that ultimately stirred him to the undertaking. Though he had known the *Nibelungenlied* from Hamburg days, and though according to the Prologue he felt even then the desire to dramatize the poem, it was Christine Hebbel's appearance

[1] Vorwort zu den Nibelungen. *Werke*, ed. cit., vol. iv, p. 341.

as Kriemhild in Raupach's *Nibelungen-Hort* that kindled the creative fire:

> Denn diesen Abend ward mein Jugendtraum
> Lebendig, alle Nibelungen traten
> An mich heran, als wär' ihr Grab gesprengt,
> Und Hagen Tronje sprach das erste Wort.

'Tine als Chriemhild' Hebbel wrote in his diary; 'eine schwarze Flamme! Gross! Uebergewaltig!'[1]

That Hebbel perceived the central problem of the Nibelungen theme to lie in the development of Kriemhild's character is plain from the original titles *Kriemhildens Leid* and *Kriemhilds Rache*, the first of which was later changed to *Siegfrieds Tod.* While the medieval epic dealt with the long sorrow following short-lived joy, with the tragic retribution exacted from a race that meets its doom unshaken—a general theme, within whose range a group of heroic figures work out their sombre destiny—the modern drama had to emphasize an individual conflict, enacted against a background representing this general theme of the old epic. Kriemhild and Hagen are the antagonists in this central conflict, which continues throughout the trilogy. In their battle, Brunhild and Siegfried play important but subordinate parts, while Gunther, his kin, and Etzel provide the necessary means of action for the two chief combatants. The main problem of the dramatist was to convert the thread of epic into the web of drama—and this Hebbel accomplished by placing Kriemhild's conflict in the centre of the action. By so doing, he emphasized the psychological motivation of her vengeance, with its stark horror and primitive cruelty. He had to make not only her action but the mode of it intelligible to a modern audience: and this was the most formidable of the problems presented by the Nibelungen theme. We have to be convinced of the necessity for the ruthless pursuance of the duel between Kriemhild and Hagen to its terrible conclusion, if the horror of that conclusion is not to prove too strong for dramatic portrayal. The epic might end in battle and murder, fire

[1] *Tagebücher*, ed. cit., vol. iii. 4244, 29 Aug. 1847.

and destruction; it was but the striking of a familiar chord:

> Mit leide was verendet des küniges hôhgezît,
> als ie diu liebe leide zaller jungeste gît.

But the drama needs more than this elegiac note to balance its more vivid presentation of disaster. Hebbel was aware of this; and on the one hand, he shows the gradual development of Kriemhild's obsession, almost to the point of madness; on the other, he suggests, throughout the trilogy, a theme which only becomes dominant at the close of *Kriemhilds Rache*. The old world ends in devastating slaughter: the glimpse of a new world is vouchsafed in a brief moment of beauty at the end. On the stage, the almost intolerable horror of the final scene of vengeance is redeemed by the figure of Dietrich von Bern, proclaiming a creed that rests upon compassion:

> Im Namen dessen, der am Kreuz erblich!

By the introduction of this theme Hebbel modernized the Nibelungen story, and in thus adapting the subject to the stage, altered it perhaps more radically than he was willing to admit.

In *Die Nibelungen*, more than in any other of his dramas, Hebbel adopts a Shakespearean freedom of technique. Confronted with the problem of dramatizing a long epic narrative, he saw himself compelled to use broader brush-strokes on the larger canvas. From the first he realized that the material was too complex for a single drama; but the various changes in form during the period of composition show clearly enough that the term 'trilogy' cannot strictly be applied. Neither *Der gehörnte Siegfried* nor *Siegfrieds Tod* has any real independence; both lead direct to *Kriemhilds Rache*, which in its turn is only intelligible on the basis of the previous parts. Kriemhild is the only one of Hebbel's heroines whose character is shown developing through a lifetime; the long period which elapses between the *Vorspiel* and *Kriemhilds Rache* is essential for the understanding of her single-minded desire for vengeance in the final part.

The *Vorspiel—Der gehörnte Siegfried*—gives a swift and skilful outline of the situation; nowhere is Hebbel's mastery of the art of exposition better demonstrated. In three successive scenes the characters of Hagen, Siegfried, and Kriemhild are sharply defined; in a fourth, the decision of Gunther to woo Brunhild is taken, and Siegfried's fatal bargain is concluded. In return for his assistance in Gunther's wooing of the warrior queen, first as guide, then with his supernatural strength and his helmet of invisibility, Siegfried is to receive the hand of Kriemhild, whose charms have won his heart at once. But meanwhile we have learnt all that we need to know of Siegfried's history, of Brunhild's strange and isolated life, of Gunther's weakness and Hagen's iron will. The stage is set for the double drama; and in spite of the minstrel Volker's warnings, the bargain is made and the expedition to Isenland determined.

Siegfrieds Tod, the first of the two five-act dramas which succeed the *Vorspiel*, is primarily concerned with the conflict of Siegfried and Brunhild. Act I is devoted to the exposition of Brunhild's situation: Frigga, her attendant, testifies to her mysterious origin and her occult powers, at the same time warning her of a danger which she dimly feels to be approaching. This warning is immediately followed by the entry of Siegfried and Gunther, with Hagen and Volker in attendance, and by their challenge to Brunhild to defend her maiden sovereignty. As ever, she is confident of victory, and bids them prepare for death; but she swears to follow Gunther as his bride, should he defeat her. The hero whose advent Frigga is awaiting—in accordance with the runes that she has read—is the wielder of the sword Balmung, and Brunhild's first greeting is intuitively addressed to Siegfried. But the latter rejects it in favour of Gunther, to whom he yields precedence as his lord. Brunhild answers Siegfried's challenge on the king's behalf by an affirmation of her mystic powers, and Frigga triumphs in confident anticipation of the issue:

> Was zag' ich noch? Und wär's der Balmungsschwinger:
> Jetzt hätte sie den Schild auch gegen ihn!
> Er fällt, wenn sie ihn liebt und doch bekämpft,
> Und sie wird kämpfen, nun sie dieses weiss. (I. 2.)

With Brunhild's awakening from her trance and her renewed acceptance of the Burgundians' challenge the act closes.

The scene changes in the second act to Worms, where Siegfried arrives to herald Gunther's return with Brunhild as his bride. His diffident exchange of greetings with Kriemhild—for Siegfried's ardent love presents a striking contrast to his self-confidence in battle or in tourney—is succeeded on Gunther's arrival by their betrothal, which fulfils the bargain between Siegfried and the king. Brunhild, at once roused from a melancholy mood, protests with startling vehemence against Kriemhild's marriage with one who is but Gunther's vassal; this, the ostensible reason for her interference, affords no real ground however for the depth of feeling she displays. Without his promised explanation she will never, she asserts, be Gunther's wife in anything but name; and an echo of her vehemence sounds in Frigga's hasty questions, when Siegfried assigns the Nibelungen treasure as a dowry for Kriemhild:

> Hat er den Nibelungenhort?

and then

> Auch die Balmungklinge?

The runic oracle is not yet clear to her; but it is plain that mystery hangs over the relations of Siegfried and Brunhild.

In the last scene of the act these relations are still further complicated. First Hagen, and then Gunther, demand of Siegfried a final service—that by virtue of the magic 'Tarnkappe' he should aid Gunther for the last time to conquer Brunhild's virgin strength. With extreme reluctance Siegfried yields to Hagen's argument:

> Doch Zauberkünste haben's angefangen
> Und Zauberkünste müssen's nun auch enden:
> So thu's denn! Soll ich knie'n?

He realizes now to the full the grave responsibility of the deception so lightly undertaken:

. . . Ich thu's nicht gern!
Wer hätt' sich das gedacht! Und dennoch lag's
So nah'! O drei Mal heilige Natur!
Mich widert's, wie noch nie in meinem Leben,
Doch was Du sagst, hat Grund und also sei's.

But it is Hagen who stresses the essential need for silence:

Nein! Nein! Kein Weib! Wir steh'n allhier zu Dreien
Und haben, hoff' ich, keine einz'ge Zunge,
Der Vierte in uns'rem Bunde sei der Tod! (II. 8.)

This note of sombre warning effectively prepares us for the crisis of the Second Part—the quarrel of the queens in the succeeding act. The deception undertaken so reluctantly fails in this essential point of secrecy: Siegfried's part in it is betrayed to Kriemhild by his unwitting retention of the girdle of Brunhild. In spite of Siegfried's vow of silence, she compels him to an explanation; and in spite of her own, she is goaded by Brunhild's outspoken disparagement of Siegfried's prowess to reveal the secret she has learnt. Not for a moment does Brunhild doubt the truth of what she says, and Frigga finds in it the explanation of the runes that seemed to lack fulfilment. Now Brunhild's only wish is vengeance; and Hagen, anticipating Gunther, vows that he will compass Siegfried's death. Only Giselher protests against the sentence, unavailingly; Gunther, confronted by Hagen with the choice between Brunhild and Siegfried, is silent, and Hagen takes this silence for consent.

In Act IV the means for Siegfried's betrayal are provided by Kriemhild herself, and the motivation of this, her second revelation of a secret, constitutes a difficult problem for the dramatist. The plot has been contrived by Hagen, who plays the major part in it. He invents a tale of broken treaties and imminent war, and so plays on Kriemhild's fears for her husband's safety that under pretence of friendship and protection he elicits the information that Siegfried has confided to her alone: the secret of the one vulnerable spot between his shoulders, where the chance fall of a leaf prevented his complete immersion in the dragon's blood.

On her revelation of this secret swift repentance follows—but too late. In the fifth act the plot is carried out: a hunting party is arranged, and Siegfried, unarmed and unsuspecting, is struck down by Hagen's spear while drinking from a forest well.

Kriemhild, early awake, finds her husband's corpse placed at her door by Hagen's order—a stroke of ferocity that goes far to justify her subsequent bitter hatred and her passionate desire for vengeance. Unhesitatingly she recognizes Hagen in the deed, and in spite of all persuasion to the contrary demands that he and all her kin should undergo the ordeal of the bier. With the spurt of blood from Siegfried's wounds as Hagen draws near, the latter's guilt is plainly recognized: when, unmoved, he seizes Balmung, Siegfried's sword, and girds it on, Kriemhild demands his life from Gunther, and curses him also, should he deny her justice. In vain the priest begs her to remember the Christian creed of forgiveness and compassion: filled with grief and bitter sense of wrong, she refuses to recognize any loyalty but that to Siegfried's memory, and to Ute's cry that in her insensate fury she will destroy her kindred she replies:

> Es mag gescheh'n! Denn hier ist's überzahlt! (V. 9.)

In this tangle of guilt and wrong, 'Kriemhildens Leid' ends; with words that sound a knell to any hope of peace, the way to *Kriemhilds Rache* is prepared.

The years that have passed since Siegfried's murder have not lessened Kriemhild's bitter hatred, nor her desire for the vengeance that has been denied her by Gunther and her kindred. At the opening of *Kriemhilds Rache*, the request of Etzel, King of the Huns, for her hand at first evokes a passionate refusal; but at the mere indication that Hagen has advised against the marriage, Kriemhild suddenly sees in it a means of attaining the vengeance that is now her only object. To it she has sacrificed even her maternal feelings, causing her son by Siegfried to be secretly conveyed to Worms for safety as an infant—and her sole wish for him is that he should grow up to avenge his father's death. Now she does not hesitate to sacrifice her own desires, and she plainly tells Etzel's envoy, Rüdeger, that her hand will only be yielded at a price. Rüdeger, when asked if she can count upon the fulfilment of any wish she may express, swears, in his own name and Etzel's, to do her will in all things; and in one swift moment, Kriemhild gives her hand to him as Etzel's proxy. Hagen, having made his vain protest, is a sombre witness of the pledge. His previous warnings have so far prevailed in Gunther's mind, however, that the king evades the duty of escorting Kriemhild to her new home—but she extracts a promise that the visit shall be subsequently paid.

Seven years elapse, between the first and second acts, before this promise is fulfilled. Then the Nibelungen, pausing on their way to Etzel's kingdom to visit Rüdeger on the banks of the Danube, appear again in their old roles—Hagen, darkly convinced of their impending doom, Gunther rejecting the thought of Kriemhild's hatred. But Volker, who is half seer as well as minstrel, is at last convinced by Hagen's vision: both are steadfastly prepared for a doom they dimly foresee. The tension of their expectation is relieved by the idyllic betrothal between Gudrun, Rüdeger's daughter, and Giselher, the youngest of the Burgundian brothers. This episode occupies the major portion of the second act, but its tender gaiety is not unclouded. Volker and Hagen hail the betrothal as a support in the contest they anticipate; and the noble king, Dietrich von Bern, warns the Nibelungen in no uncertain terms of the peril that awaits them:

> Wer weiss! Frau Kriemhild weint noch Tag und Nacht.
>
> . . . .
>
> Seid auf der Hut, Ihr stolzen Nibelungen,
> Und wähnt nicht, dass ein Jeder, der die Zunge
> Jetzt für Euch braucht, den Arm auch brauchen darf.
>
> (II. 10.)

Thus even Gunther is convinced of danger; but as Hagen steadily refuses to return to Worms alone, so he, too, refuses to be diverted from his purpose:

Ja, wenn die Norne selbst
Mit aufgehob'nem Finger mich bedräute,
Ich wiche keinen Schritt zurück. Und Du
Bist unser Tod, wenn's drunten wirklich steht,
Wie Du's uns prophezeist. Doch—
(*Er schlägt Hagen auf die Schulter*)
Komm nur, Tod!
(II. 11.)

The act ends on this defiant identification of Hagen with the figure of Death; Kriemhild's initial speech in the succeeding act implies the same dark parallel:

So wagt er's ungeladen? Hagen Tronje,
Ich kannte Dich! (III. 1.)

The terrible duel that is now to fill the stage opens with these words. Kriemhild makes her preparations with the thought of Hagen ever in her mind, to the exclusion of all else; and from her greeting to the Nibelungen in Scene 7 until the final scene of horror, there is no moment of respite in their mortal battle. At first convinced that only Hagen need be harmed, she gradually comes to realize the unbounded loyalty of these kindred to each other, and with their increasingly defiant comradeship, she, too, grows more ruthless. The Nibelungen treasure which should have been her dowry has been sunk deep in the Rhine; Hagen, her bitter foe, is still the leading spirit in the Burgundian councils; her kindred appear in armour which they refuse to lay aside, and with a retinue equipped as if for war. Kriemhild's resolve to compass Hagen's death alone recedes before these overwhelming proofs that the Nibelungen will make common cause; but at the same time, the plans she has prepared become increasingly difficult to carry out. Etzel, at first unconscious, grows aware of her determination; but he is equally determined to preserve the peace as long as the Nibelungen are his guests. But Kriemhild has no mind to wait for honourable war:

Krieg! Was soll mir der Krieg! Den hätt' ich längst
Entzünden können! Doch das wäre Lohn,

Anstatt der Strafe. Für die Schlächterei
Im dunklen Wald der off'ne Heldenkampf?
Vielleicht sogar der Sieg? Wie würd' er jubeln,
Wenn er's erlangen könnte, denn er hat
Von Jugend auf nichts Besseres gekannt!
Nein Etzel, Mord um Mord! Der Drache sitzt
Im Loch, und wenn Du Dich nicht regen willst,
Als bis er Dich gestochen hat, wie mich,
So soll er's thun!—Ja wohl, so soll er's thun! (IV. 15.)

So at the meal which follows, the child of Etzel and Kriemhild is shown, and at the same moment Dankwart comes with news that every man of the Burgundian following has been killed. To Kriemhild's cry

Das Kind! Mein Kind! . . . Er bringt es um!

Hagen responds by a swift fulfilment; and with the murder of his cherished son and heir, Etzel's scruples yield to a grim resolve of vengeance. Battle is joined in the banqueting hall, and Etzel vows that it shall be to the death:

was den Heunenkönig
Auf dieser Erde einst so furchtbar machte,
Das sollt Ihr seh'n in seinem engen Raum! (IV. 23.)

At the opening of Act V this threat has already been fulfilled. Fire and smoke fill the inner hall, and within it the remaining Nibelungen are engaged in a last desperate fight.

Wie lange soll der Jammer denn noch dauern?

Hildebrant asks of his lord, Dietrich von Bern:

So lange, fürcht' ich, bis der Letzte fiel

is the sombre answer. Dietrich is powerless to avert the catastrophe he has foreseen:

Wenn ich auch wollte, wie vermöcht' ich's wohl?
Hier hat sich Schuld in Schuld zu fest verbissen,
Als dass man noch zu Einem sagen könnte:
Tritt Du zurück! Sie stehen gleich im Recht.
Wenn sich die Rache nicht von selbst erbricht
Und sich vom letzten Brocken schaudernd wendet,
So stopft ihr Keiner mehr den grausen Schlund. (V. 5.)

And even this faint possibility fades, as Kriemhild once more appears and asks how many still remain alive. To Dietrich's catalogue of slain she has but one reply:

Und Hagen lebt!

So the fight continues. Rüdeger, against his passionate plea, is compelled by his allegiance to join it; first Gerenot, then Giselher, is reported to have fallen. At last, when Rüdeger, too, has been slain by Hagen, Dietrich mounts into the hall of battle; and to his giant strength even the might of Hagen has to yield. He and Gunther, sole survivors of the carnage, are brought down before Kriemhild as prisoners; but Hagen still refuses answer to her question about the Nibelungen treasure, alleging that as long as any of the kings still lives he has vowed never to betray its whereabouts. Kriemhild, finding one surviving servant, sends him to cut off Gunther's head, and on his return with the trophy shows it to Hagen with a renewed demand for answer to her question. But he joyfully defies her:

Unhold, ich hab' Dich wieder überlistet,
Nun ist der Ort nur Gott und mir bekannt,
Und Einer von uns Beiden sagt's Dir nicht.

Maddened by his triumph, Kriemhild seizes Balmung from his side and cuts him down, unarmed and unresisting—thus rousing Hildebrant to instant reprisal. When she, too, has fallen, Etzel and Dietrich remain, paralysed spectators of a universal judgement-day:

Nun sollt' ich richten—rächen—neue Bäche
In's Blutmeer leiten—Doch es widert mich,
Ich kann's nicht mehr—mir wird die Last zu schwer—
Herr Dietrich, nehmt mir meine Kronen ab
Und schleppt die Welt auf Eurem Rücken weiter—

And falling on the ear like distant music, Dietrich's answer:

Im Namen dessen, der am Kreuz erblich!

ends this drama of sin and retribution, guilt and vengeance.

In the general criticism of *Die Nibelungen*, two comparisons have assumed perhaps undue importance—one, which Heb bel indeed deliberately invited, with the *Nibelungenlied*; the other, which is partly a matter of chronology, with Wagner's cycle of music-dramas, *Der Ring des Nibelungen.* Neither comparison is of great assistance, however, in an evaluation of *Die Nibelungen* as a drama. Hebbel's treatment of his source has, it is true, a biographical and critical interest: the view which he took of the dramatic value of the medieval epic implied, as has already been suggested, certain restrictions on his own freedom of action, and in so far has significance for his dramatic achievement; but the comparison with Wagner's *Ring* cycle is often actually misleading.[1] Wagner not only used a different source but pursued different aims; and to compare the value of their differing achievements is not to contribute materially to the appreciation of either.

Perhaps the foremost characteristic of Hebbel's drama is the almost superhuman size of the chief figures. The poet has succeeded, at least in the characters of Hagen, Brunhild, and Kriemhild, in creating the sense of a mysterious link with unseen, daemonic powers; in their extraordinary intensity, these three figures seem to live by Will alone. In this respect they offer a striking contrast to Gunther and to Siegfried, whose actions appear rather to be determined by the will of others.

But just this heroic magnification in the characters of Brunhild, Hagen, and Kriemhild involves the dramatist in a dilemma. The human motives for their actions seem by contrast small and inappropriate. Brunhild's true reason for anger at the marriage of Siegfried and Kriemhild is little less unsatisfactory than the one that she alleges: jealousy is ill suited to her large, heroic mind. Hebbel suggests, it is true, a mysterious background to Brunhild's passionate feeling against Siegfried when Hagen says of her:

> Sie liegt in seinem Bann, und dieser Hass
> Hat seinen Grund in Liebe! . . .
> . . . Ein Zauber ist's
> Durch den sich ihr Geschlecht erhalten will,

[1] E.g. in such a study as E. Meinck, *Friedrich Hebbels und Richard Wagners Nibelungen-Trilogien* (Breslauer Beiträge zur Literaturgeschichte, Nr. 5), Leipzig, 1905.

Und der die letzte Riesin ohne Lust
Wie ohne Wahl zum letzten Riesen treibt.
(*Siegfrieds Tod*, IV. 9.)

But this explicit statement of an irrational motive only enhances Brunhild's remoteness: it does not make it more convincing. Remotely, too, she fades out of the drama. In the last two acts of *Siegfrieds Tod* we are only aware of her through others as a statuesque, unyielding figure in the background, driving them by silent compulsion to the deed of vengeance; in *Kriemhilds Rache* her epitaph is twice pronounced—once in the first act by Gunther, and once in the third act by Kriemhild's envoys on their return from the Burgundian court.

Das mild'ste Wort entlockt ihr nie ein Lächeln,
. . . .
Das härteste noch minder eine Thräne,
Sie kennt den Schmerz und auch die Lust nicht mehr.
(*Kriemhilds Rache*, I. 2.)

Gunther says of her; and to Kriemhild's question:

Habt Ihr die Königin Burgunds geseh'n?

Werbel answers:

Die sieht kein Mensch. (*Kriemhilds Rache*, III. 1.)

Silent and immovable, Brunhild is watching out her life by Siegfried's tomb.

Hagen and Kriemhild, on the other hand, grow in stature as the drama evolves. In the development of each of these two characters, the difficult moment occurs in *Siegfrieds Tod.* Hagen's action in laying Siegfried's corpse at Kriemhild's door strikes a discordant note, and the motive assigned to it in the words of Dankwart is ill-matched with his heroic stature:

Er war davon nicht abzubringen,
Und als er wiederkehrte, lacht' er auf:
Diess ist mein Dank für seinen Abschiedsgruss.
(*Siegfrieds Tod*, V. 6.)

It is indeed in the words of the dying Siegfried here referred to that incongruity is most apparent: the accusation of envy that he casts at Hagen is no more appropriate to the latter's magnificent ruthlessness than is the expression of it to Siegfried's own nature. With the single sentence:

Das that
Dein Neid!

Hebbel introduces a new element into the characterization of Hagen, and the picture presented in *Siegfrieds Tod* thus differs not a little from that in *Kriemhilds Rache.* In the second drama the barbaric grandeur of his conception of fidelity resumes full sway; it is easy to recognize the Hagen of the *Vorspiel* in this sombre prophet of an impending doom, whose very apprehensions deepen his loyalty. As the danger grows, his leadership becomes the more apparent; Gunther, the younger brothers, even Volker—whose mind is most akin to Hagen's—recede into insignificance before his gigantic strength of body and of will. Blood and destruction, battle and murder, are the Tronjer's element, but there is no smallness of revenge in the Hagen of *Kriemhilds Rache*:

So ist es recht! Was heucheln wir, Kriemhild?
Wir kennen uns. Doch merke Dir auch diess:
Gleich auf das erste Meisterstück des Hirsches,
Dem Jäger zu entrinnen, folgt das zweite,
Ihn in's Verderben mit hinab zu zieh'n,
Und Eins von Beidem glückt uns sicherlich!

(*Kriemhilds Rache*, IV. 3.)

He summons joy in battle for the last great effort:

Mein Freund, wir sind auf Deinem Todtenschiff,
Von allen zwei und dreizig Winden dient
Uns keiner mehr, ringsum die wilde See
Und über uns die rothe Wetterwolke.

. . . .

D'rum stopfe Dir die Ohren zu, wie ich,
Und lass Dein innerstes Gelüsten los,
Das ist der Todgeweihten letztes Recht.

(*Kriemhilds Rache*, III. 11.)

It is easier to believe that this is the Hagen who once begged Volker to sing the deeds only of the living:

> Nur von Lebend'gen, wenn es Dir beliebt,
> Dass man sich sagen darf: die krieg' ich noch,
> Den vor mein Schwert, und die in meinen Arm
> (*Der gehörnte Siegfried*, Sc. 1.)

than to reconcile it with the malice of his final revelation to Siegfried of the trick that has been played upon him:

> Dieser Tropf
> Glaubt noch an uns're List! (*Siegfrieds Tod*, V. 2.)

Kriemhild, too, is less clearly and convincingly drawn in *Siegfrieds Tod* than in *Kriemhilds Rache*, though the development of her character in the final part presented greater problems. But Hebbel rises to the tragic portrayal of Kriemhild's destroying vengeance with apparent ease: her obsession commands belief, her gradual implication in ever-growing destruction seems unavoidable. In *Siegfrieds Tod*, on the other hand, her double betrayal of a secret creates a certain sense of doubt; it is less convincing than the twofold revelation of Herodes' orders in *Herodes und Mariamne*, where Hebbel was faced with a somewhat similar dramatic problem. The short interlude of Kriemhild's married life has to suffice to show the change wrought in the charming maiden of the *Vorspiel*; her love for Siegfried has to be made the motive for her betrayal of his honour and his safety. The second revelation is the more easily accounted for. Kriemhild, like the others of her family, has been brought up to trust in Hagen, their most faithful friend and vassal; and when he lures her to tell him Siegfried's secret, he does it in the guise of friendship to which she is accustomed. The revulsion of feeling which immediately succeeds is the natural reaction of one who has—even with the best of motives—betrayed another's trust; and the subsequent rapid growth of her anxiety for Siegfried's safety is admirably portrayed. It is the first betrayal—the breaking of the promise, the sudden transgression of her husband's strict commands—that is more difficult to realize. She yields to the temptation of a moment, it is true;

and the provocation offered by Brunhild is great. Nevertheless, nothing in the portrait of Kriemhild has prepared us for the shock of her betrayal; and its suddenness offers a striking contrast to the extreme skill previously shown in the motivation of Siegfried's reluctant explanation to her. It was a crucial difficulty in the story provided by the *Nibelungenlied*; and with all his efforts Hebbel did not wholly succeed at this point in his characterization of Kriemhild.

Thus *Siegfrieds Tod*, in spite of many single moments of great dramatic beauty, is less satisfying than either the swift, impressionistic *Vorspiel* or the relentlessly logical *Kriemhilds Rache*. From the moment of Siegfried's death, Kriemhild's course is set. The guilt has been incurred—the spectacle of its tragic consequences is unerringly presented. From her helpless aloofness in the opening of the final part, Kriemhild grows in power and in determination, until at the last she attains inhuman stature and incarnates the spirit of vengeance itself. Her actions can then no longer be measured by the normal standards; she is, of all Hebbel's heroines, the most immoderate and titanic. So she meets her doom: Hildebrant's deed, in his primitive reaction to her monstrous violation of all feminine limitations, is but the reflection of a larger verdict—life is no longer possible for one who has so far transcended the bounds of human feeling and of human rights. Like the judgement of a tragic chorus, Dietrich's final prayer has to restore the balance of an injured world.

In comparison with these three figures of tragedy, the remaining characters of *Die Nibelungen* almost inevitably recede. They are not shadowy—we have a clear conception of Siegfried's good-humoured, naïve, and somewhat unperceptive nature, of Gunther's inherent weakness, combined with characteristic obstinacy, of Volker's imaginative and courageous mind. But they become insignificant in the gigantic drama that involves the three main actors; they are of purely human size, and are dwarfed by the comparison. *Die Nibelungen* is, it may be suggested, a drama for the stage rather than the study; once the technical difficulties are transcended, the compulsion exercised upon the spirit by the chief characters is only fully measured in dramatic representation.

The triple drama is masterly in structure. Hebbel's amazing sense for detail—Hagen's opening sentences at his decisive appearance in each part might serve as a single example of the artist's workmanship[1]—is combined with an equal feeling for clarity of outline. *Der gehörnte Siegfried* and *Siegfrieds Tod* form a double exposition to *Kriemhilds Rache*; and in none of the three plays is the action ever interrupted or diverted from its forward movement. Every episode—Kriemhild's dream, Siegfried's conquest of the Danes and Saxons, the betrothal of Gudrun and Giselher, Hagen's vision of the water-maidens—either forwards the action or heightens the suspense, while the episodic figures of the chaplain and the pilgrim reinforce the judgement of Dietrich von Bern—eventually the compensating element in the tragic catastrophe.

There can be little doubt of the dramatic skill evinced in the Nibelungen drama—the real difficulty lay in the implications of the medieval story. Hebbel maintained that the mythical foundation was inseparable from the subject, but that on it he had built a purely human tragedy. The mystic background to the characters, he asserted, conveyed the grandeur of the whole: 'dass in dem Gedicht nicht die Secunden-Uhr, die das Daseyn der Mücken und Ameisen abmisst, sondern nur die Stunden-Uhr schlägt'.[2] The inexplicable element, he reminds those who would object, is always present in the depths of human feeling and experience. And in a late letter to Engländer he once again stresses the human nature of the tragedy: 'Der Gyges ist ohne Ring möglich, die Nibelungen sind es ohne Hornhaut und Nebelkappe; prüfen Sie, Sie werden es finden'.[3] So far as the dramatic action is concerned, the poet's feeling needs little

[1] 'Nun, keine Jagd?' (*Der gehörnte Siegfried*, Sc. 1).
'Der König Gunther ward noch nie besiegt' (*Siegfrieds Tod*, i. 2).
'Nicht um die Welt!' (*Kriemhilds Rache*, i. 2), and
'Noch immer schwarz!' (*Kriemhilds Rache*, iii. 7).
'Da ist das Ende! Wie ich's mir gedacht!' (*Kriemhilds Rache*, v. 14).

[2] *Tagebücher*, ed. cit., vol. iv. 5933, 14 Aug. 1861.

[3] Letter to Sigmund Engländer, 23 Feb. 1863, *Briefe*, ed. cit., vol. vii, p. 304.

justification: the outward aids assume no undue importance, and are merely part of a dramatic convention. But in the characterization the mythical background plays a more significant part. Brunhild is not easily comprehended on purely human grounds; Hagen's actions, as recorded in the *Nibelungenlied*, imply, in part, a previous history. And when Hebbel retained the main events of the medieval story, he was confronted with psychological problems—some of which, as has been suggested, he did not wholly solve. Large and imposing achievement as it was, and as it remains, *Die Nibelungen* is less homogeneous, less completely satisfying, than either *Herodes und Mariamne* or *Gyges und sein Ring*.

With *Demetrius*—a theme ill-fated, it would seem, in the history of German drama—Hebbel turned to a more familiar type of problem than is commonly treated in his plays. The situation of Demetrius, who at the moment when he is about to crown his sudden rise to power discovers that he is not the true-born heir to the empire of the Tsars, involves an ethical conflict of a less unusual kind than that of Rhodope, or of Mariamne—he is confronted with the choice between truth and falsehood, between that which is honest and that which is expedient. It is easy to see why, with such a conflict, the subject of Demetrius appealed to Schiller. It is perhaps more surprising that Hebbel should have thought of completing that which Schiller had begun, though he recognized the divergence in their conception of the central character: 'ich [müsste ihm] freilich eine ganz andere psychologische Grundlage geben', he wrote in 1857.[1] Ultimately, however, Hebbel's play was entirely independent of its predecessor, and his Demetrius differs radically from Schiller's.

As in *Die Nibelungen*, the stage is set in a *Vorspiel*. In it the discovery of Demetrius' claim to the Russian throne is made, his decision to enforce it taken. The events narrated by Schiller's hero in the opening scene at Cracow here form the matter of the Prelude; the contrast between the youth of unknown birth—dependent on the favour of his Polish benefactor Mniczek—and the heir to a vast empire is vividly pre-

[1] *Tagebücher*, ed. cit., vol. iv. 5620, 31 Dec. 1857.

sented in Scenes 12 and 13, where Demetrius, under sentence of death, is suddenly proclaimed by monk and Cardinal, and Marina, Mniczek's daughter, accepts with gratitude his admiration, hitherto presumptuous.

The characters of Demetrius, Marina, the Polish nobles, and the scheming priests are all clearly outlined in the *Vorspiel*. In the first act of the drama itself, the Russian scene is painted—thus a double exposition is completed in the same way as in *Der gehörnte Siegfried* and the first act of *Siegfrieds Tod*. The manifesto of Demetrius is read to the Tsar Boris Godunow and his counsellors—a dramatic device which lends it a double interest—and the character of the man whom Demetrius has to overthrow is plainly shown in his reception of it. The remainder of the act is devoted to the ex-Tsarina Marfa and her situation when the news of the re-discovered heir is brought to her. Secluded in her cloister, she has at length attained a certain resignation since her loss of husband, crown, and son; but how hardly it has been won is plain from her instant reaction to the tidings brought by Otrepiep. Unable to believe that she, the mother, was deceived by a changeling, subsequently murdered and lamented as her son, she yet resolves—mainly in the present Tsar's despite—to see the youth who is now declared to have been her child and Ivan's. She rejects the cautious counsel of the Abbess:

> Du trägst kein Mutterherz in Deinem Busen,
> Und weisst nicht, was den meinen jetzt bewegt.
> Ich muss, ich muss, doch zweifle nicht, ich finde
> Den Muth, um den Betrüger zu entlarven,
> Wenn mir mein Sohn nicht in die Arme sinkt. (I. 6.)

The second act, played on the field of battle, contains the meeting of Marfa and Demetrius. The latter has so amply proved his valour as to drive his counsellors to despair by his recklessness of danger, when in the moment of rest after victory the approach of the former Tsarina is announced. But Otrepiep, who prides himself on having achieved a master-stroke in bringing Marfa to the battleground, is amazed and chagrined by the instant anger of Demetrius when he discovers that she has not come entirely of her own accord. The reception that Demetrius gives her shows so much nobility of mind and delicacy of feeling that she embraces him—though not fully convinced by her own heart that he is indeed her son. Her public acknowledgement gives a pretext to the treacherous Schuiskoi for transferring his allegiance to Demetrius—temporarily at least. But by refusing an immediate boon to Schuiskoi and by his anger at Otrepiep's manœuvres, Demetrius makes two enemies; and at the close of the act they approach each other with an obvious purpose of conspiracy, while Marfa—still uncertain of her own mind—resolves to visit the resting-place of the Tsars in Moscow and pray for enlightenment at the tomb of the child so long regarded as her own.

Act III is played in Moscow. Otrepiep seizes the opportunity offered by the funeral cortège of the Tsar Boris Godunow to spread disaffection among the people, his insinuations against Demetrius ending in a suggestion to each one to follow where Schuiskoi leads. The short episode of the old woman Barbara, who falls in trying to touch the garment of Demetrius and is bidden to visit him and ask a boon on the following day, leads to the discovery by Otrepiep from her that Marfa is visiting the vault where not only her husband but the murdered child lies buried. The consequences of her action at once become apparent: the populace is told of her tears at the child's tomb, and immediately the effect of her former acknowledgment of Demetrius is annulled. The latter meanwhile arrives at the vault to pay homage to his father's ashes; he is met by Marfa, whose uncertainty has not been dispelled, as she had hoped. She can only bless him as she goes:

> Sei glücklich, wie Du gross und edel bist!

but she is unable either to endorse or to recall her recognition of him as her son—the oracle has not spoken. Mniczek, foreseeing all the danger arising from her ambiguous actions, arrests Schuiskoi for his treasonable insinuations, and orders the coffin of the child to be removed from the vault dedicated to the Tsars; but Demetrius counteracts this order: though the child may not claim burial there by birth, his blood has bought the privilege.

Du weisst nicht, was Du thust,

Mniczek cries despairingly; but Demetrius answers:

> Ich führe Krieg mit den Lebendigen,
> Nicht mit den Todten! Lasst die Todten ruh'n! (III. 23.)

The crisis of the action follows in the fourth act. After Demetrius—unwillingly enough and only at Marina's urging—has signed Schuiskoi's death-warrant, an interview takes place between Barbara and himself. Confused by her conflicting feelings, the old woman at length, and half involuntarily, reveals the vital fact that Demetrius is indeed the son of the Tsar Ivan, but also her own child—a double substitution having been carried out at his birth by Barbara, then the Tsarina's tiring-woman. His first impulse is to call in the soldiers and proclaim both the facts and his own previous ignorance of them; but Mniczek, pleading for himself, his daughter and the Poles, finally convinces him that he is not free to follow his own wishes. When Marfa appears, begging him to avoid bloodshed by commuting Schuiskoi's sentence, Demetrius at once gives the order to repeal it.

> Es war beschlossen, eh' ich unterschrieb,
> Doch hofft' ich's zu vollbringen, wie ein Gott,
> Nun tret' ich bloss von einem Mord zurück. (IV. 12.)

Where there is no majesty, he contends, there can be no treason. While he consents to act out the part of Tsar, to sacrifice his peace of conscience for the preservation of his friends, he foresees a speedy end:

> Ich bin der Capitain von einem Schiff,
> Das scheitert; rasch in's sich're Boot mit Euch,
> Dann zünde ich die Pulverkammer an. (IV. 13.)

In these words the fate of Demetrius is indicated; the fifth act, which should show it in fulfilment, is unfinished. The eight scenes that Hebbel wrote are entirely devoted to a conspiracy against Demetrius, headed by Schuiskoi and fostered skilfully by Otrepiep. The tragic issue is plain, though the poet did not live to shape it.

It is before all else the conception of the central character which marks out this drama from Hebbel's other plays. Demetrius is of the Gyges type—but more fully developed, surer of his aim. In the *Vorspiel*, it is true, we see him young and hasty, and in the battle scenes (Act II, Scenes 2 and 4) he shows a youthful, unconsidered ardour; but for the rest, he is mature, aware of evil but strong of will and purpose to do right. The choice with which he is confronted in Act IV can scarcely be described as a temptation, for he sees all too clearly the sacrifice that his decision involves: the consciousness of right which alone affords him peace of mind has to be weighed against his debts of gratitude. No ambitious Pretender this, yielding his scruples to desire for power, but a man placed between two insistent claims, neither of which he can deny without disaster. To his personal cost, the choice is made in favour of those for whom he feels himself responsible; but no possible choice can avert the fate his own magnanimity invites. A less scrupulous man might have saved himself by the exercise of power, but Demetrius refuses to do this. His guilt is unwitting, his false situation due to the action of others; but in view of what he is, his problem is none the less insoluble. It is a striking fact that we do not revolt against this cruelty of destiny: Demetrius himself conquers his tragic fate, and compels belief in the supreme value of a generous mind.

The Demetrius sketched by Schiller, in his outline of the later acts of his unfinished play, is of an entirely different nature. The revelation of the imposture (in all probability meant for the climax in Act III) moves him to an impulse of anger, in which he strikes down the murderer of the true Demetrius—thus involving himself, by his own act, in a situation where he is forced to incur further guilt to save himself from the consequences of that act. There is a clear resemblance here to the situation of Wallenstein, and the character of Demetrius betrays an equal similarity—notably in the calculating nature of his intercourse with Marfa. He is, moreover, involved in relations with two other women, both of whom exert an important influence upon his actions. The plot outlined by Schiller is thus considerably more complex than that of Hebbel's play—though it is obviously impossible to insist on the comparison, owing to the less finished state of the earlier drama. Nevertheless, the absence of complication in Hebbel's treatment of the subject is remarkable. Marina plays a very subordinate part in the main drama; and there is no suggestion of psychological complexity in her relations with Demetrius. Marfa, on the other hand, belongs to a type of feminine character unusual in Hebbel's tragedies—perhaps the only suggestion of such a type is the figure of Ute in *Die Nibelungen*, who plays however a much less important part. The struggle in Marfa between inclination and integrity forms a parallel to the conflict in Demetrius himself; the innate honesty and truth of each draw them by instinct to each other, though this, far from lessening the uncertainty of Marfa, makes her choice more difficult. The relations between these two characters contribute in no small degree to the tragic irony of the situation; on the other hand, their delicacy heightens the sense of spiritual values in the drama.

It is possible that Hebbel might have altered *Demetrius* in some particulars (it is conceivable he might have shortened it in places); but the action is so coherent, the structure of such effective simplicity, that no material change can well be imagined. The mastery with which he paints on a large canvas is even more evident here than in *Die Nibelungen*: the battle scenes in Act II, the crowd scenes in Act V, the characterization of Polish nobles and Russian conspirators, show the poet of *Judith* in the fullest development of those dramatic powers which his first play suggested. And the figure of Demetrius himself shows us more than this. Maturity had brought a different outlook. The world of *Demetrius* is still a tragic world, and human destiny still lies in sacrifice; but blindness has been converted into sight—revolt into acceptance.

VIII

DRAMATIC TECHNIQUE

ANY detailed analysis of Hebbel's plays must in great measure demonstrate the poet's sense of dramatic effect and his mastery of dramatic means. Moreover, it is impossible to draw a rigid line of demarcation between dramatic technique and the substance of a drama, since the very substance is to some extent the outcome of the form. But Hebbel's actual methods are worthy of some general consideration. They illuminate his individual aims, and in certain ways their influence may be traced in subsequent dramatic history.

Dramatic technique must comprehend all the means used by the dramatic artist to attain his ends—the sum of the practical methods by which he expresses his meaning in dramatic form. With Hebbel, who was before all else a tragic dramatist, the chief end to be attained is a revelation of the underlying necessity for tragic development. Thus his methods of showing the interaction of character and circumstance must be stressed in any study of his technical achievement as a dramatist; the revelation of character is the key to his whole dramatic technique, from the structure of the action down to the brief stage directions.

Few readers or spectators of Hebbel's tragedies could fail to be struck by their architectural quality. Clarity of outline, ordered progress of the action, characterize them all, from *Judith* to *Demetrius*; but perhaps *Maria Magdalena* stands out amongst them as an example of austere compression and swift, relentless movement. The tragic necessity becomes more plainly visible with every scene—a process later generalized by Hebbel in his diary:

1ste Stufe künstlerischer Wirkung: es kann so seyn!
2te ,, ,, ,, es ist!
3te ,, ,, ,, es muss so seyn![1]

[1] *Tagebücher*, ed. cit., vol. iii. 4791, 1 Jan. 1851.

This entry may be compared with an earlier one made while he was still at work on *Maria Magdalena*, describing dramatic structure in a visual image: '. . . die Idee [muss] im ersten Act als zuckendes Licht, im zweiten als Stern, der mit Nebeln kämpft, im dritten als dämmernder Mond, im vierten als stralende Sonne, die Keiner mehr verläugnen kann, und im fünften als verzehrender und zerstörender Komet hervortreten. . . .'[1]

The opening acts of Hebbel's tragedies themselves illuminate this image. A gleam of light is often thrown upon a vital contrast. 'Dein Hochzeits-Kleid?' are Klara's first words to her mother in *Maria Magdalena*, dimly foreshadowing the tragic theme; and through this, the swiftest of all Hebbel's opening acts, the situation rapidly develops, till the mother's wedding-dress becomes her shroud and Klara's own marriage fatally impossible. So also do Kandaules' first words to Gyges:

> Heut sollst Du seh'n, was Lydien vermag!

suggest that pride of possession which leads him into tragic guilt, and Hagen's initial question in *Der gehörnte Siegfried*:

> Nun, keine Jagd?

draws an answer stressing the central contrast in the tragic theme:

> Es ist ja heil'ger Tag!

The main facts of the situation emerge clearly from the opening act in Hebbel's dramas, preparing the mind for a decision or event essential to the tragic sequence. Thus in the first act of *Herodes und Mariamne*, Herodes is shown in his contrasting relations with Mariamne and the outside world; the mind of Mariamne is revealed in her interview with the king, and her refusal to comply with his demand provides the occasion for his fatal decision to treat her life as one of his possessions. 'Nun lebt sie unter'm Schwert!'—he exclaims: the act closes with this decisive step. A similar development may be traced in the first act of *Gyges und sein*

[1] *Tagebücher*, ed. cit., vol. ii. 2897, 25 Nov. 1843.

Ring. The central characteristics of Kandaules on the one hand, of Rhodope on the other, are indicated in two successive scenes; the ring of Gyges, offered to Kandaules in the opening dialogue between them, occasions the king's resolve, in the last scene of the act, to satisfy his pride of possession by a secret injury to Rhodope. Here, too, the first act ends with a decision that involves the tragic outcome.

In *Kriemhilds Rache*, the resolve of Kriemhild to marry Etzel, which concludes the opening act, stands in a different relation to the action of the play; it is rather a condition of the tragic situation than a decision that invites the tragic issue. Nevertheless, the dramatic effect of Kriemhild's consent resembles that of the action taken by Herodes or Kandaules: it is a portent, the lightning flash before the coming storm.

In the whole drama of *Die Nibelungen*, the 'Vorspiel'—*Der gehörnte Siegfried*—may be said to fulfil the functions of an opening act. The situation is swiftly indicated, the characters outlined; and the Prologue concludes with the momentous bargain that is the origin of *Siegfrieds Tod* and *Kriemhilds Rache*. (Hebbel adopted a similar expedient in *Demetrius*, where the Prologue ends with the acceptance and proclamation of the new Tsar).

Where two parallel actions are involved, the first and second acts may be considered as a unit. In *Judith*, Act I is devoted to the Holofernes action and ends with the general's decision to assail Bethulia and destroy the Hebrews; Act II, which draws the contrasting picture of Judith's state of mind, closes on her challenge to Ephraim to kill Holofernes and her incipient resolve to justify the challenge when he refuses to accept it. Similarly, the first act of *Siegfrieds Tod* deals with the situation of Brunhild and her relations with Siegfried, while the second act—though mainly concerned with Siegfried and Kriemhild—ends with Siegfried's reluctant decision to fulfil his bargain with Gunther to the uttermost.

The opening act of *Agnes Bernauer*, on the other hand, offers a picture of both sides of the situation, and thus constitutes an unusually lengthy piece of exposition. In the first half, Agnes is shown in her relations with her environment—her father, her suitor, her contemporaries; in the second, Albrecht's sudden passion is portrayed, and his determination to woo her in earnest is foreshadowed in the final scene. The first act of *Genoveva* is almost equally static. In a sense, however, the decision taken by Golo at the end contributes actively to the catastrophe—intended as a test of Providence, the breakneck climb, successfully achieved, only intensifies temptation by offering a subtle argument to Golo's mind.

Hebbel's general dislike of a purely preparatory opening act is matched by his aversion to the normal 'ritardando' of the fourth act in a five-act drama. Nothing in his picture of the development of a dramatic theme is more striking than the statement that by the fourth act, the central idea must appear 'als stralende Sonne, die Keiner mehr verläugnen kann'. Instead of envisaging a retarding moment between the crisis of the third act and the catastrophe in the fifth, he sees the progress of the action rather as a continuous movement, quickening in speed as it nears the appointed end. Only in *Siegfrieds Tod* and *Kriemhilds Rache* (where the poet's close reliance on his source must not be overlooked) do we find something like the normal retardation of the action.

In *Judith*, while Act III is devoted to Judith's resolve and the great crowd scene in Bethulia, Act IV brings the chief antagonists face to face for the first time; and the spiritual conflict here evident leads directly to the ultimate conflict and catastrophe. A striking form of this progression is to be found in *Herodes und Mariamne*: the fourth act contains Mariamne's discovery of Herodes' second betrayal of her person—the climax of her spiritual tragedy; this is followed by her festival, and by the final clash between herself and Herodes on the king's return. Each of the two heroines thus plays a deliberate part at the end of the fourth act, leaving the unmasking to the fifth; but as Mariamne's inner tragedy is greater than that of Judith, so too is its issue more compelling.

In *Gyges und sein Ring* the fourth act is entirely occupied by the decisive dialogue between Gyges and the queen. The climax of the inner action is the resolve of Gyges to accept Rhodope's terms; it is preceded by the gradual unfolding of the truth, through the statement of Kandaules and the consequent explanation offered by Gyges to the queen, and is followed by a clear indication of the catastrophe:

Rhodope. Nun Brautgewand und Todtenhemd, herbei!

. . . .

(To Lesbia) Du wirst mir wohl nicht danken, armes Kind!
Und doch! Zuletzt! Ja, Lesbia, zuletzt!

The fourth act of *Demetrius* provides an interesting parallel to this. Here also the discovery of the truth marks the spiritual crisis, and Demetrius is faced with a choice that is decisive for the tragic issue; and similarly, the last words of the act prepare us for that issue.

The momentous decision of Herzog Ernst is taken in the fourth act. 'Agnes Bernauer, fahr' hin!' are the final words of the first half, before the scene changes to Straubing, where the warrant is executed. The turning-point in the drama of Herzog Ernst is here; the arrest of Agnes which follows constitutes a moment of suspense in hers—suspense that is deepened by the final words of Preising which afford a gleam of hope:

'Gott gebe, dass sie jetzt auf mich höre! Noch kann ich sie vom Tode retten und ich will's' (IV. 12).

This suggestion of a possible way of escape (which yet does not command belief) is rare in Hebbel's tragedies. The appearance of Drago's spirit at the end of the fourth act of *Genoveva* is too little related to the immediate action to be taken as a parallel—though actually it does suggest the solution which later formed the *Epilogue to Genoveva.* A more direct comparison might be made with a fleeting hope in Klara's desperate soliloquy at the end of Act II in *Maria Magdalena* (the equivalent moment in a three-act drama): 'Ich bettle ja nicht um ein Glück, ich bettle um mein Elend, um mein tiefstes Elend—mein Elend wirst Du mir geben!' (II. 6); but even this is immediately followed by such an indication of the tragic issue as occurs in *Gyges* or *Demetrius*: 'Drei Brunnen triffst Du auf dem Weg zu ihm— Dass Du mir an Keinem stehen bleibst! Noch hast Du nicht das Recht dazu!'

Retarding moments are not found at any fixed point in Hebbel's tragedies. Where they occur, their object is to make the outcome appear the more inevitable. Such is the moment between the two tests in *Herodes und Mariamne* (Act III, Sc. 6) where the outward action is suspended, but the inner conflict between Herodes and the queen grows more acute; so too in the fifth act of this drama, the explanation offered to Titus by Mariamne—while it retards the course of events—increases the force of the blow dealt to Herodes, and thus heightens the effect of the catastrophe. The most obviously retarding moment in *Maria Magdalena*—the third scene of the second act, where the merchant Wolfram arrives at Meister Anton's house and tells Klara of her brother's innocence—serves partly to explain the previous action, but mainly to deepen the tragic irony of her own situation. It is thus matched by the scene in the last act between Karl and his sister, where through an apparently slow-moving dialogue the force of Klara's determination rapidly increases till she finds in Karl's trivial request excuse for action.

Thus consideration of the structure of his plays shows that both outward events and the pause between events are used by Hebbel to further that revelation of character which forms the true action of the tragedies. This close connexion is for him the principle of dramatic exposition: the revelation of events entirely subserves the presentation of character. By this, perhaps more clearly than by any other single trait, he proves himself a major dramatist.

Every dramatic author has to evolve a satisfactory mode of linking the present with the past. The problems offered by dramatic themes are variously solved, not only by different writers, but in different ages; and Hebbel's methods of exposing essential facts are of interest to the observer of modern drama.

In *Maria Magdalena* and in *Herodes und Mariamne* an event which contains tragic possibilities has already taken place before the opening of the drama, and is disclosed in the course of the action. Klara's surrender to Leonhard's demand is the key to her tragic situation; the state of affairs between them is first revealed with consummate skill in the fourth scene of Act I. The point of view of each is indicated here, to be later expanded in Klara's conversation with the Secretary (Act II, Scene 5) and in Leonhard's short monologue at the beginning of Act III. The exposition of this fact is thus only completed in the last act, when its consequences have already assumed tragic proportions, and only in the final scene is the fact placed by the Secretary in its true relation to those consequences. Meanwhile, four separate standpoints from which Klara's action may be judged have been disclosed; and in their differences we have learnt to know the essential characteristics of Klara herself, Leonhard, the Secretary, and Meister Anton.

The death of Aristobolus, compassed by Herodes before the drama opens, fulfils a similar function in *Herodes und Mariamne*. It is mainly important for its bearing on Herodes' relations with the queen, but it has at the same time a further dramatic value: Joab, Joseph, and Alexandra react in characteristic ways to the king's despotic violence, and thus the purely subjective view of Herodes' action which would ensue from its revelation by a single person is avoided. This was a method which Hebbel had tried in the second act of *Genoveva*, though with less success; there four different judgements are passed on Golo's venturesome exploit in four successive scenes—an arrangement, however, which only emphasizes the effect of epic narrative characteristic of this play. In *Herodes und Mariamne* allusions to the death of Aristobolus recur like a refrain throughout the drama from the first scene to the last. Skilfully interwoven with Joab's account of his reception by Octavian, the first hint of Herodes' responsibility for the death of Mariamne's brother elicits the king's immediate answer:

Dank, Alexandra, Dank! (I. 1.)

and his suspicion of the part played by Alexandra receives confirmation in the second act, where she is shown plotting for revenge. It is she who in her triumphant exclamation

> Ha, Aristobolus!
> Du bist gerächt, mein Sohn, und ich in Dir! (V. 8.)

evokes Herodes' final assertion of despotic power, just as, by her intrigues and hatred, she helped to lead him to the initial act of violence. The effect upon Mariamne is more complex. The very conflict in her feelings betrays her love for Herodes, and the contrast between her allusions to her brother's death in conversation with him and with Alexandra (Act I, Scene 3, and Act II, Scene 3) throws a flood of light upon her state of mind. Still more illuminating is her admission in Act III, when she reproaches Herodes for his injurious order:

> Dem Brudermord
> Hast Du das Siegel der Nothwendigkeit,
> Dem man sich beugen muss, wie man auch schaudert,
> Zwar aufgedrückt, doch es gelingt Dir nie,
> Mit diesem Siegel auch den Mord an mir
> Zu stempeln, der wird bleiben, was er ist,
> Ein Frevel, den man höchstens wiederholen,
> Doch nun und nimmer überbieten kann. (III. 3.)

But she ultimately recognizes the significance of the king's act:

> Du kannst der Schwester nicht mehr trau'n, seit Du
> Den Bruder tödtetest . . . (V. 6.)

and in her final words she relates her own death to that of Aristobolus:

> Du, Aristobolus, sei mir gegrüsst!
> Gleich bin ich bei Dir in der ew'gen Nacht! (V. 6.)

So here too the initial fact, accomplished before the drama opens, and indicating tragic possibilities, gradually acquires its full significance through the course of the action, and in the final act is related to the tragic issue.

This method, by which the gradual growth in significance of a given fact is shown, is matched in Hebbel's plays by the way in which minor facts that have some bearing on the action are revealed. In *Maria Magdalena* the cause of the bailiff's grudge against Meister Anton—issuing in the over-hasty arrest of Karl and, as a consequence, his mother's death—is explained only in the second act (Act II, Scene 3); and the incident there related emphasizes precisely that unbending rigour in Meister Anton which brings about Klara's resolve and the ensuing catastrophe. So too in *Herodes und Mariamne* the story of Herodes' youthful defiance in front of the Sanhedrim, related by Sameas in Act II, Scene 1, crowns the previous narrative of Alexandra, and reinforces effectually that quality in Herodes' character which has already led him to a fatal step, soon to be revealed to Mariamne. The jealousy of Salome, indicated at the end of the second act and more fully in the third, is explained in the fifth act, at the moment when it acquires an added importance from Salome's impassioned account of Mariamne's behaviour at her festival; the fact disclosed thus gains a further interest by its close relation to the feelings of the narrator. This method is also used effectively by Hebbel to lend vividness to a long dramatic narrative. When Judith tells Mirza the story of her marriage (in Act II, Scene 1) the facts are already partly familiar to her hearer; it is essential that we should become aware of them, but Mirza's attention must be held as well as ours. The poet solves this problem by endowing Judith's tale with a new subjective interest. Mirza, hitherto aware only of a set of facts, now learns their inner meaning and the psychological effect on Judith of her strange experience. The retrospective narrative thus gains immensely in vividness and interest: Mirza's reaction to the story as we listen to it increases its significance.

A similar mode of lending immediate importance to a dramatic narrative is found in the first act of *Siegfrieds Tod.* Frigga's relation of Brunhild's mysterious history, with its indication of the latter's supernormal powers, is linked with an insistent entreaty to her to avoid approaching danger by offering sacrifice to the ancient gods. The effect of the story on Brunhild—who shows, like Mirza, a partial acquaintance with the facts—is to intensify her own belief and to sharpen her challenge to the approaching combatants; thus the entry of the Burgundians which immediately succeeds the narrative of Frigga gains in dramatic force. In the same way, Etzel's willing obedience to Kriemhild's wishes for the reception of the Nibelungen is grounded on his satisfaction that she has borne him an heir—this, the essential fact revealed in Etzel's speech (*Kriemhilds Rache*, Act III, Scene 2) suggests to Kriemhild the powerful motive needed to incite the king to break the peace he is determined to preserve. So Etzel's retrospective account of their marriage is skilfully interwoven with Kriemhild's present problem, and offers her a mode of solving it which contributes in a direct way to the catastrophe.

Another method of increasing the effect of a dramatic narrative is to give it an unexpected issue. Whereas the speaker may intend only a partial statement of the facts, the whole situation may be unwittingly laid bare. Genoveva's discovery, from the letter brought by Tristan, that Siegfried has been wounded is a minor example of this reversal of intention; it leads to a long narrative, not in itself conspicuously interesting, but important by reason of its effect on Genoveva and, through her, on Golo. A much more subtle use of similar means occurs in *Herodes und Mariamne.* Joseph's betrayal of Herodes' orders is unintentional; he is enmeshed by his own statements, unable to extricate himself from Mariamne's questions. In this drama Hebbel was faced with the added difficulty of a repeated situation. He solved it by a sharp differentiation between the characters of Joseph and Soemus, and by an ironic reversal in the position of Mariamne. The two men act from differing motives, but arrive at the same end; neither intends to reveal the whole situation, but whereas Joseph merely becomes involved in a difficulty he has not foreseen, Soemus deliberately takes his decision in the course of his dialogue with Mariamne. She, on the other hand, is conscious of the dread possibility in the second instance as she cannot be in the first; and in her very efforts to banish it from her mind, to behave with complete loyalty, as if it did not exist, she provokes Soemus to disclose the truth. Thus the two dialogues have an issue not wholly expected by the speakers; but the audience shares the knowledge of such a possibility with one or both of the actors.

Partial acquaintance with the facts of a given situation may also be expanded in another way: an action may be reported by the characters as they follow it with the interest of spectators. This favourite dramatic device is used by Hebbel with extraordinary power in *Der gehörnte Siegfried* and in *Kriemhilds Rache.* Siegfried's prowess in a contest of strength with Hagen, Gunther, and his brothers is an important fact in the Prelude to the Nibelungen drama, where the tragic guilt of Siegfried and of Gunther is incurred by means of the former's matchless powers. Hebbel conveys this knowledge indirectly. The joint report of Ute and Kriemhild, as they watch the contest from a window, states the facts, but this statement becomes dramatically vivid for two reasons: the issue is not expected by either of the women, and as the facts emerge, Ute skilfully relates them to the feelings of Kriemhild. Thus the scene serves not only to emphasize an essential factor in the situation but also to reveal Kriemhild's growing interest in the stranger, and to give significant indications of her character. In the final act of *Kriemhilds Rache* (Scenes 1–13) the method of dramatic report is used with still greater effect, at the highest point of conflict; the last desperate stand of the Nibelungen is reported at intervals to Kriemhild, and the growing terror of the action is reflected in the heightened passion of the tragic heroine.

The reports of Alexandra, Salome, and Titus on Mariamne's behaviour at her festival portray in a similar way a tense dramatic moment. Here a mask conceals the passion in the heart of Mariamne, and the gradually increasing horror of the spectators alone reflects the real action. Their incomprehension deepens the effect on us of Mariamne's choice—while the dramatic spectators are unaware of the essential fact, the audience shares her tragic knowledge.

It is plain that in Hebbel's dramas the exposition of fact cannot be separated from the exposition of character; he never forgot the difference between the historical and the dramatic value of events. But he was also a master in the art of revealing character by other means, direct and indirect. When Hagen speaks of Siegfried in Acts IV and V of *Siegfrieds Tod*, his words not only show a certain side of Siegfried's character but, more strongly, illuminate his own.

> Ja, hätt' er Strich gehalten, wär' er sicher,
> Doch wusst' ich wohl, es werde nicht gescheh'n.
> Wenn man durchsichtig ist, wie ein Insect,
> Das roth und grün erscheint, wie seine Speise,
> So muss man sich vor Heimlichkeiten hüten,
> Denn schon das Eingeweide schwatzt sie aus!
>
> (*Siegfrieds Tod*, IV. 7.)

Hagen says of him, when he plans the murder; and when it is accomplished, he counters Siegfried's words with

> Jetzt schweigt er. Aber jetzt ist's kein Verdienst! (V. 2.)

So, too, when Klara and Karl refer to Meister Anton, their comments reveal fully as much of themselves as of their father. Klara's perception of his real feelings, so carefully concealed, is characteristic of her own tender nature; Karl's impatient parody of Meister Anton's rigid discipline betrays his instability:

> Hobeln, Sägen, Hämmern, dazwischen Essen, Trinken und Schlafen, damit wir immer fort hobeln, sägen und hämmern können, Sonntags ein Kniefall obendrein: ich danke Dir, Herr, dass ich hobeln, sägen und hämmern darf! (III. 8.)

Modern as he is in many of his methods, Hebbel still believed in the older convention of the monologue as a means of revealing character. But he considered it appropriate only in certain conditions. 'Monologe: laute Athemzüge der Seele,' he wrote in 1861;[1] their function was to express dual

[1] *Tagebücher*, ed. cit., vol. iv. 5907, 3 May 1861.

forces in the character.[1] After *Judith* and *Genoveva* he makes more sparing use of the soliloquy, until in the last tragedies it is short and tense, occurring only at a crucial moment of preparation or decision. In *Judith* three monologues are spoken by Holofernes, one by Judith, one by Mirza; but their length, together with the general character of the dialogue, creates the impression of a more extensive use. In *Genoveva* the monologue is dominant; passionately interested in the intricacies of Golo's mind, Hebbel yielded, for the only time, to the fascination of revealing a character absorbed in self-analysis. *Maria Magdalena* marks the beginning of a change. It is true that the actual number of soliloquies is greater than in *Judith*; yet they are more compressed, and the tempo is more rapid. Klara, unbearably constrained, discloses at intervals the gradually increasing pressure that drives her to her doom—but this relief of her overburdened heart appears essential to the emotional progression of the play. Leonhard's monologues heighten the contrast between the two characters: entirely concerned with the weighing of alternatives, they emphasize his insensibility as fully as Klara's reveal her dependence upon feeling. Of the five monologues spoken by Herodes, two only belong to the older, longer type. Both these express the king's doubts of Mariamne: one (I. 4) precedes the first decision, the second (III. 6) follows the important conversation before the second test. At each of these moments, Herodes is subject to conflicting impulses; in each case, his soliloquy ends in a momentous decision. The other three express, in a short, swift summary, the momentary situation; they show the result of action, not the preparation for it. The two types of monologue are plainly to be distinguished; and from now onwards Hebbel makes increasing use of the second, shorter kind. The deliberative monologue is used by Alexandra in this play (II. 2), by Herzog Ernst and Preisinger in *Agnes Bernauer* (III. 1 and 3; IV. 1 and 3), by Rhodope in *Gyges und sein Ring* (III and IV), and by Schuiskoi in *Demetrius* (II. 13); but it is the swift exposition

[1] *Tagebücher*, ed. cit., vol. ii. 2971, 27 Dec. 1843.

of a frame of mind that emerges from the soliloquies of Agnes Bernauer (V. 1), of Gyges (II) and of Kriemhild in *Kriemhilds Rache* (I. 3 and 7; III. 2; and IV. 15). In *Die Nibelungen* indeed, the short soliloquy alone is found—three times in *Siegfrieds Tod* (II. 4; IV. 7, IV. 16), and seven times in *Kriemhilds Rache* (I. 3, I. 7; II. 6; III. 2, III. 5; IV. 10, IV. 15), where often it occupies a scene of four or five lines, and except for the empty stage has almost the effect of an aside.

The dramatic convention of the monologue was obviously suited to the type of character which most frequently attracted Hebbel. He uses it fully to disclose the inner mind. Where the tempo of the play requires it, he intensifies the passion and compresses the content of soliloquy—Kriemhild only once exceeds the limit of five lines in *Kriemhilds Rache*. And neither Meister Anton, in his rigid economy of emotion, nor Mariamne, in her intense reserve, uses this form of self-expression; Hebbel did not adapt his characters to the convention.

He was inclined, however, to a less sparing use of asides—a possible substitute for the dramatic soliloquy. Here he makes considerable—occasionally excessive—demands upon the skill of the actor and the quickness of the audience. The great scene between Herodes and Mariamne depends for its effect upon the success with which both actors convey to the audience the feelings which must not be betrayed to each other. In particular, Mariamne's words

> Die Probe
> Ist keine, wenn er ahnt, was Dich bewegt!

and

> Lenk, Ewiger, sein Herz!
> . . . .
> . . . so vergess' ich, was gescheh'n;

are vital to the comprehension of her problem; but it is no less vital that Herodes—deaf with grief and indignation—should not hear them. Judith's final aside to Mirza in Act IV is important for the undertaking of the part that she is playing; here, however, in a triangular grouping, it is easier to ensure that Holofernes does not hear her explanation. In *Genoveva*, on the other hand, there is the same exaggerated use of asides as of soliloquy; in particular, the scene between Golo and Genoveva in Act II (Sc. 4) is difficult to render credible. Golo's long speeches to himself, while Genoveva stands by uncomprehending, would strain the technical powers of any actors, and not even Genoveva's words

> Ihr redet, Golo, warum nicht mit mir?
> Ich sah Euch niemals so, Ihr seid wohl krank

avail much to ease the difficult situation.[1]

But again it may be noted that Hebbel's later tragedies show less use of this device than do the earlier ones. In *Gyges und sein Ring* the swift comment of Kandaules in his conversation with Rhodope (Act III) can be conveyed with ease; in *Die Nibelungen* the short soliloquy virtually replaces murmured comment in a dialogue. Hebbel was more inclined in this drama than in any other to free the stage, for a fleeting moment, of all the characters but one, and thus create a sense of movement in the action.

He had indeed a keen sense for this kind of stage effect, and fully realized the value alike of the static and the moving group. The picture of Holofernes or Herodes at the opening of the drama is complete: dominant among a dependent company, they create an immediate sense of power and isolation. Such a static picture, but without the central figure, is also presented in the first scene of *Kriemhilds Rache*. Her absence throws the emphasis on Hagen, and on the grouping of the Nibelungen kindred, and the elaborate scenes lend double significance to the three-lined soliloquy (I. 3) that shows the tragic heroine for the first time on the stage.

But the group picture is only used by Hebbel to open these three plays, where it achieves a special end. More frequently

[1] In the theatre version this scene was cut considerably, and Genoveva's words are corrected to

> Ihr meidet meinen Blick und redet doch?

in an obvious effort to ease the actor's task (v. *Werke*, ed. cit., vol. i, p. 438. Lesarten und Anmerkungen to *Genoveva*).

the curtain rises on one or two characters, who prepare the way for the gradual filling of the stage. The conversation between Klara and her mother at the opening of *Maria Magdalena* leads to the passage of Karl in the second scene, and this is followed by two further dialogues, between Klara and Leonhard and between Leonhard and Meister Anton. In the fourth and fifth scenes the entry of one character is balanced by the exit of another; but in the last two scenes of the act the stage gradually fills, until the curtain falls upon Meister Anton's exit from a group stricken by sudden disaster into immobility. This gradual widening of the picture in the opening act may be seen, with slight differences of form, in *Genoveva* (Siegfried—Golo—Genoveva—Drago), in *Der gehörnte Siegfried* (Hagen, Gunther, Volker—Siegfried—Ute, Kriemhild), in *Siegfrieds Tod* (Brunhild, Frigga—Siegfried, Gunther, Hagen), and in the *Prologue to Demetrius* (Odowalsky, Poniatowsky—Gregory—Maschinka—Demetrius—Marina); but it is found in its most symmetrical form in *Agnes Bernauer*. Here Theobald, Agnes, Knippeldollinger, Barbara, and Caspar Bernauer make successive appearances upon the stage, while short dialogues between Agnes and Theobald punctuate their entrances and exits. Until the ninth scene the stage gradually fills; in the three succeeding ones it empties, leaving Caspar Bernauer alone for a short soliloquy before the scene completely changes.

Hebbel is equally skilful in creating an effective moment at the end of an act. Here, too, the close may be leisurely or swift. On the one hand, the stage may gradually be cleared, leaving one character whose final words are vital to the psychological action. Such a close is to be found in the third act of *Judith*, where the crowd melts away, and Delia is left to express the inner significance of its behaviour: 'Weiter haben sie keinen Trost für mich, als dass sie sagen: Er, den ich liebte, sei ein Sünder gewesen'. Or, on the other hand, the curtain may fall upon a moment of surprise or of dismay—here the emphasis is on the situation. Rhodope's revelation to Lesbia of the proof of Gyges' love is an instance of this form:

Rhodope. Und wenn mich Gyges sah: wann sah er mich?
Lesbia. (*legt sich die Hand vor die Augen*)
Rhodope. Nun sprich als Mädchen, ob er sterben muss! (III.)

The two methods are both used in *Herodes und Mariamne*, with an interesting contrast in effect. At the end of the second act, the arrival of Herodes strikes an excited group to silence:

Alexandra (*stürzt herein*) Der König!
Joseph. In der Stadt?
Alexandra. Schon in der Burg!

The curtain descends on a motionless company—to rise in the next act on the entry of the king. Interest is entirely concentrated in this final scene on the momentous event; the portrayal of its effect upon the inner action is reserved for the succeeding act. A different result is obtained by the second method in Act IV. Here the stage becomes empty gradually, and Herodes, left with Titus, draws a poignant contrast:

Zu der hab' ich einmal gesprochen:
Zwei Menschen, die sich lieben, wie sie sollen,
Können einander gar nicht überleben,

. . . .

Titus, verlach' mich nicht! So ist's! So ist's!
Allein die Menschen lieben sich nicht so! (IV. 8.)

Attention is thus riveted on the dominant motive of Herodes' action: the impression of Mariamne's exit is subservient to its effect upon the king. In this way the opening of the fifth act is prepared, and Herodes' determination foreshadowed.

Such linking of one act to another is a remarkable characteristic of *Kriemhilds Rache.* Each curtain falls upon an anticipatory phrase. The first act closes with a general indication of the future:

Mein treuer Eckewart hat mich gewiegt,
Und ob auch alle Andern mich verlassen,
Er fehlt gewiss nicht hinter meinem Sarg.

—words which (immediately following on Kriemhild's consent to a second marriage) clearly point towards the tragic end. Act II concludes with Gunther's acceptance of Hagen's gloomy prophecy:

Und Du
Bist unser Tod, wenn's drunten wirklich steht,
Wie Du's uns prophezeist. Doch—
(*Er schlägt Hagen auf die Schulter*)
Komm nur, Tod!
(*folgen den Andern.*)

And this anticipation seems immediately confirmed by Kriemhild's opening words in the next act. Hagen's defiance ends Act III:

Nein, das vom Todtenschiff!
Das Letzte, wie der Freund den Freund ersticht,
Und dann die Fackel—Das geht Morgen los,

and Act IV virtually continues the scene after an interval of a few moments. And this fourth act closes with Etzel's ominous warning:

was den Heunenkönig
Auf dieser Erde einst so furchtbar machte,
Das sollt Ihr seh'n in seinem engen Raum!

words which find an echo in Hildebrant's initial question in Act V:

Wie lange soll der Jammer denn noch dauern?

Hebbel had a vivid sense not only for architectural, but also for pictorial and musical effects. It is true that his plays—with the possible exception of *Maria Magdalena*, where the background is almost a part of the action—are little dependent on their actual stage-setting. But there are pictures, such as the dance at Augsburg in *Agnes Bernauer*, or the night scenes in Moscow in *Demetrius*, that are remarkably full of life and rich in colour. Above all, he can create a sense of movement. The grouping of the dance scene and the Regensburg tourney in *Agnes Bernauer*, the movement of the crowd in the foreground against the background of a solemn procession in the third act of *Demetrius* reveal the master-playwright. And that this skill was intuitive is amply proved by the grouping of the crowd scenes in his first play (*Judith*, Acts III and V). In

Kriemhilds Rache, the double action of the last act depends upon a more complex use of the back of the stage than in any other of Hebbel's dramas; a wonderful pictorial effect is achieved by the contrast between the moving struggle in the background and Kriemhild's relentless immobility in the foreground of the scene. A musical effect adds sharpness to this contrast: on Dietrich's tale of the slain—matching in its accumulating detail the movement of the battle—fall the hammer-strokes of Kriemhild's refrain, 'Und Hagen lebt'. Elsewhere, too, Hebbel uses a 'Leitmotiv' in the same way to give point to a dramatic moment. The scene between Frigga and Brunhild after the discovery of the secret conveys the impression of an impending fate through echo and repetition:

Brunhild. Frigga, mein Leben oder auch das seine!
Frigga. Das seine, Kind!
Brunhild. Ich ward nicht bloss verschmäht,
Ich ward verschenkt, ich ward wohl gar verhandelt!
Frigga. Verhandelt, Kind!
Brunhild. Ihm selbst zum Weib zu schlecht,
War ich der Pfenning, der ihm eins verschaffte!
Frigga. Der Pfenning, Kind!
Brunhild. Das ist noch mehr, als Mord,
Und dafür will ich Rache! Rache, Rache!
(*Siegfrieds Tod*, III. 11.)

Subtler repetitions, ironic in effect, occur in the first act of *Herodes und Mariamne*—the word 'Perlen' forms an irregular refrain throughout the first half of the king's interview with Mariamne in Act I, and the clash of wills at the end of the scene is stressed by echoed words. Ironic repetition is indeed characteristic of this play.

With all his sense for such constructive detail, Hebbel did not approve of prescribing detail for the interpretation of his characters. Rather he believed that the one rendered the other unnecessary, and he was accordingly sparing in his use of stage directions. 'Ich selbst schreibe dem Schauspieler in meinen dramatischen Arbeiten ungern etwas vor', he wrote to Kühne in 1847, 'und bestrebe mich, nach Art der Alten, ihm durch kleine Fingerzeige im Dialog selbst die Geberden, die ich zur Begleitung wünsche, leise anzudeuten. Das geht so weit, dass ich nicht einmal des Vorhangs gern erwähne. . .'[1] An important gesture may be indicated, as well as exits, entrances, and on occasion relative positions on the stage; but beyond these and the marking of asides there is little detail for actor and producer. Nor do the scenic indications state any but the salient features of the setting—a throne, the time of day, a vista of landscape in the distance (once, in *Kriemhilds Rache*, Act V, the essential structure in the background is described). Relations of time and place were emphasized in the substance of the plays, and so the poet—in contrast to the majority of modern dramatists—left the details of production alone. In this, perhaps, he was not so far wrong. At least it is clear that he demanded—and perhaps therefore obtains—the fullest collaboration of the actors; having looked after his own business, he expected them to look after theirs. It may be that Christine Hebbel's interpretations contributed something to this attitude. It is certain that his passionate interest in character, evident in almost every aspect of his own technique as a dramatist, gave him the true measure for the actor's art.

[1] *Tagebücher*, ed. cit., vol. iii. 3943, 30 Jan. 1847, and Letter to Gustav Kühne, 28 Jan. 1847, *Briefe*, ed. cit., vol. iv, p. 5.

IX

CONCEPTION OF TRAGEDY

FOR the majority of critics, the central problem presented by Hebbel's dramatic art has been the problem of his self-consciousness as an artist. The relation of his dramatic theory to his dramas, the question of priority, has perhaps been over-emphasized, from the very fact that such a wealth of material exists to provide evidence for his mental processes. It is easy to let the diary and the correspondence weigh down the scales, more difficult to isolate the impressions that result from the dramas themselves. The idea of Hebbel as a speculative thinker, embodying metaphysical conceptions in dramatic form, frequently recurs, sometimes turning discussions of his plays into philosophic arguments. Even where this point is not reached, Hebbel's characters are often enough considered less for their dramatic value than as exponents of a view which they are held to represent. The poet's own statements, there is no doubt, often tend to create an impression of a calculated intellectual basis to his dramas, of a reflective process that conditions their development. But in estimating the value of these statements, two facts must not be overlooked. The entries concerning a given drama are in general subsequent to—or at most, contemporaneous with—the actual composition of the drama; rarely do we find (except as criticism of previous versions of a theme) reflections that precede the initial stages of dramatic creation. And, secondly, against the speculative reflections of a philosophic mind, there must be weighed other statements that Hebbel makes on the creative process. 'Dichten und Denken sind verschiedene Processe, einer schliesst den anderen aus, wie ich mehr und mehr erkenne',[1] he wrote to Elise in 1843; and five years later, on an occasion when the creative mood had been disturbed, he recorded in the diary: 'Man sollte vorsichtig werden; die Stimmung des Dichters hat zu viel vom

[1] Letter to Elise Lensing, 4 Apr. 1843, *Briefe*, ed. cit., vol. ii, p. 253.

Nachtwandeln, sie wird eben so leicht gestört, wie der Traum-Zustand, worin diess geschieht. Sonderbar ist es, dass ich in einer solchen Stimmung immer Melodieen höre, und das, was ich schreibe, darnach absinge. . . .'[1] A similar statement is made in a letter to Kolbenheyer in 1854: 'Denn das dramatische Produciren ist nun einmal ein Traum- und Nachtwandeln, welches sich von allem anderen Wandeln und Wandern dadurch unterscheidet, dass man einen und denselben Weg nicht zwei Mal machen kann';[2] while to his friend Uechtritz he explained the alternation in himself of creative activity and rest: '. . . bei mir [folgt] auf eine Zeit der Production immer eine andere der grössten Abspannung, in der es mir absolut unmöglich ist, aus mir selbst heraus zu gehen. Das war bei mir von Jugend auf der Fall; ich kenne nur Springfluten oder vollständige Ebben.'[3]

Hebbel well knew the difference between a philosophy of life and dramatic creation. Only fools, he wrote in 1842, would banish metaphysics from the drama: 'Aber es ist ein grosser Unterschied, ob sich die Metaphysik aus dem Leben entwickelt, oder ob umgekehrt sich das Leben aus der Metaphysik entwickeln soll'.[4] 'Die Poesie ist Leben, nicht Denken, Umkleiden, nicht Skalpiren. . .',[5] he writes on another occasion; and in a letter to Engländer of 1863, he proclaims once again his poetic independence:

'Sie wissen, dass ich zu dem Stück [*Gyges und sein Ring*] kam, wie der Knabe zum Vogel; er fängt ihn, weil er gerade da sitzt, und sieht sich ihn erst näher an, wenn er ihn in der Hand hat, um zu erfahren, was es für ein Kerl ist. Sie wissen aber nicht, dass es mit allen meinen Stücken so ging und werden mir diess jetzt auf mein ehrliches Wort wohl glauben. Der Maria Magdalena z. B.... liegt ein Vorfall zu Grunde, den ich in München selbst erlebte.... Da wurde der dramatische "Fehde-Handschuh" gesponnen, wenn

[1] *Tagebücher*, ed. cit., vol. iii. 4435, 22 Aug. 1848.
[2] Letter to Moritz Kolbenheyer, 13 June 1854, *Briefe*, ed. cit., vol. v, p. 164.
[3] Letter to Friedrich von Uechtritz, 19 Mar. 1855, *Briefe*, ed. cit., vol. v, p. 219. Cp. also a previous letter to Uechtritz, 14 Dec. 1854, *Briefe*, ed. cit., vol. v, p. 203.
[4] *Tagebücher*, ed. cit., vol. ii. 2605, 7 Oct. 1842.
[5] Ibid. 2947, 19 Dec. 1843.

auch nicht gleich gewoben, den ich nach Hermann Hettner der ganzen Europäischen Gesellschaft hingeworfen haben soll. . . .'[1]

Thus, if Hebbel's own statements are to count, his reiterated emphasis on the unconscious nature of the creative process cannot be disregarded; we must conclude that he was well aware, in himself, of the separation between reflective thought and imaginative realization.

But if, as Hebbel maintained—and his dramas bear out the statement if they are examined with an open mind—he first conceived individual characters in individual situations, he was irresistibly impelled to reflect upon them afterwards. He recognized, as they developed, further evidence of many conclusions he had come to about life, about the relations of men to their environment. Hailing fresh proofs as he perceived them, he would note with ardour the ideas on man and man's destiny that they reinforced; seizing on that which could most easily be embodied in logical form, he was perpetually endeavouring to formulate, from his poetic intuitions, an ordered statement of man's relation to the cosmos. So a 'theory of tragedy' may be constructed from his critical essays, and (above all) from the entries in the journal; but Hebbel's tragedies are not rightly to be judged thereby. The dramatic theory should rather be tested by the dramas, than the dramas be measured by the critical reflections of their author. Theory and practice may, and often do, coincide; but their identity must not be assumed. Hebbel was, after all, a poet and a dramatist, and it is in the light of his more important achievement as an artist that his theory of art should be considered.[2] He had a naturally inquiring mind,

[1] Letter to Sigmund Engländer, 23 Feb. 1863, *Briefe*, ed. cit., vol. vii, pp. 302–3.

[2] It may seem superfluous to insist upon an argument so elementary. But the tide of Hebbel criticism has set so strongly in a metaphysical direction that emphasis upon his dramatic view of life seems necessary. Such statements as the following would appear to assume the paramount importance of Hebbel's philosophical ideas: 'Hebbels System, der Pantragismus, ist eine einseitig auf das Drama zugeschnittene Welt- und Kunstanschauung' (A. Scheunert, *Der Pantragismus als System der Weltanschauung und Ästhetik Friedrich Hebbels*, Hamburg u. Leipzig, 1903, p. 10); 'Dass [Hebbels] poetische Schöpfungen als höchst wichtige, aufklärende Beispiele für die von ihm aufgestellten Lehren zu verwerten sind, ist selbstverständlich' (op. cit., p. 17); 'Das Ziel der vorliegenden

and the whole trend of his age was towards observation and analysis; these two facts serve to explain the wealth of comment and criticism in his personal papers and in his correspondence.[1]

The centre of Hebbel's critical reflections is his conviction that human life is fundamentally tragic. While his dramas present the fate of the individual, proof and illustration of this intense personal conviction, his dramatic theory consists in the attempt to present the world drama as a whole. He was constantly endeavouring to relate the tragic experience of the human soul to a larger process, which should illumine and justify such experience. His 'theory of tragedy' is thus a series of conclusions drawn from observation of the reactions of men to the world in which they live. By temperament and circumstance combined, Hebbel was peculiarly open to tragic experience, and its necessity was his abiding conviction; for him, tragic art illuminated and transformed the isolated suffering of the individual by revealing this underlying necessity. The persistent sense of warring forces, irreconcilable and ever-present, governed Hebbel's picture of the world and human life: he knew them in his own person, as experience that could not be evaded. He saw life as a conflict of the individual against surrounding circumstance, and visualized in varying images the battle of which he was so keenly conscious. 'Alles Leben ist Kampf des Individuellen mit dem Universum'.[2] 'Das Leben ist der grosse Strom, die Individualitäten sind Tropfen, die tragischen aber Eisstücke, die wieder zerschmolzen werden müssen und sich, damit dies möglich sey, an einander abreissen und zerstossen'.[3] 'Leben

Untersuchung war es . . . zu zeigen, wie das gesamte Hebbelsche Gedankensystem von einer alles befruchtenden Grundidee ausgehend, unabhängig von fremden Einflüssen, sich organisch aus sich selbst entwickelt, um schliesslich in einem neuen Dramatypus dem Ganzen den krönenden Abschluss zu geben' (F. Zinkernagel, *Die Grundlagen der Hebbelschen Tragödie*, Berlin, 1904, p. v).

[1] It may here be noted that Hebbel's critical essays embody ideas which are, for the most part, expressed more clearly in the *Tagebücher*, where he wrote naturally and freely; entries in the diary are therefore chosen for quotation, wherever possible, in preference to the more involved and elaborate statements in the formal essays.

[2] *Tagebücher*, ed. cit., vol. ii. 2129, 13 Sept. 1840.

[3] Ibid. 2664, 6 Mar. 1843.

ist Verharren im Angemessenen', he writes to Emil Rousseau. 'Ein Theil des Lebens ist *Ufer* (Gott und Natur) ein anderer (Mensch und Menschheit) ist *Strom*. Wo und wie spiegeln sie sich, tränken und durchdringen sie sich gegenseitig? Dies scheint mir die grosse Frage von Anbeginn, die dem Dichter der Genius vorlegt'.[1] And in a letter to Rousseau's sister in 1843, he indicates the function of tragic art: 'Das Leben ist eine furchtbare Nothwendigkeit, die auf Treu und Glauben angenommen werden muss, die aber Keiner begreift, und die tragische Kunst, die, indem sie das individuelle Leben der Idee gegenüber vernichtet, sich zugleich darüber erhebt, ist der leuchtendste Blitz des menschlichen Bewusstseyns, der aber freilich Nichts erhellen kann, was er nicht zugleich verzehrte'.[2]

The individual, in Hebbel's conception of the world-drama, is irresistibly driven to assert those qualities which make him individual. But this emphasis, this self-assertion, is incompatible with the preservation of a general balance; and herein lies the necessity for tragedy. The stronger the character, the more inevitably must the conflict between the two interests arise; the higher the differentiation of the individual, the more certain is his defeat. 'Die Helden stürzen, weil sie sich überheben'.[3] 'Maasslosigkeit' is the inevitable guilt incurred by the tragic individual in his relation to the whole;[4] and the universe is necessarily victor in the involuntary contest.

This belief was not held without a struggle. 'Wozu dieser Fluch der Kraft?' Hebbel, himself a strong man, cries in 1842.[5] 'Was ist das? Sobald der Mensch sich fühlt und sich aufrichtet, empfindet er etwas, wie einen Druck von oben, und doch lebt er nur so weit, als er sich fühlt. Es ist, als ob er sich aus einem Abgrund erhöbe und von unbekannter Hand immer wieder hinein gestossen würde.'[6] But the tempera-

[1] Letter to Emil Rousseau, 30 Dec. 1836, *Briefe*, ed. cit., vol. i, p. 140.

[2] Letter to Charlotte Rousseau, 7 July 1843, *Briefe*, ed. cit., vol. ii, p. 272, and *Tagebücher*, ed. cit., vol. ii. 2721.

[3] Ibid. 2578, 29 July 1842.

[4] Ibid. 3158, 13 June 1844.

[5] Ibid. 2578, 29 July 1842.

[6] Ibid. 2078, 13 Aug. 1840.

mental conviction was reinforced by observation and experience. On the one hand, the poet—child of a century whose main discoveries were the fruit of close and dispassionate scrutiny of facts—examined the selective processes of the natural world and saw their issue: 'Das Gute selbst kann Feind des Guten seyn, die Rose kann die Lilie verdrängen wollen, Beide sind existenzberechtigt, aber nur Eins hat Existenz.'[1] The processes of Nature continue, while the single existence is submerged. Like autumn leaves that early fall and wither, but fertilize the products of a new year, so the life of the individual contributes to that of the universe; and as the leaf that falls is of little account in the total sum, so too is the man who suffers: 'der Baum hat der Blätter im Ueberfluss und die Welt der Menschen'.[2] In such an image Hebbel saw the general relation of individual effort to the whole. And his own experience, both in conflict with circumstances and in a tragic sex-relationship, revealed to him a mode of individual self-assertion. A temperamental inability to compromise, a continuous early struggle for existence, and Hebbel's relation with Elise Lensing, formed the basis of experience from which sprang his conception of tragedy.

It is in the relations of the individual effort to the world-process, and in those of individual men and women to each other, that the tragic conflict manifests itself in Hebbel's dramas. In either case, the tragic guilt of the individual is the same. Judith and Holofernes, Mariamne and Herodes, Golo and Kandaules, transgress their limitations and incur the penalty. All these, in varying degree, are guilty of a tragic self-assertion. But such characters as Genoveva, Agnes Bernauer, Klara, or Rhodope, do not actively provoke their fate. In placing these as central figures in their dramas, Hebbel widens the range of tragic character and tragic conflict. Their tragic guilt consists in their outstanding quality; by virtue of this alone they invite their destiny. Genoveva's charity, Agnes Bernauer's beauty, are as abnormal as Holofernes' strength or Golo's passion; and all incur a tragic fate.

[1] *Tagebücher*, ed. cit., vol. i. 1823, 7 Dec. 1839.
[2] *Tagebücher*, ed. cit., vol. ii. 2881, 21 Nov. 1843.

Thus not only the fight against outward circumstance, not only the battle of good and evil in the human soul, but the conflict of good with good, the sacrifice and downfall of the innocent, are Hebbel's tragic themes. Tragic guilt and ethical guilt need not be identical. Such a figure as that of Agnes Bernauer is an extreme type of the innocent victim, whose only flaw is an excess of quality; the very characteristics of beauty and integrity that raise her above the average human level render her death more inevitable in the given situation.

Such tragic themes as that of *Herodes und Mariamne*—the conflict of two dominant natures—strike us perhaps as more familiar than those of this second type, where the central figure contributes less actively to the catastrophe. There is little doubt that the spectacle of such passive suffering as that of Agnes, Klara, or Genoveva corresponds to those problems of undeserved misfortune and innocent sacrifice which proclaim themselves insistently in human life. But in their effort to present the picture of an ordered universe, the poet and the dramatist have for the most part chosen characters in situations where the connexion between action and catastrophe is closer—the very term 'poetic justice' bears witness to such a connexion.

It is here that Hebbel's vision of the world is most clearly conditioned by the age in which he lived. Much has been said of the relation between his conception of the world-order and contemporary philosophic thought.[1] But it is at least equally close to the scientific thought of the mid-nineteenth century, when scientist and social historian alike were emphasizing the relations of man to his environment and the influence of that environment upon his personal life. In both fields of observation there is a common spectacle: highly differentiated individuals, while they may ultimately contribute to the advancement of the type, or of the community,

[1] In the diary for 1844, Hebbel noted his discovery that Hegel's conception of tragic guilt was like his own. 'Hätt' ich's gewusst', he adds, 'als ich gegen Herrn Heiberg schrieb!' (*Tagebücher*, ed. cit., vol. ii. 3088 (and *Anmerkung*), 25 Mar. 1844). He had already written *Genoveva* and *Maria Magdalena* when this entry was made.

may themselves be compelled, by their very individual quality, to succumb before the pressure of the average. Thus the individual unit that is far in advance of the normal type may be doomed to immediate failure, though its ultimate value may be great, apart from individual failure or success. Development, in fact, proceeds by the preservation of 'balance in Nature': the continuance of any living organism depends upon the maintenance of a delicate equilibrium.[1]

Hebbel's dramas, presenting a stern vision of humanity at grips with a relentless process, imply a similar picture of balance in the cosmos. He was little concerned with the average individual, who by compromise and caution leads a sheltered life—little interested in spiritual safety. He was, on the contrary, passionately concerned with those who walk dangerously, who disturb the balance and incur the penalty. Excess, of whatever kind, brings retribution. Herodes, dominant in virtue of his spacious conceptions and his strength, is immoderate in his disregard of the personality of others. Agnes, equally dominant in virtue of her qualities, also oversets the balance, and pays toll with her life for being what she is. Her relation to her age and type determine her doom; guiltless in any ethical sense, she is a source of danger to the

[1] In this connexion two passages may be quoted from an early nineteenth-century biologist, which suggest an interesting, though probably a fortuitous parallel: 'Bewegung ist Stöhrung des Gleichgewichts entgegengesetzter Kräfte. Diese Stöhrung aber ist nur dadurch möglich, dass die eine der letztern wächst, indem die andere abnimmt' (G. R. Treviranus, *Biologie*, vol. i, pp. 28–9, Göttingen, 1802). Applying this to a general conception of development, the author continues: 'Hat die Zufälligkeit der äussern Einwirkungen, bey welchen die eigenthümliche Thätigkeit der lebenden Organismen unverändert fortdauert, Gränzen, und zieht jede Uebertretung dieser Gränzen die Zerstöhrung jener Organismen nach sich, so ist zwar keine *fortdauernde* Stöhrung des allgemeinen Organismus von Seiten eines lebenden Individuums möglich. Allein schon die *erste* Uebertretung dieser Gränzen wird Unordnungen in dem erstern nach sich ziehen. . . . Wir müssen annehmen, *dass jede Abweichung eines lebenden Individuums von der zur Erhaltung des allgemeinen Organismus nöthigen Thätigkeit eine entgegengesetzte Veränderung desselben nach sich zieht, und dass die auf die Uebertretung der erwähnten Gränzen folgende Zerstöhrung eines Individuums immer durch diese entgegengesetzte Veränderung geschieht.* Ein Uebermass von Thätigkeit muss durch ein Minus, ein Minus durch ein Plus, und *eine* anomalische Abweichung derselben durch eine andere, nach entgegengesetzter Richtung gehende anomalische Abweichung wieder gut gemacht werden' (*op. cit.*, vol. i, pp. 67–8). This work of Treviranus was published in parts between 1802 and 1822.

whole. The idea of guilt that is not sin, of flaw that is not fault, is one familiar to the later conception of evolution; it also issues naturally, and almost unavoidably, from Hebbel's picture of balance in the cosmic process. Thus tragic guilt implies that the individual stands in a relation to his environment that renders compromise impossible. This relation may involve widely varying degrees of personal ethical responsibility: the essential factor is that it should admit of no alternative. 'Nothwendigkeit', as Hebbel terms it, is identical with tragic guilt. In the moment when an individual disturbs or deviates from the normal order by an assertion of supernormal character, a reaction is necessitated, an opposing force must restore the balance: 'die auf die Uebertretung der . . . Gränzen folgende Zerstöhrung eines Individuums geschieht immer durch diese entgegengesetzte Veränderung.'[1]

If Hebbel's conception of tragic fate resembles the conclusions of a scientific observer, watching the selective processes of the natural world, the answer that he suggests to our demand for justice, or compensation, offers a further parallel. He points away from the individual to the general process. The majority of his characters do not attain to inner harmony. Holofernes is murdered in his power, and Judith remains, with her problem unsolved. Klara sacrifices herself to save her father, but she gropes in the dark for any other justification of her doom: 'Wär's um mich allein—ich wollt's ja tragen, ich wollt's geduldig hinnehmen, als verdiente Strafe für, *ich weiss nicht was*, wenn die Welt mich in meinem Elend mit Füssen träte, statt mir beizustehen. . . . Aber ich bin's nicht allein, und leichter find' ich am jüngsten Tag noch eine Antwort auf des Richters Frage: warum hast Du Dich selbst umgebracht? als auf die: warum hast Du Deinen Vater so weit getrieben?' (III. 2). Herodes, unchanged by tragic experience, clings but the more firmly to that despotic power which betrayed him into dealing a mortal injury to Mariamne. Agnes Bernauer, choosing death rather than the renunciation of Albrecht's love, questions in her last words the justice of her sentence: 'Thut mir, wie Ihr müsst und dürft, ich will's

[1] G. R. Treviranus, loc. cit.

leiden. Bald weiss ich, ob's mit Recht geschah! (V. 3). These figures, considered by themselves, suggest no sense of harmony.

Mariamne, on the other hand, chooses death deliberately, seeing in it both vengeance and the solution of her own problem. By following this deep instinct of her being, by leaving to Herodes a legacy of remorse to avenge her injured spirit, she may perhaps be said to attain a kind of harmony within herself, as she meets death with stoic pride. In the logic of her action she finally asserts the value of her personality. In a different manner, Golo, too, arrives at a solution, when he chooses death as an atonement for his crime against Genoveva.

But such a measure of self-harmony is not generally portrayed in Hebbel's tragic characters. Only in one drama—*Gyges und sein Ring*—do we find all the chief actors arriving at a solution of their problem. Hebbel was indeed convinced that harmony, or 'Versöhnung' was to be sought elsewhere than in the individual character. Beyond and above the individual case, in the unity and continuity of the whole process, he sees the reconciliation of the tragic dissonance. 'Die Versöhnung im Tragischen geschieht im Interesse der *Gesammtheit*, nicht in dem des *Einzelnen*, des Helden. . . .'[1] he wrote in 1843; and fifteen months later: 'Dass in der dramatischen Kunst die Versöhnung immer über den Kreis des speciellen Dramas hinaus fällt, werden Wenige begreifen.'[2] For a rhetorical glossing over of the tragic catastrophe he had no use; early in 1843 he wrote of Oehlenschläger: 'Er will Versöhnung im Drama—wer will sie nicht? Ich kann sie nur darin nicht finden, dass der Held, oder der Dichter für ihn, seine gefalteten Hände über die Wunde legt und sie dadurch verdeckt!'[3]—a characteristically uncompromising utterance. 'Es ist thörigt', he wrote a little later, 'von dem Dichter das zu verlangen, was Gott selbst nicht darbietet, Versöhnung und Ausgleichung der Dissonanzen. Aber allerdings kann man fodern, dass er die Dissonanzen selbst gebe und nicht in

[1] *Tagebücher*, ed. cit., vol. ii. 2664, 6 Mar. 1843.

[2] Ibid. 3168, 25 June 1844.

[3] Ibid. 2635, 5 Jan. 1843.

der Mitte zwischen dem Zufälligen und dem Nothwendigen stehen bleibe. So darf er jeden Character zu Grunde gehen lassen, aber er muss uns zugleich zeigen, dass der Untergang unvermeidlich, dass er, wie der Tod, mit der Geburt selbst gesetzt ist'.[1]

By temperament and conviction, Hebbel saw the life of the individual as an essentially tragic phenomenon. By its force, the single unit contributes to the forward movement of the whole, but is itself submerged. There *is* a balance that gives meaning to the cosmic process; but only in the contemplation of the whole can the tragedy of the individual be seen in a perspective which reveals its purpose and significance. The wound, Hebbel writes, can only be healed 'durch den Nachweis, dass sie für die erhöhte Gesundheit nothwendig war'.[2]

'Diejenigen, die vom Tragödien-Dichter verlangen, dass er nicht bloss die sittliche Idee retten, sondern zugleich auch den Helden vor dem Untergang bewahren soll, fordern eigentlich etwas eben so Unvernünftiges, als wenn sie vom Arzt verlangten, dass er den Organismus nicht bloss von einer Krankheit befreien, sondern die Krankheit selbst auch, als eine individuelle Modification des allgemeinen Lebensprocesses, respectiren und also am Leben erhalten solle.'[3]

The mood of the scientific observer is here plainly to be recognized.

Thus, though Judith and Holofernes are both in their different ways defeated, Bethulia, the Hebrew city, is saved. Though Genoveva's tragic suffering continues and Golo dies in torment, his deliberate choice of death suggests the vindication of fundamental human values. If Klara's actual sacrifice was vain, the motive force of love inspiring it is vital to the world, and 'Maria Magdalena' indicates its meaning. Though neither Mariamne nor Herodes solves the problem presented by their relationship, the pageant-like passing of the Kings of Orient heralds a new world to which Herodes, with all his tenacious grasp of power, must yield. And when

[1] *Tagebücher*, ed. cit., vol. ii, 2776, 29 Aug. 1843.
[2] Ibid. 2845, 11 Nov. 1843.
[3] *Tagebücher*, ed. cit., vol. iii, 3892, 10 Jan. 1847.

Siegfried and Brunhild, in their abnormal strength and courage, have wrought each other's doom, and Kriemhild, transformed into a destroying Fury, has been herself destroyed, Dietrich survives to usher in a new order, and suggests the victory of the world-process as it fulfils itself.

It has often been asserted that in this final suggestion of the relation between individual suffering and the larger process Hebbel was superimposing on the dramatic situation a metaphysical idea. But the implied reproach can hardly be maintained in face of the profound dramatic effect produced by the concluding scenes of *Herodes und Mariamne* and *Die Nibelungen.* The poet here was far from being led astray by the speculative critic: on the contrary, he triumphantly justifies, in these swift, suggestive scenes, his own imaginative power.

Two of Hebbel's major dramas suggest the solution of the dramatic problem in a different way. In *Agnes Bernauer* a logical reconciliation is offered at the end; in *Gyges und sein Ring* the tragic characters themselves attain to inner harmony through sacrifice. There is a striking contrast in the effect of the two plays. Both solutions rest on the recognition of tragic guilt; but whereas Albrecht yields to a logical argument after the death of Agnes—the innocent sacrifice—Rhodope, Gyges, and Kandaules all come to recognize before the end that their personal desires must be surrendered. Kandaules acknowledges his fault and atones for it with his life; Gyges expiates his half-unwitting crime by obedience to Rhodope's will; Rhodope herself fulfils the sacrifice by choosing death when atonement has been made. In Hebbel's other great dramas, the balance is restored by the cosmic process, overpowering or disregarding the wills of men: it is the world-process that inevitably conquers, though in the strength of the individual opposing it lies the basic value of human life. But in *Gyges und sein Ring* the spirit of man, transcending its limitation of one-sidedness, aids the restoration of harmony by an active recognition of governing necessity. Herein lies man's essential freedom—to acquiesce voluntarily in the laws that condition the world-process. By this acquiescence the tragic individual can arrive at the inner solution of his problem; the human mind can attain, through tragic experience, a serene and perfect poise.

It is not insignificant that *Gyges und sein Ring* is the first of Hebbel's dramas to create this impression of attained serenity. With that unswerving honesty which was the native characteristic of his mind, he refused to suggest a solution until he had experienced it. 'Ich weiss nicht, ob ich mich irre', he wrote in 1847, 'aber mir däucht es eine Sünde wider den heiligen Geist der Wahrheit, wenn der Dichter seinem Kunstwerk eine Versöhnung mit der menschlichen Situation und den Weltzuständen überhaupt, einzuhauchen sucht, von der er selbst noch fern ist. Mir scheint, dass das Kunstwerk dann jeden Werth verliert.'[1] By 1854, the year of Elise Lensing's death, the tragic relation which had filled his early years as a dramatist had also reached solution. The mark of that relation is plainly visible in Hebbel's earlier dramas. The individual conflict is felt in terms of sex; here the poet himself knew, in its acutest form, the will to power, the encroachment of one personality upon another, the assertion of the individual right to be. The expiation (if expiation were appropriate) of Hebbel's relations with Elise Lensing might well be found in the stern conception of tragedy which possessed his mind—and were it so, she might rest satisfied with such a monument.

But there is a distinct progression in the line of Hebbel's heroines. Judith in her active transgression of a woman's sphere, Genoveva and Klara in their feminine role of passive sufferers, arouse less interest and admiration than does the commanding figure of Mariamne, who both acts and suffers. Agnes, even more completely a passive heroine than Klara, is yet a more absorbing personality. In Rhodope, her immediate successor, Hebbel's ideal of womanhood seems to be expressed; and if the poet's experience with Elise Lensing is of paramount importance for his choice of tragic themes, his marriage to Christine Enghaus would equally seem to have had no small influence on his portrayal of feminine character. Rhodope presents, more fully than any other of

[1] *Tagebücher*, ed. cit., vol. iii. 4150, 19 Apr. 1847.

his heroines, Hebbel's conception of purely feminine qualities. Her weapons are not found in any other armoury; her logic does not belong to any system of philosophy. Her intuition is certain, her knowledge innate; and she convinces by the very absence of all argument. In no way does she transgress her limitations as a woman and as an individual: and it is by following her own deep feeling that she brings both Gyges and Kandaules to appreciate it, and obey her will.

Kriemhild in *Die Nibelungen* is a militant character in the fullest sense. But her activity, violating all bounds of sex and nature, belonged to the data provided by the *Nibelungenlied*, and Hebbel had less freedom here than in the creation of any other female character. Thus she belongs to the group of active combatants; but the dramatist shows her developing, under the most cruel stress, from a gentle woman into a being of abnormal stature and gigantic will, possessed of only one idea. By this excessive development of the individual will, Kriemhild too invites her fate; she is struck down by the hand of a vassal, crudely stirred to action by her unnatural deeds of vengeance. By a kind of inversion, she represents Hebbel's deep conviction: 'Durch Dulden Thun: Idee des Weibes'.[1] 'Im Gemüth', he wrote later, 'wurzelt die Kraft des [weiblichen] Geschlechts'.[2]

Thus from Judith to Rhodope, the heroines of Hebbel's major dramas emphasize ethical values. In *Demetrius*, for the first time, the women characters are of less moment than the hero. The problem of Demetrius must be solved by him alone; Marina does not, Marfa cannot, aid him in his inner conflict. It is at least conceivable that *Gyges und sein Ring* marked the close of Hebbel's long preoccupation with feminine character and the dualism of sex; that in the sympathy that is finally attained, in their several relations, between Gyges, Kandaules, and Rhodope, the poet too found peace.

'Die Ideen sind im Drama dasselbe, was der Contra-Punct in der Musik; Nichts an sich, aber Grundbedingung für

[1] *Tagebucher*, ed. cit., vol. i. 1516, 24 Feb. 1839.
[2] *Tagebücher*, ed. cit., vol. iii. 3635, 30 June 1846.

Alles.'[1] Hebbel could hardly have summed up more exactly than in this observation the characteristic of his dramatic work—the relation of the conscious to the unconscious artist. In the fascinating pursuit of observing his subtle mind assimilating and converting its experience, we may be tempted to forget that the second process of the two took place in the depths, where it could not be recorded. But the tragedies, if they are allowed to speak in their own tongue, will vindicate the dramatic poet. Through character and situation Hebbel offers us a vision of humanity at odds with fate—the picture of the universe as he saw it with a poet's eyes. That he was primarily attracted by the abnormal character and the unusual situation is undeniable; but by virtue of his own experience and a profound imaginative mind, he endowed them with a wider significance, suggesting the universal in the individual instance. '... Der dramatische Dichter', he wrote '[muss] sich in demselben Sinn auf jede Species menschlicher Charactere einlassen, wie der Naturforscher auf jede Thier- und Pflanzengattung, gleichviel, ob sie schön oder hässlich, giftig oder heilsam ist, indem er die Totalität darzustellen hat!'[2] The characters of his tragedies, from Judith to Demetrius, go far to substantiate this claim.

The universal process, as Hebbel sees it, is stern and unrelenting; the individual life is of little moment in the course of Nature and of human history. The Dithmarschen mason's poet son knew that the world was no forcing-house for tender plants; but he arrived, after great travail, at a belief in the abiding value of effort. 'Wir müssen nicht klagen, dass Alles vergänglich sey. Das Vergänglichste, wenn es uns wahrhaft berührt, weckt in uns ein Unvergängliches'.[3] An intuitive certainty rather than a logical conclusion, this early belief was the mainspring of Hebbel's personal life; in his life's work its justification may be found.

[1] *Tagebücher*, ed. cit., vol. iv. 5695, 1 Apr. 1859.
[2] *Tagebücher*, ed. cit., vol. iii. 4908, 27 June 1851.
[3] *Tagebücher*, ed. cit., vol. i. 585, 17 Jan. 1837.

I. CHRONOLOGICAL LIST OF DRAMAS

Title.	*Date of Completion.*	*Publication.*	*Date of first Performance.*
Judith.	28 Jan. 1840. (*Tagebücher*, ed. cit., ii. 1893.)	(a) *Judith.* Ein *Trauerpiel* (*sic*) in drei Acten. 'Als Manuscript gedruckt'. 1840. (b) *Judith.* Eine Tragödie in fünf Acten. Hamburg, 1841.	6 July 1840. Berlin. Hoftheater.
Genoveva.	1 Mar. 1841. (*Tb.*, ed. cit., ii. 2282.)	*Genoveva.* Eine Tragödie in fünf Acten. Hamburg, 1843.	13 May 1849. Prag (translated). 20 Jan. 1854. Wien. Burgtheater ('Magellona').
Der Diamant.	29 Nov. 1841. (*Tb.* ed. cit., ii. 2392.)	*Der Diamant.* Eine Komödie in fünf Acten. Hamburg, 1847.	1852. Kremsier.
Maria Magdalena.	4 Dec. 1843. (*Tb.*, ed. cit., ii. 2910.)	*Maria Magdalene.*[1] Ein bürgerliches Trauerspiel in drei Akten. Hamburg, 1844.	13 Mar. 1846. Königsberg.
Ein Trauerspiel in Sizilien.	9 Jan. 1847. (*Tb.*, ed. cit., iii. 3890.)	In *Ausgewählte Romane, Novellen, Dramen, Erzählungen u. Gedichte*, Neue Folge, Iter Bd. Leipzig, 1847. No. 162. Bd. IV.	28 Oct. 1907. Hamburg. Deutsches Schauspielhaus.
Julia.	23 Oct. 1847. (*Tb.*, ed. cit., iii. 4312.)	*Julia.* Ein Trauerspiel in drei Acten. 'Als Manuscript für Bühnen'. Wien [1848].	1903. München. Schauspielhaus.
Herodes und Mariamne.	14 Nov. 1848. (*Tb.*, ed. cit., iii. 4461.)	*Herodes und Mariamne.* Eine Tragödie in fünf Acten. Wien, 1850.	19 Apr. 1849. Wien. Hofburgtheater.
Der Rubin.	19 May 1849. (*Tb.*, ed. cit., iii. 4592.)	*Der Rubin.* Ein Märchen-Lustspiel in drei Acten. Leipzig, 1851.	21 Nov. 1849. Wien. Hofburgtheater.
Michel Angelo.	18 Dec. 1850. (*Tb.*, ed. cit., iii. 4758.)	*Michel Angelo.* Ein Drama in zwei Akten. 'Manuscript für Bühnen'. (Prutz: *Deutsches Museum*, Leipzig, 1851).	1 Apr. 1861. Wien. Quaitheater.
Epilog zur Genoveva.	21 Jan. 1851. (*Tb.*, ed. cit., iii. 4811.)	In *Europa*. Chronik der gebildeten Welt. 19 Feb. 1852. Nr. 15.	(v. under *Genoveva.*)
Agnes Bernauer.	24 Dec. 1851. (*Tb.*, ed. cit., iii. 4982.)	*Agnes Bernauer.* Ein deutsches Trauerspiel in fünf Aufzügen. Wien, 1852.	25 Mar. 1852. München. Hoftheater.

[1] The form Magdalene appeared in the first edition and thus established itself. Hebbel himself refers to Maria Magdalena, with one exception, throughout the *Tagebücher*. v. also note in *Werke*, ed. cit., vol. ii (Lesarten u. Anmerkungen), p. 372.

Title.	*Date of Completion.*	*Publication.*	*Date of first Performance.*
Gyges und sein Ring.	14 Nov. 1854. (*Tb.*, ed. cit., iv. 5348.)	*Gyges und sein Ring.* Eine Tragödie in fünf Acten. Den Bühnen gegenüber Manuscript. Wien, 1856.	25 Apr. 1889. Wien. Hofburg-theater.
Die Nibelungen.	22 Mar. 1860. (*Tb.*, ed. cit., iv. 5798.)	*Die Nibelungen.* Ein deutsches Trauerspiel in drei Abtheilungen. Iter Bd. (*Der gehörnte Siegfried*, *Siegfrieds Tod*), Hamburg 1862. IIter Bd. (*Kriemhilds Rache*). Wien [1862].	I and II, 31 Jan. 1861. I and II, 16 May 1861. III, 18 May 1861, Weimar.
Demetrius.		*Demetrius.* Eine Tragödie (Nachgelassenes Werk). Hamburg, 1864.	

II. POEMS AND LYRICS

Gedichte. Hamburg, 1842.
Neue Gedichte. Leipzig, 1848.
Gedichte. Gesamt-Ausgabe stark vermehrt und verbessert. Stuttgart und Augsburg, 1857.
Mutter und Kind. Ein Gedicht in sieben Gesängen. Hamburg, 1859.

III. COLLECTED TALES

Erzählungen und Novellen. Pest, 1855.

Note.—For more detailed chronological information the reader is referred to H. Wütschke, *Hebbel-Bibliographie*, Berlin, 1910 (Veröffentlichungen der Deutschen Bibliographischen Gesellschaft, Bd. 6. 1907) and to *Werke*, ed. cit., vol. xii, pp. 404 ff. (Hebbel-Bibliothek.)

SELECT BIBLIOGRAPHY

I. *Works, Diaries, and Correspondence*

F. HEBBEL. *Sämtliche Werke.* Historisch-kritische Ausgabe besorgt von R. M. Werner. Berlin, 1901 ff.
Ite Abteilung: Werke. 12 vols.
IIte Abteilung: Tagebücher. 4 vols.
IIIte Abteilung: Briefe. 8 vols.

—— *Sämtliche Werke*, her. von H. Krumm. Hamburg, 1891–2. 12 vols.

Friedrich Hebbels Briefwechsel mit Freunden und berühmten Zeitgenossen, her. von F. Bamberg. Berlin, 1890–2. 2 vols.

Elise Lensing. Briefe an Friedrich und Christine Hebbel, her. von R. Kardel. Berlin und Leipzig, 1928.

Hebbel-Dokumente. Unveröffentlichtes aus dem Nachlass. her. von R. Kardel. Heide 1931.

II. *General*

BORNSTEIN, P. *Friedrich Hebbels Persönlichkeit.* Gespräche, Urteile, Erinnerungen. 2 vols. Berlin, 1924.

—— *Friedrich Hebbel.* Ein Bild seines Lebens, auf Grund der Zeugnisse entworfen. (Deutsche Buch-Gemeinschaft). Berlin.

—— *Hebbels 'Herodes und Mariamne'.* Vortrag. Hamburg und Leipzig, 1904.

CAMPBELL, T. M. *The Life and Works of F. Hebbel.* Boston, 1919.

DOSENHEIMER, E. *Das zentrale Problem in der Tragödie Friedrich Hebbels.* Halle, 1925.

EBHARDT, R. *Hebbel als Novellist.* Berlin, 1916.

GEORGY, E. A. *Die Tragödie Friedrich Hebbels nach ihrem Ideengehalt.* 2te Auflage. Leipzig, 1911.

—— *Das Tragische bei Friedrich Hebbel.* Leipzig, 1922.

GUBELMANN, A. *Studies in the Lyric Poems of Friedrich Hebbel.* New Haven, 1912.

Hebbel-Kalender für 1905. Ein Jahrbuch herausgegeben von R. M. Werner u. W. Block. Berlin, 1904.

KUH, E. *Biographie Friedrich Hebbels.* 3te unveränderte Auflage. Wien und Leipzig, 1912. 2 vols.

LAHNSTEIN, E. *Das Problem der Tragik in Hebbels Frühzeit.* Stuttgart, 1909.

LAHNSTEIN, E. *Hebbels Jugenddramen und ihre Probleme.* Berlin, 1911.

MEINCK, E. *Friedrich Hebbels und Richard Wagners Nibelungen-Trilogien.* (Breslauer Beiträge zur Literaturgeschichte, 5.) Leipzig, 1905.

MEYER-BENFEY, H. *Hebbels Dramen.* Göttingen, 1913.

PETSCH, R. *Zur Einführung in das Studium Friedrich Hebbels.* Germanisch-Romanische Monatsschrift, i. 1909 (pp. 20 ff.).

REES, G. B. *Friedrich Hebbel as a dramatic Artist.* London, 1930.

SCHEUNERT, A. *Der junge Hebbel.* Weltanschauung und früheste Jugendwerke. (Beiträge zur Ästhetik her. T. Lipps u. R.M. Werner, 12.) Hamburg und Leipzig, 1908.

SCHMITT, S. *Hebbels Dramatechnik.* (Schriften der Literarhistorischen Gesellschaft Bonn, 1.) Dortmund, 1907.

TIBAL, A. *Hebbel. Sa vie et ses œuvres de 1813 à 1845.* Paris, 1911.

WALZEL, O. *Hebbelprobleme.* Leipzig, 1909.

WERNER, R. M. *Hebbel. Ein Lebensbild.* (Geisteshelden 47/48). Berlin, 1905.

WÜTSCHKE, H. *Hebbel-Bibliographie.* (Veröffentlichungen der Deutschen Bibliographischen Gesellschaft, 6. 1907.) Berlin, 1910.

ZINKERNAGEL, F. *Die Grundlagen der Hebbelschen Tragödie.* Berlin, 1904.

INDEX

The principal references are in heavy type.

Bamberg, Felix, 97, 108, 110, 111, 122, 132, 134, 138, 140, 142, 143, 144, 189, 207.
'Beppy' (Josepha Schwarz), 25, 26, 27, 124, 125.
Bruyck, Karl Debrois van, 188, 190.

Campe, Hebbel's relations with, 27, 28, 48, 49, 56, 58, 59, 60, 61, 62, 93, 102, 103, 108, 123, 124, 129, 192.
Copenhagen, 62, 91, 92, 94, 95, 96, 103, 105, 113, 125.
— residence in, 92–4.
— Danish grant, 9, 62, 91, 94, 95, 98, 99, 101, 102, 104, 107.

Dethlefsen, Franz Christian, 5, 6.
Dingelstedt, Franz, Hebbel's relations with, 181, 187, 191.
Dithmarschen, 1, 2, 10, 93.
Dramatic production, unconscious nature of, 124, 193, 255–7, 269.
Dramatic technique, 67, 70, 72, 114, 143, 151, 153, 180, 214, 215, 228, 234, **235–54**.
— 'Analytic' technique, 119–20, 240, 241, 242, 243, 246.
— asides, 80, 248–9.
— exposition, 72, 215, 236, 237, 238, 240, 246.
— monologues, 74, 80, 85, 153, 154, 246–8.
— stage directions, 253–4.

Enghaus, Christine, *v.* Hebbel, Christine.
Engländer, Sigmund, Hebbel's relations with, 49, 124, 133, 183, 192, 228, 256.
Evolutionary process, relation of Hebbel's conception of tragedy to, 66, 86, **177–8,** 258, 259, 260, **261–3,** 264, 265, 266, 269.

Gmunden, Lake (Orth), Hebbel's home at, 44, 185, 186, 192, 212.
Goethe, 13, 38, 91, 101, 103, 194.
Gurlitt, Ludwig, Hebbel's relations with, 107, 108, 111, 112, 127.
Gutzkow, Hebbel's relations with, 28, 56.

Hamburg, 9, 10, 11, 19, 28, 30, 56, 57, 61, 62, 94, 95, 97, 99, 101, 102, 105, 107, 109, 110, 113, 130, 131, 137, 183, 192, 211.
Hamburg, first residence in, 12–16.
— return to, 30, 33, 34.
— second residence in, 56–62.
— third residence in, 94–6.
Hebbel, Anje Margarete, 2, 4–5, 6, 16, 29.
HEBBEL, CHRISTIAN FRIEDERICH:
Life:
material for, 2.
birth, 1, 2.
childhood, 2–6.
schooling, 4, 5.
apprenticeship to Kirchspielvogt, 6–7, 10, 11.
first residence in Hamburg, 12–16.
connexion with Elise Lensing, **14–15, 30–4, 58–9, 75–6,** 95, 96, 97, **98–107, 109–10, 111–13, 129–32, 183–4.**
residence in Heidelberg, 16–19.
residence in Munich, 19–34.
second residence in Hamburg, 56–62.
residence in Copenhagen, 92–4.
third residence in Hamburg, 94–6.
residence in Paris, 96–103.
residence in Italy, 103–10.
arrival in Vienna, 110.
marriage to Christine Enghaus, 113.
mode of life in Vienna, 127, 128, 134, 181, 182, 188, 192.
connexion with the Burgtheater, 127, 135, 136, 181, 183, 191, 192.
summer residence on Lake Gmunden, 185, 192.
approach of last illness, 192–3.
death, 193.
Works:
Abfertigung eines ästhetischen Kannegiessers, 137.
Aufzeichnungen aus meinem Leben, 2, 3.
Agnes Bernauer, 86, 138, **170–80,** 181, 182, 183, 205, 237, 238, 239, 247, 248, 250, 252, 260, 261, 262, 263, 266, 267, 270.
von Törring's *Agnes Bernauerinn*, 172.
Demetrius, 187, 188, 193, **229–34,** 235, 237, 239, 240, 247, 250, 252, 268, 269, 271.
Schiller's *Demetrius*, 187, 229, 233–4.
Der deutsche Philister, 23.
Der Diamant, 23, 24, 60, 61, **88–91,** 125, 132, 139, 169, 187, 270.
Prolog, **89–91.**

Hebbel, Christian Friederich
Works (*contd.*):
Der Rubin (comedy), 54, 136, 138, **168–70,** 270.
Der Steinwurf oder *Opfer um Opfer*, 187.
Die Nibelungen, 127, 179, 184, 185, 186, 187, 188, 191, 192, 193, 194, 208, 209, **212–29,** 230, 234, 236, 237, 238, 243–4, 245, 246, 248, 249, 250, 251, 252, 253, 254, 266, 268, 271.
Nibelungenlied, 184, 186, 209, 212, 213, 214, 223, 227, 228, 229, 238.
Prolog, 127–8, 212, 213.
Raupach's *Nibelungenhort*, 127, 213.
Wagner's *Der Ring des Nibelungen*, 223.
Ein Trauerspiel in Sizilien, 113, 132, 137, **138–40,** 143, 270.
Genoveva, 24, 25, 58, 59, 61, **73–88,** 121, 143, 144, 171, 175, 176, 183, 187, 198, 205, 238, 239, 241, 244, 247, 249, 250, 260, 261, 264, 265, 267, 270.
'Maler' Müller's *Golo und Genoveva*, 25, 74, 75, 76.
Raupach's *Genoveva*, 59.
Tieck's *Leben und Tod der heiligen Genoveva*, 74, 75, 76, 77, 86.
Nachspiel zu Genoveva, 84, **87–8,** 138, 175, 239, 270.
Gyges und sein Ring, 44, 124, 138, 144, 166, 168, 170, 174, 175, 179, 182, 183, 184, 186, 193, **194–208,** 212, 228, 229, 233, 236, 237, 239, 240, 247, 248, 249, 250, 251, 256, 260, 264, 266, 267, 268, 271.
Herodotus' version, 195, 196, 198, 199, 202, 205.
Herodes und Mariamne, 55, 59, 133, 134, 135, 136, 137, 138, 143, **144–68,** 170, 171, 174, 175, 179, 194, 195, 196, 205, 212, 226, 229, 236, 238, 240, 241, 242, 243, 244, 245, 247, 248, 249, 251, 253, 260, 261, 262, 263, 264, 265, 266, 267, 270.
Josephus' version, 145, **146–8,** 149, 150, 151.
Judith, 23, 24, 25, 49, 57, 58, 59, **63–73,** 74, 86, 88, 96, 110, 113, 114, 127, 135, 143, 144, 151, 171, 175, 179, 187, 234, 235, 237, 238, 243, 247, 248, 249, 250, 252, 260, 263, 265, 267, 268, 269, 270.
apocryphal tale, 63–4, 66, 74.
Jungfrau von Orleans, 22, 23, 65.
Napoleon, 24–5, 65.
theatre version, 57, 73, 96, 135.
Julia, 108, 113, 132, 135, 136, 137, 138, **140–3,** 270.
Lyric poems, 7, 8, 9, 10, 13, 18, 24, 27, 28, **35–46,** 56, 60, 62, 91, 93, 100, 108, 109, 133, 181, 186, 187, 212, 271.
ballad form, 36, 37, 41, 42, 43.
Maria Magdalena, 3, 24, 44, 47, 61, 88, 93, 94, 97, 101, 102, 103, 107, **113–22,** 123, **124–6,** 132, 135, 138, 140, 143, 144, 175, 179, 187, 205, 235, 236, 239, 240, 241, 243, 246, 247, 248, 250, 252, 256, 260, 261, 263, 265, 267, 270.
Vorwort, 102, 122–4, 125, 138.
Mein Wort über das Drama (and *Ein Wort über das Drama*), 95, 96, 123.
Michel Angelo, 137, 138, 270.
Moloch, 61, 125, 136.
Mutter und Kind, 185, 186, 187, **209–12,** 271.
Novellen, 18, 22, 35, **46–55,** 89, 133, 140, 271.
Anna, **47,** 48, 49.
Barbier Zitterlein, 22, **46–7,** 48, 49.
Der Rubin, 48, 49, 54, 168.
Der Schneidermeister Nepomuk Schlägel auf der Freudenjagd, 48, 49, **51,** 89.
Die beiden Vagabunden, 48, 49.
Die Kuh, 48, 49, **54–5.**
Die Obermedicinalräthin, 48.
Ein Abend in Strassburg, 48.
Eine Nacht im Jägerhause, 47, 48, 49, 50.
Herr Haidvogel und seine Familie ('Herr Weiss'), 47, 48, 49.
Matteo, 48, 49, 50.
Pauls merkwürdigste Nacht ('Johann'), 47, 48, 49, 50.
Schnock, 30, 48, 49, **51–4,** 56.
Tagebücher, 2, **12–13,** 17, 18, 24, 25, 58, 62, 92, 94, 95, 98, 106, 111, 123, 137, 170, 181, 182, 183, 186, 189, 191, 193, 255, 257, 258 (note), (and quotations *passim*).
Hebbel, Christine, 31, 110, 111, 112, 113, 125, 126, 127, 128, 129, 130, 131, 133, 135, 136, 144, 181, 182, 183, 185, 188, 189, 191, 209, 212, 213, 254, 267.
Hebbel, Emil ('Ariel'), 128, 129, 133.
Hebbel, Ernst, 102, 105, 109, 128, 129, 133.
Hebbel, Karl, 129 (and note), 130, 131.
Hebbel, Klaus Friedrich, 2, 3, 4, 5, 6, 185.

Hebbel, Maximilian Friedrich ('Max'), 58, 98.
poem on, 40, 100.
Hebbel, Tine ('Titi'), 131, 132, 133, 182.
Heiberg, J. L., Hebbel's relations with, 73, 95, 96, 261 (note 1).
Heidelberg, 1–2, 16, 17, 18, 19.
Heine, Hebbel's relations with, 97.
Hoffmann, E. T. A., 7, 46, 54.
Hettner, Hermann, Hebbel's relations with, 108, 257.
Humour, definitions of, 50, 51.

Italy, 49, 94, 102, 103, 132, 139, 181.
— residence in Rome, **103–8,** 110, 111.
— residence in Naples, 103, **108–9.**

Kleist, influence of, 7, 41, 46, 47.
Kuh, Emil, Hebbel's relations with, 2, **188–90,** 191.

Laube, Hebbel's relations with, 136 170, 182, 183, 191.
Lensing, Elise, 14, 15, 16, 17, 19, 21, 22, 23, 26, 28, 29, 30, 31, 32, 33, 34, 38, 40, 41, 47, 53, 56, 58, 59, 61, 75, 76, 92, 93, 94, 95, 96, 97, 98, 99, 100, 101, 102, 103, 104, 105, 106, 107, 109, 110, 111, 112, 113, 128, 129, 130, 131, 132, 133, 137, 182, 183, 184, 209, 255, 260, 267.

Marriage, views on:
— in relation to Elise Lensing, 32, 33, 98, 99, 101, 104, 105, 106, 107, 109, 110, 111, 112, 130, 131.
— to Christine Enghaus, 110, 111, 112, 113, 127, 128, 130, 132, 144, 267.
Metaphysics, relation to drama, 255, 256, 257 (and note), 266.
Mohr, J. J., Kirchspielvogt in Wesselburen, 6, 7, 11.
Müller, 'Maler', Criticism of, 25, 74, 75, 76.
Munich, 16, 19, 20, 21, 24, 25, 26, 27, 28, 29, 30, 33, 34, 38, 60, 64, 74, 76, 105, 113, 124, 125, 181, 256.
Music, early interest in, 5–6, 25.

Nature, feeling for, 1–2, 17, 18, 25, 36, 38, 39, 43, 44, 45, 46, 103, 185, 211–12, 260, 263.

Oehlenschläger, Hebbel's relations with, 9, 10, 92, 93, 94, 96, 102.
— criticism of, 264.

Paris, 6, 94, 95, 96, 97, 99, 102, 103, 104, 106, 113, 122, 127.
— residence in, **96–103.**

Revolution of 1848, 133, 134, 135.
— counter-revolution, 134.
Richter, Jean Paul Friedrich, Influence of, 53.
Rousseau, Emil, 17, 26, 27, 28, 29, 40, 62, 188, 259.

Schiller, influence of, 7, 8, 13, 23, 35, 36, 37.
Demetrius, 187, 188, 193, 229, **233–4.**
Jungfrau von Orleans, 22, 23, 65.
Schleswig-Holstein, dependent states of, 1, 9–10.
Schoppe, Amalia, 10, 11, 14, 15, 16, 30, 56, 57, 58.
Schröder, Emma, Hebbel's relations with, 58, 75.
Schwarz, Anton, 25, 124.
Schwarz, Josepha, v. 'Beppy'.

Theatre, early interest in, 9.
Tieck, Hebbel's relations with, 30, 48, 49, 56.
— criticism of, 60, 74, 75, 76, 77, 86.
Tragedy, Hebbel's theory of, 66, 67, 168, 177, 178, 227, 257, 258, 259, 260, 261, 262, 263, 264, 265, 266, 269.
Tragic individual, Hebbel's conception of the, 66, 67, 86, 121, 167, 168, 177, 178, 205, 208, 227, 233, 258, 259, 260, 261, 262, 263, 264, 265, 266, 267, 268, 269.

Uhland, Hebbel's relations with, 8, 9, 10, 18, 19, 27, 57, 187.
— influence of, 7, 8, 36, 37.

Vienna, life in, 127, 128, 132, 133, 134, 135, 136, 181, 182, 183, 185, 186, 188, 191, 192, 193.

Wagner (*Der Ring des Nibelungen*), 223.
Wesselburen, 1, 2, 3, 4, 5, 8–9, 16.
Weimar, relations with, 181, 187, 188, 191, 192.